Hospitality Promotion and Advertisement Management

HOSPITALITY PROMOTION AND ADVERTISEMENT MANAGEMENT

Bhavi Chhaya

CENTRUM PRESS
NEW DELHI-110002 (INDIA)

CENTRUM PRESS
H.O.: 4360/4, Ansari Road, Daryaganj,
New Delhi-110002 (India)
Tel: 23278000, 23261597, 23255577, 23286875
B.O.: No. 1015, Ist Main Road, BSK IIIrd Stage,
IIIrd Phase, IIIrd Block, Bengaluru-560085 (INDIA)
Tel: 080-41723429
Email: centrumpress@gmail.com
Visit us at: www.centrumpress.com

Hospitality Promotion and Advertisement Management

First Edition, 2013

ISBN 978-93-81460-13-9

PRINTED IN INDIA

Printed at Balaji Offset, Delhi.

Contents

Preface

Advertising, marketing, promotions, public relations, and sales managers coordinate their companies' market research, marketing strategy, sales, advertising, promotion, pricing, product development, and public relations activities. In small firms the owner or chief executive officer might assume all advertising, promotions, marketing, sales, and public relations responsibilities. In large firms, which may offer numerous products and services nationally or even worldwide, an executive vice president directs overall advertising, marketing, promotions, sales, and public relations policies. Advertising managers direct a firm's or group's advertising and promotional campaign.

They can be found in advertising agencies that put together advertising campaigns for clients, in media firms that sell advertising space or time, and in companies that advertise heavily. They work with sales staff and others to generate ideas for the campaign, oversee a creative staff that develops the advertising, and work with the finance department to prepare a budget and cost estimates for the campaign. Often, these managers serve as liaisons between the firm requiring the advertising and an advertising or promotion agency that actually develops and places the ads. In larger firms with an extensive advertising department, different advertising managers may oversee in-house accounts and creative and media services departments. The *account executive* manages account services departments in companies and assesses the need for advertising. In advertising agencies, account executives maintain the accounts of clients whereas the creative services department develops the subject matter and presentation of advertising. The *creative director* oversees the copy chief, art director, and associated staff. The *media director* oversees planning groups that select the communication medium—for example, radio, television, newspapers, magazines, the Internet, or outdoor signs—that will disseminate the advertising.

Marketing managers work with advertising and promotion managers to promote the firm's or organization's products and services. With the help of lower level managers, including *product development managers* and *market research managers,* marketing managers estimate the demand for products and services offered by the firm and its competitors and identify potential markets for the firm's products. Marketing managers also develop pricing strategies to help firms maximize profits and market share while ensuring that the firms' customers are satisfied. In collaboration with sales, product development, and other managers, they monitor trends that indicate the need for new products and services and they oversee product development.

Promotions managers direct promotions programs that combine advertising with purchasing incentives to increase sales. Often, the programs are executed through the use of direct mail, inserts in newspapers, Internet advertisements, in-store displays, product endorsements, or other special events. Purchasing incentives may include discounts, samples, gifts, rebates, coupons, sweepstakes, and contests.

This approach will provide a solid foundation this subject on which the student will continue to build during the remainder of his or her professional life and most certainly during the remainder of his or her professional education.

—Author

1

Destination Promotions in Hospitality Sector

Destination marketing facilitates the achievement of tourism policy, which should be coordinated with the regional development strategic plan. Marketing of destinations should also guide the tourism impacts optimisation and the maximisation of benefits for the region. In order to appreciate the complexity of destination marketing this paper explains the destination concept and attempts to synthesise several models for strategic marketing and management of destinations.

Destination as an Amalgam of Tourism Services and Experiences

Destinations are amalgams of tourism products, offering an integrated experience to consumers.

Traditionally, destinations are regarded as well-defined geographical areas, such as a country, an island or a town. However, it is increasingly recognised that a destination can also a perceptual concept, which can be interpreted subjectively by consumers, depending on their travel itinerary, cultural background, purpose of visit, educational level and past experience. For example, London can be a destination for a German business traveller, whilst Europe may be the destination for a leisure Japanese tourist who packs six European countries in a two week tour. Some travellers will consider a cruise ship to be their destination, while others on the same cruise may perceive the ports visited during the trip as their destination. Often destinations are artificially divided by geographical and political barriers, which fail to take into consideration consumer preferences or tourism industry functions. An example of that is the Alps shared by France, Austria, Switzerland, Italy by often perceived and consumed as part of the same product by skiers. For the purpose of this paper destinations are considered to be a defined geographical region which is understood by its visitors as a unique entity, with a political and legislative framework for tourism marketing and planning. This definition enables Destination Management Organisations (DMOs) to be accountable for the planning and marketing of the region and to have the power and resources to undertake action towards achieving its strategic objectives.

Destinations offer an amalgam of tourism products and services, which are consumed under the brand name of the destination.

Leiper (1995) explains that destinations are places towards which people travel and where they choose to stay for a while in order to experience certain features or characteristics-a perceived attraction of some sort. Cooper et al (1998) define destinations as the focus of facilities and services designed to meet the needs of the tourists. Therefore, a destination can be regarded as a combination (or even as a brand) of all products, services and ultimately experiences provided locally. It also enables us to assess the impact of tourism regionally, as well as manage demand and supply in order to maximise benefits for all stakeholders.

Six As Framework for the analysis of tourism destinations;

- Attractions (natural, man-made, artificial, purpose built, heritage, special events)
- Accessibility (entire transportation system comprising of routes, terminals and vehicles)
- Amenities (accommodation and catering facilities, retailing, other tourist services)
- Available packages (pre-arranged packages by intermediaries and principals)
- Activities (all activities available at the destination and what consumers will do during their visit)

- Ancillary services (services used by tourists such as banks, telecommunications, post, newsagents, hospitals, etc)

Although there is plenty of literature on destination planning and development of facilities, there are few textbooks examining destination marketing and even fewer illustrate destinations as an experience-provider for tourists and locals.

This is also reflected in the academic literature published in journals and other scientific publications.

The inadequacy of destination marketing literature probably illustrates the interest of researchers in the impacts of tourism on destinations. Hence, the management and marketing of destinations is often left to industry people and consultants and it is not frequently discussed in the literature or in academic debates. The competitive nature of destination marketing also prevents involved parties from publishing their strategies and marketing plans. In addition, there is an apparent difference between the marketing and planning tourism literature.

Traditionally marketing concentrates on increasing visitation and treats tourism like any other commodity. This approach fails to recognise the unique needs and limitations of each destination as well as their particular geographical, environmental and socio-cultural characteristics. In contrast, planning literature concentrates more on the impacts of tourism and on limiting tourism development, often ignoring the market dynamics and the requirements of entrepreneurs at the destination and the place of origin explains that companies and governments in tourism have applied only part of the marketing mix to tourism, i.e., promotion, with little attention being paid to the other components of marketing. However, if tourism is to survive by generating satisfaction among interacting tourists and hosts, it must adopt societal marketing strategies. This involves carefully monitoring tourist satisfaction levels and using these as part of the criteria for success, rather than increasing numbers of tourists; continually monitoring host reactions to tourists, for host-tourist interaction is an important component of the tourist experience; and being aware that infrastructure development of tourism resort areas has implications for the types of tourists that will be attracted.

The Strategic Purpose of Destinations and their Management and Marketing

Destinations are some of the most difficult entities to manage and market, due to the complexity of the relationships of local stakeholders (Sautter and Leisen,1999). Managing and marketing destinations is also challenging because of the variety of stakeholders involved in the development and production of tourism products. The destination experience is essentially comprised of regions, resources and amalgams of tourism facilities and services, which often do not belong to individuals. Instead they represent a collection of both professional and personal interests of all the people who live and work in the area. Managing often conflicting stakeholders' interests makes controlling and marketing destinations as a whole extremely challenging. Hence, strategies and actions should take into account the wishes of all stakeholders, namely indigenous people, businesses and investors, tourists, tour operators and intermediaries, and interest groups. Perhaps the most difficult problem is ensuring the rational use of zero-priced public goods, such as landscapes, mountains, and the sea for the benefit of all stakeholders and at the same time preserving the resources for future generations. Conflicts can easily develop, especially when some (perhaps greedy) stakeholders exploit resources for short-term benefits. A compromise encompassing all these interests is extremely difficult if not impossible, but is the key to long term success.

And yet tourists perceive the destination as a brand comprising of a collection of suppliers and services. Before visiting they develop an image about destinations as well as a set of expectations based on previous experience, word of mouth, press reports, advertising, and common beliefs. During their holiday, they "consume" destinations as a comprehensive experience, without often realising that each element of the product are produced and managed by individual players. Most service providers are small and medium-sized tourism enterprises which have a wide range of strengths and weaknesses whilst are also characterised by their independent nature. Tourists' overall experience is composed of numerous small encounters with a variety of tourism principals, such as taxi drivers, hoteliers, waiters, as well as with elements of the local attractions such as museums, theatres, beaches, theme parks etc. Their overall impression develops their image of a destination after their visitation. As a consequence there is much overlapping between strategic marketing of the destination as a whole and of each individual supplier at the region. Hence, the competitiveness of each player is often interrelated and almost indistinguishable from one another.

As consumers increasingly value environmental resources they are prepared to pay for them premium prices. Hence, local resources become a central asset for destinations and tourism suppliers and their sustainability a core function of tourism marketing. Middleton and Hawkins state that "a marketing perspective is essentially an overall management orientation reflecting corporate attitudes that, in the case of travel and tourism, must balance the interests of shareholders/owners with the long-run environmental interests of a destination and at the same time meet the demands and expectations of customers".

DMOs tend to be part of the local, regional or national government and have political and legislative power as well as the financial means to manage resources rationally and to ensure that all stakeholders can benefit in the long term. Destination management and marketing should act as tools and facilitators to achieve a complex range of strategic objectives, which will ultimately need to satisfy the needs and wants of stakeholders. The development and implementation of strategic objectives at destinations depends on relationships between stakeholders and thus the implementation of the key generic strategic objectives will be determined by the dynamics of the actors on this wheel.

Naturally each stakeholder aims to maximise the benefits emerging for themselves. Inevitably, the interests of some stakeholders may be conflicting with others and thus some of the four key strategic objectives may be jeopardised. This is often a result of some stakeholder trying to enhance its benefit at the expense of others.

For example a tour operator may try to reduce the prices paid to local suppliers in order to increase its profit margin and remain competitive in the marketplace. It is imperative, therefore, for DMOs to use legislative and management tools during planning and management of destinations in order to ensure that the benefits of tourism activity is shared fairly between all stakeholders and that sustainable practices safeguard the regeneration of resources utilised for the production of tourism. Failure to ensure and maintain a balance effectively jeopardises relationships between stakeholders, and threatens the achievement of the strategic objectives and the long term competitiveness and prosperity of destinations.

Strategic management and marketing objectives for destinations;

- Enhance the long term prosperity of local people
- Delight visitors by maximising their satisfaction
- Maximise profitability of local enterprises and maximise multiplier effects
- Optimise tourism impacts by ensuring a sustainable balance between economic benefits and socio-cultural and environmental costs

Hence, tourism marketing should not only be regarded as a tool for attracting more visitors to a region, as it has been the case for most destinations. Instead, tourism marketing should operate as a mechanism to facilitate regional development objectives and to rationalise the provision of tourism in order to ensure that the strategic objectives of destinations are achieved. Tourism marketing should also ensure equitable returns-on-resources-utilised for the production and delivery of tourism products, as well as the regeneration of these resources. It should also provide suitable gains to all stakeholders involved in the tourism system. Hence, marketing should be used as a strategic mechanism in coordination with planning and management rather than a sales tool. Destinations may also involve de-marketing, i.e. the discouragement of certain market segments from visiting the destination during certain periods, through a range of prohibitive measures or by charging premium prices. Examples of these techniques include:

- visitor management techniques in theme parks which divert people from congested attractions to less busy ones by using a leading story/attraction;

- towns like Cambridge, which aims to attract only visitors who stay overnight and to discourage excursionists who contribute little to the local economy by controlling their parking processes; _ Mauritius which provides high quality resort accommodation and does not allow charter flights, therefore promoting high expenditure tourism; or
- Venice, which deters more visitors by charging premium prices for all services offered and recently initiated negative advertisement to reduce mass tourism.

In this way marketing is used as a mechanism to achieve strategic objectives of destination regions and thus, should be guided by the policies for regional development.

Main Markets and Destination Choice

Understanding destination types and characteristics is of paramount importance for its marketing. Each destination can only match certain types of demand and hence tourism marketers need to appreciate travel motivations in order to develop appropriate offerings and brand destinations for

the right target markets. In addition, destinations should be aware not only of the needs and wants of the active demand but also of the potential markets they can attract. It can then develop a product portfolio, which will enable the optimisation of benefits and adapt their marketing mix to their target markets. Consumer behaviour studies indicate that a wide range of criteria is used to select tourism products. These criteria are altered according to the purpose and features of the trip, elements of the external environment, the characteristics of the traveller and the particularities and attributes of destinations.

Classifying travel behavior and segmentation becomes increasingly more difficult as modern travellers combine pleasure with business, in order to take time and cost advantage. There are therefore endless variations between the two principle classifications of travel activities, i.e. business and leisure trips. However, leisure trips may include elements, characteristics and motivations of business travel and vice versa. Incentive travelling, extended conference stays and business meetings during leisure travel makes the distinction between the two categories increasingly blurred. Nevertheless the two principle categories are fairly identifiable and they are treated differently in this text for simplifying the concepts and marketing responses.

Business trips are fairly inflexible and it is often difficult for travellers to select their destinations.

Business travel, often referred to as MICE (Meetings-Incentives-Conferences-Exhibitions), is normally determined by business opportunities and involvement of the traveller with organisations at the destination. Perhaps more flexibility can be exercised by travellers attending optional meetings, which provide benefits but are not strictly essential to their business such as conferences, exhibitions, incentives, familiarization trips etc (Davidson 1994). Even though business tourism is much more

restricted in terms of choice, destinations providing a high degree of efficiency and safety, as well as elegance and leisure opportunities tend to be preferred for conferences and incentive travel. Business travel is seasonal, as people do not generally travel less during the holiday seasons, i.e. summer months and public holidays. Nevertheless, business tourism provide much higher revenue for enterprises as consumers are willing to pay more for their inflexible schedules and also destinations can increase their multiplier effects as some particular forms of business tourism use a much greater spectrum of local services than leisure tourism. Convenient transportation connections with major cities around the world, smooth arrangements at the destination and adequate provision of business related amenities are therefore very important. Urban destinations in developed countries with strong economic activity and vibrant markets tend to receive the majority of business traffic, as a result of the business meetings taking place locally. The location of meeting partners, host organisations, as well as company policy may determine the selection of destinations for business travel. In addition, corporate rates, membership of loyalty clubs (i.e. frequent flyer or frequent guest) as well as the availability of service providers are some additional criteria used to identify suitable destinations and service providers for the MICE market.

Leisure travellers, on the other hand, use a much more complex set of criteria in selecting their destination. They have a much higher price elasticity and therefore, price is a key element in the decision making process. In addition, leisure travellers are often time sensitive as families with children cannot travel during school time, creating the seasonality problem for the industry. However, different market segments have dissimilar seasonality patterns. For example, pensioners and elderly people tend to travel during the low season to benefit from discounts, whilst Scandinavian tourists tend to stay home during the summer months in order to enjoy the whether. School children and University students go on field research trips or excursions during the low season. Therefore, destinations have to identify the seasonality patterns of their various markets and attract compatible segments, which will enable them to maximise their total yield (both average expenditure and occupancy levels). It is also important to understand other factors that influence the decision of consumers to purchase. The social status and peer groups of consumers often influence what is acceptable and desirable as a destination. Travel intermediaries also play a significant role in determining the destination decision of consumers by using a wide range of promotional techniques and often channeling travellers to destinations and principals who offer higher remuneration for them.

This will also enable destinations to manage their resources according and attract the right market segments in order to optimize their impacts.

Nevertheless for both leisure and business markets, perhaps the most important criterion for selecting to visit or not to visit a destination is its image. Image is the set of expectations and perceptions a prospective traveller has of a destination. Past experience of the destination or the companies involved (i.e. airlines, hotels, tour operators); descriptions by friends and relatives; general information; and marketing campaigns develop these expectations and perception which may be true or imaginary representations. Interestingly, the sustainability of local resources becomes one of the most important elements of destination image, as a growing section of the market is not prepared to tolerate over-developed tourism destinations and diverts to more environmentally advanced regions. The degree of consumer satisfaction will depend on the assessment of the perceived overall experience of the destination versus anticipated expectations and perceptions. Developing the right image for destinations will therefore determine their ability to satisfy visitors as it will allow them to develop realistic and fulfil-able expectations.

Types of Destinations, Target Markets and Marketing Strategies Required

Developing a destination typology is a difficult task, as different visitors use destinations for different purposes. Nevertheless most destinations can be classified in several categories which represent their principle attractiveness. Understanding and appreciating the type of destination enables marketers to develop a suitable destination marketing mixes and deliver them to the appropriate target markets.

Urban destinations have been involved in tourism since the early years of the civilisation. People used to travel to cities and towns to meet politicians and business associates. Sports organisations, such as the Olympic Games in ancient Greece also generated tourism activity in main cities. People also travelled to cities on pilgrimage for religious purposes, as this is where all major cathedrals, mosques and temples were usually located. Urban destinations have also been attracting business travellers attending meetings, conferences and exhibitions. Most urban destinations are well equipped with conference and exhibition halls and transportation and accommodation infrastructure to facilitate the organisation of larger events. Urban destinations also attract leisure travellers, especially during periods of low business travelling activity, such as weekends and school holidays. Suppliers and facilities aim to reduce seasonality by developing the number of leisure visitors, despite the fact that they can only charge a fraction of the price they charge business travellers. On the other hand, leisure travellers can take advantage of some of the unique facilities and services of urban destinations to enjoy short-breaks or extended weekends.

London for example provides a wide range of heritage attractions as well as a wide range of entertainment opportunities such as theatre, concerts, bars, theme restaurants, discos etc.

Barcelona offers excellent conference facilities, combined with a culturally interesting and relaxed atmosphere. New York is highly regarded for shopping, sight seeing and theatre going. Urban destinations also attract education and health tourists, as they are generally equipped with good educational establishments and hospitals. Increasingly urban resorts take advantage of their industrial heritage and use obsolete industrial sites as educational experiences and leisure facilities. The Docklands in Liverpool and coal mines in Skipton are good examples of these facilities.

Seaside destinations and resorts traditionally serve tourists on holidays. Travellers from Northern regions and climates tend to spend a proportion of their annual holiday in the South where they can enjoy sunshine as well as sea sports. Seaside resorts nearby the place of residence were replaced by international destinations as a result of the emergence of mass tourism since the 1970s. For example, in the UK traditional resorts such Blackpool, Scarborough, Bournemouth and Brighton were replaced by the Spanish Costas through the development of package holidays. Typically European leisure travellers will take their annual holiday at Mediterranean seaside resorts, whilst Northern Americans visit Southern regions such as Florida,

California and the Caribbean. As the product in traditional seaside resorts matures, new long haul and exotic destinations, often in less developed countries attract sophisticated travellers who are looking for authentic and off-the-track experiences. The globalization experienced reduces distances and enables people to travel further afield. Examples include destinations such as Goa and Bali which take advantage of developments in transportation and attract travellers. Examples of seaside destinations and resorts can be identified globally.

Alpine destinations attract leisure travellers for winter sports, such as skiing, as well as holidaymakers who appreciate natural attractions in all seasons. They also attract activity holidaymakers such as naturalists, mountain cyclists, walkers etc. Although the majority of alpine sports are for recreational purposes a wide range of expeditions and challenges are organised for mountains such as the Everest or the Alps. Lakes may also offer facilities for sea sports such as surfing and skiing. Although the majority of alpine resorts are in near proximity to urban centres and thus can easily be accessed by private car, several are still unexplored and offer authentic experiences for travellers. Lakes and scenic landscapes make alpine resorts increasingly more popular for conference and incentive tourists and thus a certain business travelling activity can be observed in the last few years. The development of important business, political and economic meetings, such as the Davos Forum, attract a new market segment and expand the season for winter resorts. As a result a wide range of marketing and planning implications emerge to allow alpine areas to benefit from tourism and yet to ensure the sustainability of their resources.

Destinations in authentic (often Third World) countries are often off the beaten track. Tourists enjoy authentic experiences in places which have experienced limited tourism development.

Emerging destinations in Asia, South America and Africa attract a small number of adventurous tourists who are prepared to forego their comfort in order to interact with local communities and unspoiled surroundings. Although these regions may develop at a later stage to mass tourism destinations, they need to be planned properly in order to sustain their resources. They often lack the required infrastructure to deliver tourism services.

Finally certain destinations are branded unique-exotic-exclusive as they are regarded to offer a unique and precious experience. As a result, these destinations are promoted as "one-in-a-lifetime" experience and they are promoted premium prices. Examples include Bhutan, Mauritius, and Seychelles.

In some destinations, there are several mechanisms controlling the number of visitors, often through managing their transportation and accommodating capacity or immigration procedures and visa allowances.

These destinations focus on the non-charter and non-mass traveller reducing their visitation but maximising their income per visitor. They often epitomise the dream of the average traveller and thus are packaged and priced as prestigious products, for instance for weddings, honeymoons, anniversaries or a special occasion trip, or for incentive travel.

Marketing Research: Identifying Market Segments for Destination Products

Marketing research is used extensively by destination marketers to identify the types of customers that can be attracted (active demand), as well as the prospective visitors (suppressed demand) who do not visit for a variety of reasons (Athiyaman, 1997). Approaching the right target market and providing the most appropriate combination of local tourism products and services is the secret for successful destinations. Product design and formulation should therefore be based on research. As tourism bundles are formulated ad-hoc to satisfy specific consumer requests, a dynamic marketing research process will enable destinations to provide unique products by initiating local partnerships between all suppliers to address the needs of demand. Destination image is also developed through marketing research, which guides promotional activities towards branding and amending the brand values of the region. The effectiveness of promotional campaigns can be assessed so that the most cost-effective media is used to approach and persuade target markets to visit the destination.

Contribution of marketing research to destination marketing;

- Identification of the main attributes anticipated by each market segment
- Design and attributes required for tourism products and services
- Evaluation and development of destination image
- Segmentation of market and development of corresponding marketing mixes
- Opening new markets and reducing dependency on existing ones
- Evaluation of the elasticity of demand for each market segment
- Reduction of seasonality by matching market segments
- Examination of reasons deterring people (suppressed demand) from visiting destinations
- Assessment of compatibility with other target markets

- Examination of alternative distribution channels
- Assessment of tourism impacts to the destination and selecting the right segments
- Evaluation of marketing effectiveness and selection of media for promotion.

Marketing Destinations: Strategies and Practices

Developing a marketing strategy and mix for destinations is a complex process, mainly because there are many independent stakeholders and principals involved. Destinations cannot be managed or marketed as enterprises, due to the dynamics of interests and benefits sought by stakeholders. In addition, most destinations are amalgams of independent SMTEs, which already follow their own marketing strategies. Although DMOs have traditionally taken marketing responsibility for the destination product, they fail to control marketing activities and mixes of individual players and hence can only coordinate and guide, rather than undertake a comprehensive marketing strategy. Perhaps the most important challenge for destination marketing therefore is to bring all individual partners together to compete rather than to cooperate and to pool resources towards developing an integrated marketing mix and delivery system.

The international tourist industry is becoming an increasingly competitive marketplace where only the best-managed destinations are likely to prosper. Comprehensive strategic business plans therefore need to address all factors that have an impact on the product. Tourism strategies should not only concentrate on visitation, but also include the entire range of impacts such as overcrowding, environmental problems, visitor safety and security, seasonality problems, and sensitivity to local culture (Evans, et al 1995). This will enable destinations to develop comprehensive strategies to fulfil all strategic objectives.

The Position of Destinations and their Marketing

Perhaps one additional complication to tourism marketing is that in most cases destinations have already a rich history and legacy development which needs to be taken into consideration when developing tourism marketing strategies. Not only consumers develop certain images and views about places, but also previous development often provides several limits for marketing to address as well as stakeholders who need to be respected and consulted. Understanding therefore the stage and roots of tourism development is critical for development a strategy. One of the most widely used tools for undertaking this task is the destination life cycle. The main utility of the destination life cycle is to facilitate the understanding the evolution of tourist products and destinations and it to provide guidance for strategic decision taking. Cooper suggests that the life cycle concept illustrates that destinations experience a "birth to death" cycle and that the life cycle model has gained attention in tourism and hospitality as an explanatory tool.

Although in tourism life cycle analysis is often seen as a useful conceptualisation tool for destination area development, in hospitality management it is beginning to be used as a guide for strategic planning. However the main problems relate to identifying turning points, stages, length of stages and level of aggregation. Despite the many criticisms of the life cycle concept, it is quite critical for marketers to appreciate the stage of development of resort areas. A number of researchers have used the cycle as a framework for analysing changing destinations.

The different stages destinations are going through during their life cycle and illustrates how that effects their tourism impacts. This also illustrates that different stages of the life cycle require different marketing strategies and planning actions. This is largely due to the differences between demand and supply experienced at different levels. In the early stages demand exceeds supply whilst this relationship is reversed in the maturity and consolidation stages. As a result, marketing strategies should focus on building awareness and promoting the destination product on the early stages of the circle while they probably have to deal with image alteration and re-design and re-launch the product at the later stages. The entire marketing mix therefore will need to be differentiated to accommodate the needs of destinations at each stage of their life cycle. In addition, destinations experience different environmental and socio-cultural impacts during the different faces. As a result they need to use marketing to encourage sustainable practices for both consumers and industry as well as to communicate their environmental and socio-cultural policies.

Porter's Generic Strategies

Three main strategies proposed by Porter (1980) aimed to "outperform other firms in an industry", i.e.:

- Overall cost leadership, where organisations are required to minimise their costs, based on mass production and strict cost control of the main business functions;
- differentiation of products or services offered by "creating something that is perceived industrywide as being unique";
- focus on a "particular buyer group, segment of the product line or geographical market" and achieve either cost leadership or product differentiation.

This is well-developed generic model, which is widely used to all industries. It provides clear guidance for decision makers to position their products in order to maximise profitability and improve their competitiveness. However, this model fails to address the specific needs of tourism and in particular the scarcity of resources at the destination level. Therefore, similarly with commodities this model suggests unlimited resources are available to reproduce endless number of products. This is particularly the case for the cost leadership strategy where organisations are urged to increase their volume and to reduce their profit margin. Unfortunately environmental resources, both natural (e.g. coral reefs or mountain landscapes) and man-made (e.g. archaeological sites or architectural structures) have a limited capacity which they can accommodate. Resources in tourism are irreplaceable once destroyed and therefore a strategy should ensure that their use is limited to the degree that does not threat their sustainability in the long term. Once this is understood and appreciated, Porter's model enables tourism marketers to focus on differentiation strategies and to develop their mix accordingly. However, several destinations, which are on the consolidation phase of their life cycle, have exceeded the maximum capacity which would have enabled them to sustain their resources. Their ability to promote differentiated tourism products has also been jeopardised, as over-development has exploited and damaged their resources. This is experienced in some mass tourism destinations, such as Benidorm and Costa Brava in Spain, or Faliraki and Malia in Greece.

Once destinations have reached that stage there is limited choice. The majority try to attract more mass tourism so they can increase their profitability through volume. Increasingly however some regions aim to renovate their properties and facilities and re-launch their offerings. The Calvia example in Mallorca, which decided to demolish three hotels in order to improve public areas and to enhance the quality of its products set new best practices which may be followed by other regions.

Gilbert's Strategic Framework

Based on the above rational the second strategic framework introduced by Gilbert argues that destinations can classified on a continuum between a "status" and a "commodity" area. "Status areas" achieve intentional demand as a result of the unique product attributes perceived by the tourism market. These unique attributes may be genuine or imaginative and thus, a destination is regarded as irreplaceable, which increases consumers' loyalty and willingness to pay.

In the "commodity status" case, destinations are substitutable, very sensitive to price and economic changes, while consumers have a low awareness of any unique benefits or attributes. Thus, travellers base their decision to visit the area merely on price, while the demand for the destination is incidental and destinations are unable to attract high spenders. Despite the fact that the sustainability of resources is not discussed explicitly by the model, it is quite evident that "status areas" manage their resources as product attributes and therefore are appreciated by consumers who are willing to pay more.

Gilbert (1990) asserts that destinations should attempt to become "status areas", rather than a "commodity area" one, in order to improve their image, loyalty and economic benefits. It is suggested that destinations should differentiate their tourism products in order to achieve a unique "tourist product benefit". This will enable them to establish their position in the international market, and attract both high spenders and loyal tourists, who appreciate the uniqueness of their resources and offerings. Although the model clearly differentiates destinations to distinctive categories it fails to recognise that the majority of destinations lay between the two ends of the continuum.

It also fails to relate to the different stages of the life cycle and to the inevitability experienced in several regions where destinations are launched as status areas and gradually slip to commodity status (Buhalis,1999a). Nevertheless the model clearly contributes to tourism marketing by correlating product attributes with willingness to pay and also by illustrating clearly that destinations should decide on what direction they should plan and manage their resources and facilities.

Poon's Flexible Specialisation

A third strategic approach for tourism is proposed by Poon (1989 and 1993), based on the concept of "flexible specialisation" of the tourism business. Poon examines the tourism industry processes and proposes a strategy to enable tourism organisations to improve their competitiveness.

Commodity Area rigidly packaged". "The main sources of flexibility for service firms lie in the organisation, management, marketing, distribution and other forms of interaction and interrelationships among guests, hotels, suppliers, distributors. What is important however is not each of these stand-alone aspects but how they are coupled to create competitive advantages and hence, capabilities to move with the market".

This is a timely model, which predicted the impact of information technology on the both decision making and consumer behaviour. Industry innovation is critical in this strategy and the utilisation of new technology provides the opportunity to customise products according to customers' specific requirements. Hence destinations can organise their assets and attributes in such a way which will enable them to specialise their tourism product according to particular demand needs.

Although Poon's model revolutionised tourism thinking it is still difficult to implement at the destination level. The majority of infrastructure and superstructure is based on fixed assets, which cannot be altered easily and therefore they have a limited degree of flexibility. This is more evident at destinations at the consolidation stages, which are unable to reinvent themselves and approach new markets.

Nevertheless, the model clearly contributes to the field by encouraging tourism organisations and destinations to challenge existing strategies and practices and to forcing them to approach new tourism with new tools introduced by technology. Concentrating on core functions and outsourcing all peripheral activities to networks of virtual co-operations should enable destinations and enterprises to innovate and to adapt to the needs of consumers constantly.

Aviation Promotion

Aviation Promotion Program

The Aviation Promotion Program helps stimulate aeronautical activity and promote aviation across the state by raising awareness in the business and public sectors about the programs and services provided and the economic benefits generated by Virginia airports. The program provides funding to airport sponsors for the promotion of commercial aviation services and general aviation activities. The Virginia Aviation Board has delegated the authority to review and approve funding requests for the Aviation Promotion Program to the Virginia Department of Aviation.

Project Eligibility

Promotion programs should feature public relations activities, advertising, educational activities, publications, and the development of business and financial plans. Programs for general aviation airports can cover a wide spectrum of projects based on the diverse needs of each community and an airport's target audience. Funding for a new project can only be requested after an existing grant agreement is closed.

Eligible projects for the Aviation Promotion Program include:

- airport flight guides
- newsletters

- annual reports
- promotional videos
- on-line services
- brochures and fliers
- print media, billboards, and sign boards
- air time on radio and television
- airport and aviation displays
- aviation educational activities
- acquisition of educational supplies
- business and financial plans that must include a description of the business, financial data, and supporting documents that verify up-to-date master and airport layout plans
- items or services that are contracted for the public's use and benefit at special events such as airport appreciation days, fly-ins, and air shows
- meetings specifically held for promotional activities, including administrative, legal, and incidental costs incurred in completing a project.

Ineligible projects include:

- a promotional item or activity that has the specific purpose of attracting business or passengers from another Virginia airport, including advertising or activities referencing the name, services, or economic advantages of one airport over a neighbouring Virginia airport
- the purchase, lease purchase, or long-term lease of office equipment, presentation equipment, audio-visual equipment, vehicles, uniforms, or similar items
- the physical enhancement, beautification, decoration, or improvement of airport facilities
- a promotional item, service, or event that is not available to the public
- the promotion of privately owned businesses as sole beneficiary of a promotional effort.

State Participation

For the Aviation Promotion Program, the VAB established a $25,000 annual ceiling per airport on state financial participation for air carrier airports and a $10,000 annual ceiling per airport for general aviation airports.

Careers in Tourism

Travel and Tourism one of the world's largest foreign exchange earner among industries, provides employment directly to millions of people worldwide and indirectly through many associated service industries.

A very wide industry, it includes Government tourism departments, Immigration and customs services, travel agencies, airlines, tour operators, hotels etc and many associated service industries such as airline catering or laundry services, Guides, Interpreters, Tourism promotion and sales etc. Travel and Tourism enterprises include major internationals with a workforce of thousands, to the small private travel agent with a handful of employees.

Work in the travel and tourism industry is essentially concerned with providing services for people who are away from home, on business or holiday. Travel can be leisure travel involving package tours, pilgrim travel, adventure travel etc or purely business. Work at every functional level in the industry involves dealing directly with people.

Travel agents assess the needs of tourists and businessmen and help them make the best possible travel arrangements from the many travel options available. Also, many major cruise lines, resorts, and specialty travel groups use travel agents to promote travel packages to the millions of people who travel every year.

Travel company personnel must be up-to-date on current rules and regulations and documentation required, in areas like cargo, ticketing and passports, visas etc. so as to correctly advise their clients, and to take care of the paperwork when necessary. Besides this, all tourism staff in marketing, counter sales, or guide services, should be knowledgeable about the places their clients visit, in terms of general background, how to get there connections by air, rail and road and the facilities available.

In India, Travel and tourism, as an industry, has been somewhat slower to take off than in many other places. However, with increasing worldwide interest in travel, and with the Government's encouragement of its activities, it is undergoing massive expansion and improvement.

This forecasts a bright future for all those who choose to make a career of travel and tourism. Young people with drive and a capacity for hard work can rise to top positions very quickly in travel and tourism or even head their own agencies. A job in the industry gives good returns as well as perks including opportunity to see many locales at low prices.

Eligibility: The eligibility criteria for admission to Travel and Tourism courses at the undergraduate level is, higher secondary examination pass. Job Prospectus: Job prospectus both in public and private sector's, are bright. However, the best prospectus for qualified tourism professionals are in the private sector with travel agencies, tour operators, airlines, hotels, transport and cargo companies etc.

Remuneration : Jobs in the travel and tourism industry offer good remuneration and perquisites, which include free travel for employees and their families. Salaries can vary somewhat within the industry and are higher in foreign airlines and agencies.

Travel and Tourism Competitiveness

The *Travel and Tourism Competitiveness Report* was first published in 2007 by the World Economic Forum. The 2007 report covered 124 major and emerging economies.

The 2008 report covered 130 countries, and the 2009 report expanded to 133 countries. The index is a measurement of the factors that make it attractive to develop business in the travel and tourism industry of individual countries, rather than a measure of a country attractiveness as a tourist destination.

The report ranks selected nations according to the Travel and Tourism Competitiveness Index (TTCI), which scores from 1 to 6 the performance of a given country in each specific subindex. The overall index is made of three main subindexes: (1) regulatory framework; (2) business environment and infrastructure; and (3) human, cultural, and natural resources.

The Report also includes a specific Country Profile for each of the nations evaluated, with each of the scores received to estimate its TTCI, and complementary information regarding key economic indicators from the World Bank, and country indicators from the World Travel and Tourism Council.

Variables

For the 2008 index, each of the three main subindexes is made of the scoring of the following 14 variables, called pillars in the TTC Report. Several changes were introduced in the 2008 TTCI in the definition of the variables as compared to the definitions of the 2007 TTCI.

First, the "environmental regulation" pillar was improved with help from the IUCN and the UNWTO, and for the 2008 index was re-named the "environmental sustainability" pillar to *"better reflect its components and to capture the increasingly recognized importance of sustainability in the sector's development."*

Second, the original pillar "natural and cultural resources" was divided into two separate subcomponents: "natural resources" and "cultural resources", thus, allowing to differentiate those countries which do not necessarily have the same strengths or weaknesses in these two different resources.

In general, the model was improved with better data and new concepts were introduced.

Travel and Tourism-related Policy and Business Decision Making

Tourism Infrastructure in India

Tourism plays a vital role in the economic development of a country. Tourism is the second largest foreign exchange earner in India. The tourism industry employs a large number of people, both skilled and unskilled. It promotes national integration and international brotherhood.

India has fascinated people from all over the world with her secularism and her culture. There are historical monuments, beaches, places of religious interests, hill resorts, etc. that attract tourists. Every region is identified with its handicraft, fairs, folk dances, music and its people. The Departments of Tourism promotes international and domestic tourism in the country. The Tourism Advisory Board recommends measures for promotion of tourist traffic in India. Indian tourism is adversely affected by terrorism, tours and pollution. Sincere efforts could help to further develop the Indian tourism industry.

Tourism is one of the fastest growing industries of the world. It plays vital role in the economic development of a country. India is one of the popular tourist destination in Asia. Bounded by the Himalayan ranges in the north and surrounded, on three sides by water (Arabian sea, Bay of Bengal and Indian Ocean), India offers a wide array of places to see and things to do. The enchanting backwaters, hill stations and landscapes make India a beautiful country. Historical monuments, forts etc. add to the grandeur of the country. They attract tourists from all over the world.

Tourism is the second largest foreign exchange earner in India. The tourism industry employs a large number of people, both skilled and unskilled. Hostels, travel agencies, transport including airlines benefit a lot from this industry. Tourism promotes national integration and international understanding. It generates foreign exchange, it promotes cultural activities. Tourism also promotes the traditional handicrafts sector. The tourist gets an insight into the rich and diverse cultural heritage of India.

India has a composite culture. There is a harmonious blend of art, religion and philosophy. Thought India has been subjected to a serious of invasions, she has retained her originality even after absorbing the best of external influences. Religions like Christianity, Buddhism, Islam, Hinduism, Jainism, Sikhism and Zoroastrianism etc. has co-existed in India. India has fascinated people from all over the world with her secularism and her culture.

The diverse geographical locales of India delight the tourists. The monuments, museums, forts, sanctuaries, places of religious interest, palaces, etc. offer a treat to the eyes. Every region is identified with its handicrafts, fairs, folk dances, music and its people. Some of the places that attract a huge number of tourists are Agra, Jaipur, Jhansi, Hyderabad, Nalanda, Mysore, Delhi, Mahabaleshwar, Aurangabad etc. Hardwar, Ujjain, Shirdi, Varanasi, Allahabad, Puri, Ajmer, Amritsar, Vaishno Devi, Badrinath, Kedarnath, Rameshwaram etc. are places of religious importance. Srinagar, Kullu, Manali, Dehradun, Nainital, Darjeeling, Ooty etc. are famous hill resorts.

The Department of Tourism was formed to promote international and domestic tourism in the country. It provides infrastructure and carries out publicity campaigns. It provides information aimed at promotion of tourist sites in the world market. It formulates policies and programmes for the promotion of tourism in India. It has officers in India and abroad. The Indian Institute of Tourism and Travel Management, The National Council for Hotel management and Catering technology etc. provide professionally trained personnel to the industry.

The Tourism Advisory Board recommends measures for promotion of tourist traffic in India. It reviews the tourist trends and suggests appropriate measures. Some of the places, havelis and castles have been converted into heritage hotels. In these hotels, the tourists get the experience the exotic lifestyle of the bygone era. The exotic train 'palace on wheel's which travels through Rajasthan attracts a lot of foreign tourists. The Indian Tourism Development Corporation (ITDC) organizes entertainment programmes like folk dances and songs and provides shopping facilities. Today many private companies like Sita Travels, Club Mahindra etc. arrange domestic as well as foreign tours.

With the growth of urban professional middle class, the tourism in India is flourishing, Many states have taken necessary steps to promote tourism. Goa promotes water sports like sailing, scuba diving and rafting. Kashmir offers the pleasure of winter sports like skiing and mountaineering. Kerala has introduced the concept of houseboats in its lagoons. Himachal Pradesh has developed winter sports in the state. In 2005 The Indian Tourism Development Corporation (ITDC) stared a campaign called 'Incredible India' to encourage tourism in India. For a better growth, the department divided different places in different section like 'spiritual tourism,' 'spa tourism', 'Eco-tourism' and 'adventure tourism'. Things have now started looking bright for the Indian tourism industry.

However the Indian tourism industry has been hit by pollution. The effluents emitted by the Mathura Refinery has led to the decolonization of the Taj Mahal in Agra. The condition of many or our monuments is deteriorating due to the negligence of the concerned authorities. On the other hand, beaches have become the dumping grounds of garbage and waste left by tourists. This nuisance should be properly monitored.

Terrorism nowadays has become a global problem. Our country is also not an exception. The terrorism in Jammu and Kashmir, Maoists attacks in West Bengal and Bihar, Bodo agitations in north eastern hill areas greatly affect the tourism in our country. Kashmir is the paradise for domestic and international tourists. The terrorism in this valley not only affects the life of the common people but also the tourism, which is very important for the economy of the sate. Necessary steps should be taken by the state government as well as central government to prevent this menace.

The tourist infrastructure in India should be strengthened. Airports and railway stations should provide information to the tourists about the tourist destination. Government owned hotels should be properly managed. The Government should also take steps for the maintenance for the tourist destination. Steps should be taken to restore the ancient splendour of the monuments. Sincere efforts could help to further develop the Indian tourism industry.

Medical Tourism

Today India is emerging as a favoured place of medal treatment. Our country has witnessed a remarkable growth in the service of hospital and well-qualified doctors, which has not only attracted the patient population from neighbouring counties but also from the Middle East and the West.

As the concept of medical tourism continues to gain momentum in India, the Ministry of Health and Family Welfare, with the help of the Ministry of Tourism, is taking numerous initiatives in order to maintain international standards in medical facilities. With some of the best hospitals in the world, Delhi is competing with foreign countries. Even there are countries where critical patients may have to wait for months. But in Delhi, any kind of treatment is available in the shortest possible time.

The cost of treatment is substantially less than those in developed countries. Besides personalized nursing care, Delhi is superb place to rejuvenate. Our country also integrate traditional medical concepts Ayurveda, Unani and Homeopathy with complimentary therapies like Yoga, Acupuncture and Aroma therapies progress the process of healing.

Infrastructure: Key to Accessible Tourism in India

The travel and tourism industry in India is being exposed to the need and opportunity of Accessible Tourism. While this aspect was touched upon in the previous cover story, the important step forward, once the awareness is created, is for the industry to start formulating and implementing plans to tap this segment. However, the moot question which arises is, are we ready to provide services for this particular segment?

The needs of Accessible Tourism, broadly defined as a set of services and facilities for individuals with specific needs that may include the disabled, elderly people, pregnant women, parents with children or people with temporary disabilities, has been voiced by the American Society of Travel Agents (ASTA) India and various Non-Government Organisations (NGOs) like Samartayam (a civic body and National Centre for Accessible Environments), Access Ability (Universal Design and Disability Employment Specialist), Svayam (organisation for people with reduced mobility), National Association of the Blind, etc. These NGOs have been working with civic and government agencies and various other corporate houses to press home the needs of this segment and to create the required infrastructure.

In India, the first step towards Accessible Tourism will involve making public infrastructure accessible to people with reduced mobility.

Hospitality Sector

The Ministry of Tourism (MoT) has listed some amenities for the disabled as criteria in order to obtain four-star or five-star classification for hotels. These include, one room for physically challenged, easily accessible lifts, four-star and above hotels should have bathrooms for physically challenged, ramps with anti-slip floors and handrails at the entrance, wheelchair access with suitable table in at least one restaurant, facilities for visually impaired persons, public rest rooms to have low height urinal (24 inches maximum) and exclusive parking for PwDs near the entrance.

There are no budget hotels that have accessible rooms or supporting infrastructure. MoT will soon make provisions for the two-star and three-star hotels to be accessible as well. However, information is lacking and it is always word of mouth, which the disabled community has to depend on. Hotels with accessible features should provide this information on their websites.

Transport Sector

"Inaccessible railways, road transportation, airways and transit infrastructure is a deterrent not only for travellers with disabilities but also for the elderly, children and travellers with temporary disabilities like a fractured leg or arm, etc. "Indian carriers do not allow two wheelchair travellers to sit together, refuse to take responsibility for the disabled travellers, charge travellers for stretchers and ambulifts and lack in developments like seat numbers in Braille, etc. Such lack of infrastructure can discourage tourists for repeat visits to India.

The Railway Ministry has announced projects for provision of world-class facilities at metro railway stations. The new design concept will have all the Universal Design features in place that will make railway stations accessible to people with reduced mobility. Even local transport like accessible taxi services, trains are needed. However, efforts are being made, though on a small scale and on a private level like Tata Group working with Samarthyam to provide low floor buses in Delhi, Chandigarh, Indore, Ahmedabad and Mumbai

Tourist Sites

"Unfortunately all the tourist attraction sites, as well as historical monuments remain inaccessible to most people with reduced mobility. Historical monuments because of their status of protected monuments under the Archaeological Survey of India were never really considered for incorporating changes to make them accessible to all," stated Kavita Agarwal. Qutab Minar is one of the tourist sites in India which has ramps for tourists on wheelchairs.

"Universal Design is the need of the hour, especially in countries like India. With India on the brink of exponential growth in infrastructure development this is the right time to take up the issues related to barrier free and inclusive public infrastructure and transportation.

The organisations involved in the development of tourism at the Centre are Ministry of Tourism, Indian Institute of Tourism and Travel Management, National Council for Hotel Management and Catering Technology, India Tourism Development Corporation Limited, Indian Institute of Skiing and Mountaineering and National Institute of Water Sports.

The Ministry of Tourism is responsible for formulation and implementation of policies and programmes for the development of tourism within the country and for attracting foreign tourists to India by way of developing tourism infrastructure, publicity and promotion, dissemination of information, coordination and supervision of activities of various segments of industry such as hotels, travel agencies, tour operators, etc.

There are 20 field offices of the Ministry of Tourism in India and 13 in other countries to undertake both developmental and promotional activities. While the overseas offices are in constant contact with tourists, travel intermediaries and media to promote tourism in India, the field offices in India provide facilitation services to tourists and coordinate with the State Governments on tourism infrastructural development. The main objectives of the overseas tourist offices are to position India in the tourism generating markets as a preferred tourism destination, to promote various Indian tourism products vis-a-vis competition faced from various destinations and to increase India's share of the global tourism market. These objectives are met through an integrated marketing strategy and synergised promotional activities undertaken in association with the Travel Trade and State Governments.

India Tourism Development Corporation Development Limited

India Tourism Development Corporation (ITDC) came into existence in October 1966 with the objective of developing and expanding tourism infrastructure in the country and thereby promoting India as a tourist destination. Working on the philosophy of public sector, ITDC succeeded in achieving its objectives by promoting the largest hotel chain in India and providing all tourist services, i.e. accommodation, catering, transport, in-house travel agency, duty free shopping, entertainment, publicity, consultancy, etc., under a single window. It also offers consultancy services from concept to commissioning in the tourism field both for private as well as public sector.

In pursuance of the disinvestment policy of the Government, 18 hotels have been disinvested. Keeping in view the changed scenario, the Corporation has suitably been restructured so that it continues to fulfil its original mandate for tourism development in the country. Besides consolidating and expanding its existing business areas, ITDC has made diversification into new avenues/ innovative services like full-fledged money changer services and Western Union Money Transfer, Training Consultancy in hospitality sector, event management and consultancy and execution of tourism and engineering projects.

India Tourism Development Corporation (ITDC) came into existence in October 1966 with the objective of developing and expanding tourism infrastructure in the country and thereby promoting India as a tourist destination. Working on the philosophy of public sector, ITDC succeeded in achieving its objectives by promoting the largest hotel chain in India and providing all tourist services, i.e. Accommodation, Catering, Transport, in-house Travel Agency, Duty Free Shopping, Entertainment, Publicity, Consultancy, etc., under a single window. It also offers consultancy services from concept to commissioning in the tourism field both for private as well as public sector.

In pursuance of the disinvestment policy of the Government, 18 hotels have been disinvested. Keeping in view the changed scenario, the Corporation has suitably been restructured so that it continues to fulfil its original mandate for tourism development in the country. Besides consolidating and expanding its existing business areas, ITDC has made diversification into new avenues/ innovative services like full-fledged Money Changer Services and Western Union Money Transfer, Training Consultancy in hospitality sector, event management and consultancy and execution of tourism and engineering projects.

ITDC has been a pioneering tourism organisation which provides all the tourist services/facilities under one roof. ITDC's present network consists of 8 Ashok Group Hotels, 7 Joint Venture Hotels including one under construction, two Restaurants (including one Airport Restaurant), 13 Transport Units, 1 Tourist Service Station, 37 Duty Free Shops at International as well as Domestic Custom Airports, 1 Tax Free outlet, 1 Sound & Light Show and 4 Catering Outlets. Besides, ITDC is also managing a Hotel at Bharatpur and a Tourist Complex at Kosi and a SEL show at Sabarmati, Ahmedabad owned by the Department of Tourism.

The Ashok International Trade Division of ITDC offers world class duty free shopping facilities to international travellers at its 38 outlets, earning crucial foreign exchange for the country and showcasing Indian products to the world.

The Ashok Travels and Tours (ATT) handles work relating to Domestic/International ticketing, hotel booking and tour packages, car and coach rentals, money changing services, money transfer services, overseas insurance and organizing exhibitions.

The Ashok Reservation and Marketing Services (ARMS) Division of ITDC, which is mainly responsible for marketing of Ashok Group of Hotels, participated in national/international events like ITB Berlin to ensure direct interaction with Foreign Tour Operators to promote various services of ITDC.

The Ashok Institute of Hospitality & Tourism Management (AIH&TM) of ITDC has been associated with the pioneering efforts in human resource development for more than three decades. Awarded the ISO-9001-2000 Certification, the institute conducts 18 months Craft/Certificate courses in the field of Culinary Skill Development, besides providing training to management trainees/ apprentices and organising Executive Development programmes for the officials of ITDC. Under an MOU signed with the prestigious Kurukshetra University, the AIH&TM started 4-year Bachelor's Degree Course in International Hospitality Business Management from August 2004.

Hotel Management and Food Craft Institutes

The Ministry of Tourism has accorded high priority to the development of manpower to meet the growing needs of Hotels, Restaurants and other Hospitality-based Industries. For this purpose, 21 Institutes of Hotel Management and Catering Technology and 10 Food Craft Institutes (3 of these are now also State IHMS) have been set up in the country. In addition to the above, four more Institutes of Hotel Management are in the pipeline at Uttarakhand (Dehradun), Jharkhand (Jamshedpur), Chhattisgarh (Raipur) and Haryana (Kurukshetra). These Institutes conduct Degree courses in the field of Hotel Management, Catering Technology and Applied Nutrition and Craft Courses in Food and Beverage Services, Accommodation Operations, Dietetics and Hospital Food Service, Food Production and Patisserie, House Keeping, Front Office, etc. IHM's Mumbai, Bangalore and Pusa (New Delhi) have started 2 Years M.Sc Hospitality courses also. Food Craft Institutes conduct Craft Courses for duration ranging from six months to one year for operational staff. All these training Institutes are affiliated to the National Council for Hotel Management Catering Technology and Applied Nutrition (NCHMCT) at apex level which regulates academics for all these Institutes.

Capacity Building for Service Providers (CBSP)

In the year 2002, the Ministry launched a programme called CBSP to train the persons engaged in small hotels, dhabas, eating joints, restaurants, etc., and also handling tourists like Immigration staff, airport staff, security/Police personnel, guides, taxi operators, bus drivers, etc. The objective was to provide short term training to improve their etiquette, behaviour and attitude towards tourists.

The scope of this scheme has been further enlarged and the training programmes of 3/6 months duration have been added for skill development of existing as well as fresh service providers.

Under this scheme, a new programme called 'Project Priyadarshini' was also launched in 2005 aimed at imparting training to women in taxi driving/operation, entrepreneurship like setting up souvenir kiosks, etc, to adopt tourism as their profession.

Hotel Accommodation

The hotel sector forms one of the most important segments of the tourism industry with high potential for employment generation and foreign exchange earnings. To give impetus to this sector, the government provides concessions under EXIM Policy and other incentives. The Industrial Policy has now placed hotels and tourism related activities as a priority industry. Foreign investment and collaborations are now facilitated under the new economic policy. Automatic approval is available for foreign direct investment upto 100 per cent in Hotel and Tourism sector.

Travel Trade

The Department of Tourism has a scheme of approving Travel Agents, Tour Operators, Adventure Tour Operators and Tourist Transport Operators. During 2005, keeping in view the spurt in Domestic Tourism, a new category for the recognition of Domestic Tour Operators has been introduced. The aims and objectives of this scheme are to encourage quality, standard and service in these categories so as to promote tourism in India. The Travel Trade Division also interacts with the travel trade associations like Travel Agents Association of India (TAAI), Indian Association of Tour Operators (IATO), Indian Tourist Transport Operators Associations,(ITTA), etc., and other agencies like India Convention Promotion Bureau, Pacific Asia Travel Association (PATA), etc.

The Travel Trade Division also deals with all matters pertaining to the regulation and training of tourist guides at Regional level and also co-ordinates with other Ministries such as Civil Aviation, Culture, Railways, Surface Transport, External Affairs and Home Affairs on various issues to improve the facilities for the tourists visiting various destinations in India.

Celebration of Various Tourism Events

A number of events and road shows have been organised during 2005-06 for spreading awareness about India Tourism in domestic and international tourism market to attract more tourists to India. The major events organised by the Ministry in collaboration with various State Tourism Departments are: Golf open tournament, Srinagar; Sindhu Darshan at Leh; Heritage Festival, New Delhi; All India Crafts Mela, Hyderabad; Heritage International Festival, Jaipur; India International Boat Show, Kochi; Paragliding Show and Tourism Conclave in Himachal Pradesh; Mega Folk Festival "Virasat" in Dehradun; Prithivi 05-Global Eco-Meet, Kochi; Domestic and International Photo Exhibition "A Confluence of Cultures" and Essay and Photographic competition on "What Tourism Means To Me" on World Tourism Day on 27 September (every year); India National Tourism Day on 17 March 2006; Designer's Night Bazar, Surajkund Crafts Mela, Haryana; 3 Global Interline Golf Championship, Photo Exhibition, Eco-Tourism Marketing Meet; Mussorie (Uttarakhand), WTTC, Himalayan Run and Trek and Photo Exhibition on Hindu, Buddhist and Islamic monuments of Kashmir.

The Ministry of Tourism also participated in various travel and tourism events, trade fairs and exhibitions in India and abroad. The important fairs and exhibitions are Tourism Travel Fair in New Delhi, Mumbai, Bangaluru, Chennai and SATTE (South Asia Tourism and Travel Expo), New Delhi.

India Tourism offices located in 20 cities in India also participated at local important fairs. The Ministry of Tourism participated in several overseas travel and tourism trade fairs, notably World Travel Market, London; ITB (International Tourism Bourse), Berlin; Arabian Travel Market (ATM), Dubai; EIBTM, Spain; IMEX, Frankfurt; Pata Travel Mart, Malaysia; FITUR, Spain; and World Travel Fair, Shanghai.

India Tourism offices located in 13 overseas cities also participated in various travel and tourism fairs.

National Tourism Policy 2002

A National Tourism Policy-2002 was announced by the Government with, inter-alia attempts to position India as a global brand to take advantage of the burgeoning global travel and trade and the vast untapped potential of India as a destination.

Tourism in 10th Five Year Plan

In order to further accelerate the development of tourism in the country, the thrusts during the 10th Five Year Plan has been to:

Position Tourism as a Major Engine of Economic Growth

Harness the direct and multiplier effects of tourism for employment generation and economic development

Provide Impetus to Rural Tourism

Provide a major thrust to domestic tourism which will act as a spring board for growth and expansion of international tourism

Position India as a global brand to take advantage of the burgeoning global travel and trade and the vast untapped potential of India as a destination

Acknowledge the critical role of private sector with government working as an active facilitator and catalyst

Create and develop integrated tourism circuits based on India's unique civilisation, heritage and culture in partnership with states, private sector and other agencies

Ensure that the tourist to India gets physically invigorated, mentally rejuvenated, culturally enriched, spiritually elevated and "feels India within him".

By 2020, Tourism in India could Contribute Rs 8,50,000 Crores to the GDP

In other words, every man, woman and child could become richer by Rs 7,000. India has yet to realise its full potential from tourism. The Travel and Tourism industry holds tremendous potential for India's economy. It can provide impetus to other industries, create millions of new jobs and generate enough wealth to help pay off the international debt. That is why we have included Tourism amongst the Core Sectors of the Indian Economy.

Incredible India !

India is probably the only country that offers various categories of tourism. These include history tourism, adventure tourism, medical tourism (ayurveda and other forms of Indian medications), spiritual tourism, beach tourism (India has the longest coastline in the East) etc.

Explore India-choose the locales of your choice, and see what each state has to offer. Lose yourself in the wonder that is India. Meander through lands steeped in chivalry and pageantry that begin before recorded history. Explore modern cities that have grown organically from the roots of a multi-hued past. Make a pilgrimage to holy shrines that echo with tales of antiquity. Frolic on a vast array of golden beaches that dot an enviable coastline, washed by two seas and an ocean. Sport with adventure in style. Let the jungle lure you to a fascinating world at a diverse array of wildlife sanctuaries and national parks....... this is the wonder that is India.

India on the World Map

The Indian tourism industry has not had it so good since the early 1990s. Though the India economy had slowed, it was still growing faster than the rest of the world. In 2009, the country is seen rising 6.5 percent, compared to the world output, which is seen falling 0.4 percent. With Indian economy growing at around 7% per annum and rise in disposable incomes of Indians, an increasing number of people are going on holiday trips within the country and abroad resulting in the tourism industry growing wings.

It is fast turning into a volume game where an ever-burgeoning number of participants are pushing up revenues of industry players (hotels, tour operators, airlines, shipping lines, etc). Thus, the tourism sector is expected to perform very well in future and the industry offers an interesting investment opportunity for long-term investors.

The Indian tourism sector is seen generating $42.8 billion by 2017, a 42 percent surge from 2007, according to an industry research note by auditing and consulting firm Deloitte Touche. Despite the challenges being faced in terms of a slowing economy, sluggish demand and security concerns, the country was fighting back and tourism developments were taking place, it said." Although there will inevitably be some short-to medium-term set backs, the long-term outlook remains positive," it said." Despite the deepening world economic crisis, India's economy remains in decent shape and is still experiencing some of the strongest growth rates in the world," the Deloitte report said.

Despite the numerous problems, tourism industry was the second-largest foreign exchange earner for India. Realising the potential in India, international and domestic hotel chains were rushing to cash in on it. According to the global authority for hotel real estate, Lodging Econometrics, there were 73,793 hotel rooms in the pipeline of which 11,207 were due to open in 2009 and 22,522 in 2010, it said.

International tourists account for a little over 5 million visitors, while domestic market is seen at more than 500 million. Limited infrastructure pose a constraint to the free flow of tourists, but the Indian government is addressing the issue through upgradation of existing airports and building new ones.

Medical tourism was poised for rapid development in the future and India is busy developing first-class facilities to attract this multi-billion dollar niche market. The government has already relaxed the criteria to receive a visa for medical tourism.

It is also considering other incentives such as offering air travel and accommodation for foreign tourists who visit India for the third time. It may also pick up the bill for tour operators promoting domestic and medical tourism and is mulling income tax exemption for hoteliers if they invest 50 percent of profits into infrastructure. Tourist arrivals in the country slowed throughout 2008, after rising 13 percent year-on-year from 2005-2007, due to a slowdown in the main source markets for India, the U.S. and U.K., which account for more than 15 percent of all inbound tourists.

India : An Idea who's Time has Come

Conde Nast ranked her amongst the top 10 tourist destinations. JBIC ranked her as the fifth most attractive investment destination. The World Social Forum, AdAsia, World Bamboo Congress, Commonwealth Games, Laureus World Sports Academy Global Submit, F1 alongwith some of the biggest expos and conferences of the world chose her to play host.

Presenting India to you Readers. The subcontinent to whose splendour, diversity and world-class facilities the world has finally woken up to. Away from threats, untouched by SARS and politically stable India is the flavor of the season. Take a fresh look at her flourishing economy (double digit growth in third quarter of 2003-2004), geographically strategic location, faith fortified by major software firms to make it a global backup hub for software, the staggering figure of over 366 national/international level expos and about 100 congress already scheduled for leap year 2004 (of which over 50 in January alone), her forex reserves, her rising Sensex, rapidly growing consumer markets, presence of world's finest and choicest brands and the exceptional growth in interest from FIIs, to understand why India offers a feel good factor. Truly, India is one of the most exciting emerging markets in the world.

The Scene Till Now

Some major international events like 9/11, US-led war against terror and SARS hit the tourism industry over the past few years. Cutting down of routes by domestic airlines and increase in airfares last year also led to a fall in the movement of people in the country. The Mumbai terror attacks, targetting two premium hotels, also tarnished the country's reputation, drastically reducing hotel occupancy levels, and affecting year-end travel. The adverse travel advisories by many countries to their citizens too contributed to a significant slowdown in tourism in India.

There were other negatives too. Consider this-Expenses per night of stay for a tourist in India during the SE Asian currency crisis was $100 whereas it was around $35-40 in the SE Asian countries. This hurt Indian tourism. Though this discrepancy has come down, still there is some gap. Some of the reasons for this are high luxury and entertainment taxes and high landing charges applicable in Indian airports.

Costs are also high because tourism is a state subject. Each state separately spends on tourism and tourism related activities, whereas if these funds were spent in a cohesive manner by a nodal agency to showcase the entire country as one destination, the results would probably have been far more spectacular. Currently, the centre is only allocating finances for tourism projects. But the government is trying to convince states on the benefits of bringing tourism under the aegis of the Central government on to the concurrent subject on to the concurrent list.

Government Policy Initiatives

Keenly aware of the unfolding boom in the tourism industry, the government is lending a hand to the growth of the industry. In the Union Budget for 2003-04, government has extended infrastructure status to tourism, thus opening the doors to cheap, long-term funds to help finance tourism infrastructure.

Outlay for tourism for the Tenth Five Year Plan is Rs. 2900 Crore. For the financial year 2003-04 the outlay is Rs 325 crore. This is up sharply from Rs 150 crore allocated in the previous financial year. State governments such as Kerala lay a lot of stress on boosting tourism. The state has an outlay of Rs. 74.25 crore for the financial year 2003-04.

The Government of India has extended the benefits of Section of the Income Tax Act, 1961 to institutions financing hotels of three-star category and above. A top level executive of Travel Finance Corporation of India (TFCI) is all smiles as he says, "This has benefited TFCI as the company has a major part of its portfolio in the exempted category." And this smile is now strongly percolating down to all tourism industry players in the country.

The divestment of government's stake in government run hotels is another step in the right direction. Professionals are increasingly stepping in to take over this service-oriented industry. Global best practices, cost cuts and service with a smile are fast turning a norm.

Going Forward-Destination India

India is now chalking up one of its strongest growth charts in a long time. As the Indian economy continues to open up in an effort to integrate with the world economy, benefits of doing business with and in India are increasing. With the results, hundreds of thousands of jobs are moving to the Indian shores from the West. This brings in its wake transit travellers, business travellers, business meets and holiday seekers. This is resulting in greater room occupancies and average room revenues (ARRs) in the country. ARRs have moved up from Rs. 3200-3400 last year to Rs 4000-4200 this year. Room occupancy rates have shot up from 75-80% in 2002 to over 90% now. Infact, in Bangalore it is now estimated at 100%.

International Tourism in India

Tourist Arrivals on Track for Target

Data released by India's Ministry of Tourism in November 2008 indicate that foreign vistitor arrivalscontinued to grow strongly in the first 10 months of the year, despite the slowing global economy. Intotal, 4.32 million visitors arrived in India between January and October, up by 9.4% y-o-y. This was also positive for foreign exchange earnings, which rose by a higher 17.1% y-o-y to total INR40,712 crore overthe period.

This growth rate represents a slight slowdown from double digit arrivals growth in the first two quartersof the year. However, given the global economic slowdown and the regional diversion effect of the Beijing Olympics in August, we view growth of 9.4% y-o-y as highly positive. Indeed, given that tourism arrivals within the region as a whole are beginning to slow, it is encouraging that India continues to post such strong sector growth. We view this relative resilience as the result of long-established links between India and its chief tourism markets, the US and the UK. In addition, visits by Indian nationals living abroad, which traditionally spike during the Western hemisphere summer season, have also offered support to arrivals figures. As such, we remain positive regarding the prospects for full-year growth, and maintain our forecast for arrivals of 5.2 million. Looking ahead, we expect tourist arrivals to continue tomoderate in 2009, as the global economic slowdown weighs on the global travel and tourism industry.

However, we expect India to continue to be one of the top global performers, with sector growth likely toremain one of the highest in the Asia-Pacific region.

India Focuses on Cruise Sector Potential

The government is seeking to encourage stronger growth in the cruise sector, in order to exploit the potential of India's long coastline. Tourism Secretary Shilabhadra Banerjee announced that the government is targeting stop-off arrivals of 10 million by 2010. Banerjee added that achieving this targetwould imply an inflow of US$9 billion in revenue, and the creation of 15 million new jobs. While this target appears somewhat optimistic, especially given the deteriorating global tourism environment, boosting India's cruise sector would offer valuable support to the industry. India has avaried and extensive coastline, which to date has not been exploited in terms of cruise potential. As such, the government has stated that it will seek to improve cruise infrastructure, encouraging a diversification from concentration on cargo ports to those more oriented towards tourism. As part of this plan, it will setup cruise terminals at Chennai, Mumbai, Goa and Kochi, and reform the tax on bunkers systems to provide more incentives for investment in the cruise industry.

International Tourism in India

Strategic Significance, Gaps and Vulnerabilities

India initiated economic reforms as an aftermath of a serious foreign exchange crisis. The number and the pace of reforms have been increasing ever since. The scope of external liberalization has increased many-fold in several fields, with difficult with drawl conditions under WTO agreements. Despite all these efforts, the Balance of Trade continues to be adverse, and so is the case with balance in the current account, if the private transfers were not supporting the same. Even then the Balance of Payment position can not be said to be satisfactory, if one takes into account the transfers in capital account and the external debt position, the latter having crossed U.S. $ 100 billion mark in the year 2002.

The importance of it for India can be realised from the fact that a 2.5% share in even one year can wipe off India's total external debt and an increase by 0.25% share can more than off set the adverse balance of trade, and ease foreign exchange pressure on the economy.

If India wishes to negotiate and open Tourism sector further to benefit from the international tourism business, it has to think strategically and gear up internally to develop appropriate physical, human resource, and other organisational infrastructure in an integrated manner, which can meet the varied needs of international tourists. Failing this, if the tourism sector is opened further for the external players, India may become only a minor tool in the value creation process in the international tourism business in India. It must prepare for playing the role of the main player, who not only helps in enhancing the value creation, but also captures and controls the value created. The major benefits otherwise would be captured by other international players.

To understand the strategic gaps and vulnerability, it is necessary to revisit three basic concepts, the concepts of (tourism) business, strategic management and value creation, value capture and value control in the (tourism) business.

Needless to add, tourists do not go to destination to gain theoretical or visual knowledge of it; which they can do even by being at their place, thanks to technological development in the present internet era. They come to experience it, personally, in the total setting. In this context the *arrangements of foods, stay (and travel) too can add to* attractiveness, if they are unique, tasty (comfortable) and hygienic (safe and affordable). It may be noted that *as the distance between the place of origin and the* destination (place of interest) increases, tourist tends to visit larger number of sites/spend larger number of day to maximise satisfaction from *the amount of money and time spent*. It is rare for an international tourist to come and see just one place, spending thousands of rupees (equivalent) and several days in travel. *He then starts seeking package* of places of interest. Packages are sought not only in terms of sites, but also services (stay, food and travel etc.), cities/ states and groups of people to enhance pleasure together and guard against lack of familiarity.

There are *other needs too, which are not easily realised* such as availability of necessary amount of money as and where required. The tourist needs to know the details of the site, its attractiveness *as well definitiveness and the ease of making arrangements* for travel, stay and food. Over and above this, the requirements of certainty, reliability and prompt information about *disturbance causing events also assume significance for him*. An additional demand arises on account of differences in languages. The above *does not purport to be a comprehensive and exhaustive, but* only an indicative list of all the needs of tourists emanating from different origins and conveys the variation in the nature and magnitude of requires *as the distance between place of origin and destination increases.* These need to be elaborated and prioritized through research studies.

The significance of the above *discussion lies in the fact that these* requirements of the tourists get determined by the definition of target in *terms of place of origin and the demographic variables of tourists.* The requirements of tourist from Kenya would be different from those of Sweden, the requirements of senior citizens as tourists would be different from the adolescents. *The preparation required to be made for attracting* tourists and catering to their needs at the destination may go haywire, if *the customer requirements are not properly defined before hand.*

The *uniqueness of tourism business lies in the fact that it is not a single* service, but involves a large variety of different, exclusive and specialized *services,* which can be provided by different group catering to hospitality, transport and travel, unique, attractive site etc. *There is thus, an additional task or business: that of integration of these services.* For example, the tourist would like to know about the places he may like visit, and as he goes to decide it, he wants whether accommodation and travel reservation within his budget are possible and if so, could he have them confirmed. Any loose link in the entire value chain of services needed by him, may jeopardize his plan and pleasure. *He is willing to pay the price for the role of integrator is ensuring certainty and reliability.* The *success of tourism business perhaps depends as much, if not more, on this integration aspect,* as the quality and variety of the specialized saves of transport, accommodation etc.

Value Creation, Value Capture and Value Control in Tourism

Business

The value chain of tourism business starts from the activity of identifying the customer, presenting them the attractiveness of destination in an interactive manner, helping him in travel, accommodation & other reservations, helping in money transfer etc, and actually taking to and entertaining him at the destination site, besides taking care at nodal, transit points. The total money spent by a tourist is the total value created in the tourism business. Income from impulse purchases like specialities, memoirs etc. and *all other money spent by him on account of his "pleasure travel" constitute the total value added* in the tourism business.

The sharing or capture of the total value created by different service providers depends not only upon the absolute quality of service provided by individual supplier, but their ability to control it. It is much the same way as in the case of computer hardware sales. Out of a total price of a PC say Rs. 40,000, half of it is captured by the supplier of processors and mother board etc. With every effort to assemble and sell a PC, the sale of processor is assured. Though a high amount of efforts are required to assemble and sell PCs, the major value is captured by processor supplier and it can strategically control the entire sales.

The same may turnout to be the case of Tourism also if due care is not taken to develop adequate safeguards measures when the sector is opened for the foreign players. Further discussion on the issue is deferred to a later section.

Strategic Management

The concept of strategic management can help in analysis of strategic gaps with reference to management of International Tourism in India. Strategic Management can be understood by looking at the types of managerial decisions. Ansoff has classified the organisational decisions into three broad categories; namely, the strategic, the administrative and the operating decisions. The strategic decisions (covered under strategy formulation) are concerned with the issue of setting the direction in which the organisation will move or the course that the organisation would follow in the future. These cover the decisions regarding the organisation's mission, objectives and the strategies (i.e., the product/ market scope).

The administrative decisions (commonly referred to as strategy implementation), on the other and relate to the task of gearing, up the existing setup i.e., physical, human and organisational infrastructure to meet the requirement of business/operations in the future. Typically they cover such issues as the resource allocation, changes in the organisational structure, systems, skills technology, organisation culture and key functional policies. Taken together they cover the entire scope of strategic management function. Finally, there are operating decisions concerning various transactions or the actual operations. Strategic management deals with decisions that fall in the strategic and administrative decision categories mentioned above. Strategic management may be defined as a stream of decisions and actions which lead to the development of effective strategy or strategies to help achieve corporate objectives.

Strategic management may thus be called as a process by which the top management determines the long term direction and performance of organisation, by ensuring that careful formulation, proper implementation and continuous evaluation of strategy takes place.

It is necessary here to explain the concept of corporate strategy. Corporate strategy can be defined as "a statement of organisation mission, objectives, strategy, policies and major plans and programmes of actions, described in a way that conveys what business we are in and why are we in this business". This definition brings out the need for organisational clarity about the mission, objectives and strategies, to integrate or unify the organisational efforts. Corporate strategy may, thus, be understood as the outcome of strategic formulation process.

The Strategic Gaps

Gaps in the Concept of Business

As mentioned earlier, the strategic management forces the management to be clear on what business an organisation is in. Strategic management concerns with two significant discussions related to a future of an organisation. These are:

(i) What business the organisation would be in the future (in terms of produces market scope) and why?

(ii) How it proposes to gear up to meet the requirements of physical infrastructures, human resources (skills, style etc.) and organisational resources (structures, systems, shared values etc.) of the future business?

As elaborated in an earlier section, the value system of tourism industry tends to encompasses all the services required from the place of origin of the international tourist to the destination. The total gamut of services that need to be provided can be broadly classified into two categories.

A. Promotional and developmental (to induce, attract bring tourists from his place of origin to the state of destination).

B. To cater to his requirements once they reach the place, to help them gain memorable experience of the visit.

The *first major strategic gap that is stunning one, is observed in the concept of business itself.* At present, the country seems to be geared only for entertaining the international tourists on their arrival, focusing on activities related to "B" part mentioned above, *rather than focusing equally* on inducing and attracting international tourist to India.

A visit to tourist developments corporations will reveal the glaring nature of this gap. An international tourist can not know and get the services *relating to "A" part from the place of his origin.* The websites of different tourist corporation are not integrated even for information, leave alone providing other services, like booking/reservation of accommodation, air/rail ticketing etc. Each website seems to be quite independent of other and does not provide information in an integrated, building block manner.

Customer Segmentation Gaps

The international tourists are taken as a homogeneous group. The word "international" is thus used loosely rather than identifying and focusing on different geographic and demographic segments to develop appropriate infrastructure to uniquely meet the requirements of different tourists segments. This is exemplified by the publicity material that is available in English Hindi or other vernacular language which can not meet the requirements of a nature German, Swiss, French, Italian, Spanish Swede, Dutch or other European tourists. *One may be surprised to learn that the* hotels, reservation and such other agencies may not even know from where is the potential market, USA, Europe, Japan, Kenya or Singapore. A knowledge of the fact that the biggest chunk in the international tourism is constituted by European tourists, may considerably help in sharpening and focusing strategy. Efforts are made to design Buddha Circuit, Taj Circuit etc. But these may not be items of common/ equal level of interest to international tourist from Japan and Europe. Same is the case of lack of understanding about their demographic patterns. For example, there seems to be no cognition of the fact that there are different segments by age group and that the requirements of each age group is different.

Lack of Clarity on Objectives

The individual services providers like hotels, airlines etc. cater to tourist alright, but they can not be sure of attracting them because all by themselves they can not determine it. The tourism development corporations were expected to do the job. *But a typical list of objectives would indicate that* they had various activities listed to entertain the tourist ones they come to *country.* There is no mention that they wish to earn foreign exchange and bring more tourists from different parts of the globe. They thus reduce themselves to play the role of individual service provider, concerned primary with increase in their capacity utilisation through variety of customers, rather than gearing up to bring the international tourists here.

Gap in Integration Value Chain Activities

The essence of strategic management is not only futuristic but also ensuring integration; ensuring that the requirement of infrastructures and operations for international tourism in India are properly taken care of. Presently there seem to be lot of gaps in the inter-linkages between various services. *The* hospitality industry (hotels etc.) treat tourism more as an as add on *activity.* The local site seeing is some what better connected in physical terms, but *there is little standardisation and assurance of quality of service.* The international money transfer facility is not provided by any domestic agency. *The list of certified hotels and guest houses is not available to the* tourists except though foreign travel agencies There is little or no interconnectivity *across various service providers and across the states.* The international tourist has to decide various arrangements before commencement of journey. But at present an international tourist *may not* even know about tourist facilities available at different sites, directly from *any domestic, Indian travel agent and other players*. He has to reach the country before he decides finer details.

There is no integrated system to system to let international tourist get successive levels of information. There is no single agency to take care of missing links and ensure integration of various services as a cohesive whole, rather than presenting services in a fragmented manner.

Objectives of A State Tourism Development Corporation

- To promote, take over, develop, start, purchase, construct, take on lease, maintain, manage and operate hotels, restaurants, motels, travellers' lodges, guest houses and other places for the purpose of boarding, lodging and stay of the tourists; canteens, cafeteria, places of tourist interest like wild life sanctuaries, beauty and recreational places like parks, avenues and galleries, handicrafts emporia, establishments, undertaking enterprises and such other activities of any description with a view to develop, facilitate and promote tourism in the stat.
- To enter into any arrangement for taking over any or all of the assets and liabilities of any department of the state government or of the Government of India connected with the development of tourism and in particular as a going concern all or any of the Tourists' Homes/State government Guest Houses/Travellers' bungalows and catering establishments already established and maintained by the state Government or by the Government of India in various places and to run the same with the object of promoting tourism.
- To establish and manage transport units, travel and transport counters, import, purchase, lease and run or otherwise operate buses, coaches, trucks, launches, ropeways, aircraft, helicopters, inland, waterways and other modes of transport and to act as travel agents I for airlines, railways, shipping companies etc.
- To provide, arrange or conduct entertainment for tourists by way of cultural shows, dances, music concerts, cabarets,

ballets, film shows, sports and games, son-et-lumiere spectacles and others.

- To provide or arrange shopping facilities for tourists, establish or manage shops including duty free shops, emporia and other places for selling travel requisites and other articles of tourist interest.
- To carryon the business of restaurant keepers, wine and spirit merchants, licensed victualers, theatrical agents, box office keepers, concert room proprietors, hotel keepers, dramatic and musical publishers and printers and any other business, which can be carried on in connection with any of those objects as may seem calculated to render profitable any of the company's property and rights for the time being.
- To establish art galleries for the exhibition of paintings, engravings, sculptures, jewellery and other works of art and to buy, sell and deal in works of art of all kinds.
- To acquire land and construct, develop and maintain wayside amenities and picnic spots.
- To organise or conduct all inclusive tours by roads, rail, sea, air or otherwise and to enter into agreements for this purpose.

The task of ensuring appropriate integration is not so difficult in the present internet era, But major players who can effectively play the role of *integrator* such as State Bank of India, Bank of Baroda, etc. who have large network of branches both in India and abroad and also have close interaction with railways, airways, hotels etc. for other businesses, *are feeling shy of entering the tourism business* and playing critical integrative role and really make tourism a money spinning and foreign exchange earner.

Strategic Vulnerability

The fact that tourism world wide is a U.S.$ 4 trillion business, opens up great opportunity for India to benefit from it in terms of earning foreign exchange and mitigate adverse balance of trade account. *An increase of* 0.25% share in the international tourism business can overcome the pressure of earning foreign exchange that has to be arranged through high interest bearing bonds and deposits, which add to self perpetuating *crisis.*

The potential business may be lost if India does not gear up to bridge the strategic gaps mentioned above. Worse still these potential may be exploited to the hill by the foreign players by bridging the gaps. Despite huge international tourism business in India, the country may not benefit in terms of getting foreign exchange as the same may be appropriated by *them.* The booking of international travel may be done by foreign carriers and exchange and commission associated with transfer of money may be appropriated by the international players like American Express, Thomas Cook etc, using Indian labour only. Even the booking of hotels may be done in foreign country and the foreign exchange may not flow to India. *A big* chunk of total value created in the tourism business in the form of travel, accommodated money transfer, even shopping may be captured by the strong armed multinational player with world wide network and Indian service providers reduced to play only second fiddle.

Some recent *studies show that the country has not gained benefits as expected by opening of Indian economy* in terms of reducing international trade gap, technological capability building and globalization or enhanced global competitiveness and ability to earn foreign exchange on its own. The same may happen in the tourism sector if it opened without necessary ground work.

Action Strategies

International tourism is an *extremely tempting proposition in terms of* potential of business especially foreign exchange earnings, for opening of tourism sector in the next round of negotiations. It may, however, turnout *to be a mirage* if the sector is opened without adequate preparation to gear up the strategic gaps. India currently is not geared to reap the advantage of first movers. Hence must avoid straight jacket opening. *It has to fine tune* this gearing up with speed of opening tourism sector as per the provisions *of negotiations at WTO. It has to carefully examine when and how much* to open through (almost irreversible) specific commitments and what should be limitations put into effect to achieve this fine tuning.

The preparations for exploitation of international tourism business *require* as much attention of the government and industry as of the academicians. The governments need to play the first level integrator role in terms of setting priorities and expectations from the international tourism business. It has to play the role of promoters, persuading different providers (to bridge the gaps), who have not come forward to play the role like the banks. The industry has to *develop mechanisms to ensure strong linkages among various service providers to make it an integrated whole,* rather than behaving like a large number disjointed service providers. The academicians have to *provide strong analytical support through research* studies for identification of missing links in providing various services, *pointing conceptual confusion in mission, objectives and strategies*. In a nutshell the international tourism business has to be considered in its entirety by the three major contributors.

Issues for Future Research

The paper highlights the need for several types of in-depth studies required to gear up for benefiting from the growing international tourism business. Firstly, there is a need for *study of international tourists needs (especially those related to the promotional and developmental aspects* explained in section 3 of the paper) coming from different geographical areas. There is also a need for *studying the appropriateness of existing infrastructure in* light of the needs identified to understand the degree to which the present *infrastructure is adequate or inadequate*. Only the in-depth studies can show whether there is need to focus more on utilisation of infrastructure already created rather than creating new ones. The country has paid a huge price in the race for creating assets in the nineties in various sectors of industry leading to excessive infrastructure created in the industry sector as a whole. The mistake does not need to be repeated once again in this sector. There is also a need for validating the *strategic gaps identified in the concept of business*. This will help in identifying to what extent the thrust of tourism strategy in India has been a lopsided one; focusing mainly on entertaining the international tourists who have come to India vs. bringing them to India and its different states. *Studies are also required to ascertain* the nature and level of efforts and investment required for bringing the *international tourists to India.*

Further, *studies are also required to clarify* the strategic focus of tourism industry; how much domestic and how much international tourism and why?

Studies are also required to clarify the assumption of considering all the *international tourists as a homogeneous group*. Are there demographic segments that can help in designing the infrastructure in a better manner to meet specific and varied requirements of different segments?

There is yet another set of studies required to *identify the missing links in* the tourism business at the country, state and city level that need to be *taken care of*? There is also a need for ascertaining *whether tourism in* general, and international tourism in particular, is being consider as an integrated business or an assortment of hospitality, entertainment and *travel businesses by various players in the field*. If so, what is the consequence of it in terms of loss of tourism business in general, and international tourism business in India, in particular.

Last but not the least, there is a need for studies to understand *how much of* the value created in the international tourism in India is being captured and retained (especially the foreign currency part) in India and how much of it is captured and repatriated out of India by the international players. This is important as if due care is not taken then India may not benefit in terms of foreign exchange earning from this lucrative sector, what is a key consideration in negotiation at WTO for opening this sector.

2

Destination Image Promotions

Introduction

The unprecedented growth in the tourism industry during the last fifty years has created major challenges in tourism marketing. As more and more areas of the world are developed for tourism, the destination choices available to consumers continue to expand. Furthermore, today's consumers, facilitated by increased leisure time, rising levels of disposable income and more efficient transportation networks, have the means to choose from among this much larger variety of destinations. As a result, tourism marketers are now faced with influencing consumer decision making in an increasingly complex and competitive global marketplace.

One of the most significant marketing challenges arising from this situation is the need for an effective destination positioning strategy. In order to be successfully promoted in the targeted markets, a destination must be favourably differentiated from its competition, or positively positioned, in the minds of the consumers. A key component of this positioning process is the creation and management of a distinctive and appealing perception, or image, of the destination.

Tourism has been long accepted as an economic activity of attracting tourists and catering to their needs, which has rapidly grown into the world's largest industry and surpassing other important sectors such as automobiles, steel, agriculture and so forth. As demand for tourism increased, more and more areas developed for tourism and the choices of destination available to tourists continue to expand. As a result, destinations compete, and this phenomenon would lead to a fierce competition between tourism destinations. In this case, to be successfully promoted in targeted market, a destination must be favourably differentiated from its competition and has strong image to be positioned in the mind of the tourists. Thus, destination image play an important role in making the tourism destination viable for long-term tourism business Tourists today have to be enticed since the tourism destination is an intensely competitive and many destinations competing with one and another to attract the same potential tourists.

Therefore, a better understanding of destination image is vital in order to develop appropriate marketing strategies that based on tourists' perception and behaviour so that more competitive destinations' products are delivered to current and potential tourists.

The research of destination image can be traced back to the early of 1970s. In this era, images signify a pretesting of the destination which, can be referred as transpose representation of the destination into potential tourist's mind. Natural environment or beautiful beaches are the images held that likely to detract or contribute to the important role in tourism development and this become the concerns of Hunt study. His influential work has been expanding and later, several studies also highlighted the aspect of image and travel behaviour such as Mayo (1973), Gunn (1972), which since then and after 30 years, destination image become the most researched topics in the field of tourism.

Factors that Influencing the Destination Image Formation

The understanding of image formation is a one way to develop a competitive image or good impression of tourist destinations to the market. A positive image of tourist destination is considered as pulling factors among the flood of total impression that attract visitors to the destination. However, there are several types of factors that vital in the destination image formation which is pushing the tourists to the destination. Previous section has explained the importance of variety and types of information sources in image formation. Thus, this section attempts to highlight personal factors which refer to individual's personal characteristics, as well as psychological characteristics which influence destination image formation. On top of that, the differences in tourists' cultural values and past travel experiences are also important factor to be included.

Past Travel Experience

Previous studies have shown a significant effect on what tourist has perceived and acted based on previous experiences. According to Perdue (1985), past travel experience explain the reason why repeat visitors only visit several or specific destination. It is because of specific intention or certain level of knowledge that pulled them to the destination again. On the other hand, first time visitors travelled to more destination and visited more attractions than repeat visitors (Oppermann, 1997).

This was supported by Fakeye and Crompton (1999) study that shows repeat visitors rated attraction-based images significantly higher than first-timer or even the potential tourists. Potential tourists have limited knowledge about the attributes of a particular destination and they have no previous experience, while previous visits affect familiarity with the destination.

For instance, Millman and Pizam (1995) found that individuals with past experience at a destination had a more positive image of the destination, and is more likely to revisit compared with individuals who were aware of, but had never experienced in the destination. They also found that individuals with no awareness of a destination were similar in their intention to visit compared with individuals with some level of destination awareness. This has enlightened that past experience reduces the risk of unfamiliarity of the environment and unsatisfactory experience which in turn result in accepting or rejecting a destination in a choice set.

Destination awareness is about knowledge or how much the tourist knows about the destination product. This term of awareness was used in purchasing and consumption behaviour which reveals whether the consumer has experienced or familiar with the product, and followed by repeat purchase.

In this case, for repeat visitation to be occurred there must lead to a first trial or first visit. Nevertheless, the awareness may not always lead to purchasing behaviour. In other words, information collected by tourists is not necessarily influence their travel behaviour perhaps there are many situational factors that may affect tourists travel behaviour. If satisfaction occurs as the result from the first visit, repeat visitation will follow.

Personal background characteristic, psychological factors and cultural values Every individual is different in nature. Personal characteristic, psychological factors and cultural values do affect the formation of image. The amount of external stimuli which is being exposed to the tourist determines the level of beliefs toward the attributes of the destination. Nevertheless, the internal factors such as sociodemographic characteristics perhaps lead to the various developments of mental picture about the destination, which produces their own version of images prior to individual's needs, motivation, knowledge, preferences and other personal characteristics.

A tourist destination can be described as a combination of services, resources and experiences. The destination image is basically measured through the cognitive-affective dimension which tells what images should be promoted based on what tourist has perceived or preferred. On the other hand, the amount of external stimuli which is being exposed to the tourist as well as, the motivational aspects that took place will initiate the action based on the image preferred.

The development of mental images will be later modified during the actual contact of the destination. As a result, the outcome of the experience affects the overall perception of the destination. This influences the post-decision for the future selection of holiday or visitation whether revisited or rejected.

The proposed theoretical framework identified the process as discussed in the literature. The question remains on how this process being examined as a complete cycle of image preference. This involve before the tourist making visit, during and after visitation as well as, the next process in intention to revisit. Therefore, this paper proposed a theoretical framework that need for further inquiries based on the given phenomenon.

Measures of Physical Attractiveness

Definition

To define a Tourist Attraction is not simple. Here are two definitions:

1. A physical or cultural feature of a particular place that individual travellers or tourists perceive as capable of meeting one or more of their specific leisure-related needs. Such features may be ambient in nature (e.g. climate, culture, vegetation or scenery), or they may be specific to a location, such as a theatre performance, a museum or a waterfall.
2. Positive or favourable attributes of an area for a given activity or set of activities as desired by a given customer or market, including climate, scenery, activities, culture.
   (a) Man made attractions are physical structures (Sydney Harbour Bridge) or events (Olympics).
   (b) Natural attractions are physical phenomena deemed unusual and /or beautiful (Bungle Bungles).
   (c) Secondary attractions have tourist appeal, but are not the primary reason for visiting a location.
   (d) A negative attraction is an attribute of an area that tends to make some customer or market choose not to visit as for example pollution or crime.

Types of Attractions

There are basically two types of attractions:

- Built Attractions.
- Natural Attractions.

In attempting to embrace the core values of these definitions, Tourism Western Australia has developed the following set of essential and desirable recognition criteria for assessing a Tourist Attraction. The use of these criteria will ensure that uniform standards provide a fair and equitable assessment of all Tourist Attractions. A Tourist Attraction will need to meet all of the essential recognition criteria before a recommendation is made to Main

Roads Western Australia or a local government for the erection of appropriate road signs.

Built Attractions – Recognition Criteria

Essential Criteria

Most importantly:

- Tourism must clearly be an important part of the business In addition, the attraction must:
  * Provide a substantive tourist experience in addition to, or part of, the commercial establishment's normal activities.
  * Have all relevant State and Local Government licenses and approvals to operate as a commercial tourist attraction including health, planning, parking and disabled access facilities.
  * Be a member of a recognised local tourism organisation.
  * Be open on weekends and thiee other days of the week including public holidays.
- Clearly display opening times (if not open 7 days):
  * At the entrance to the property or establishment.
  * In brochures and all promotional mediums (advertisements, web sites, etc.).
- Be open at least between 10am and 4pm.
- Produce a leaflet or brochure describing the attraction.
- Be distinctly signed at the property line so that the attraction can be easily identified.
- Be clean and well presented at all times.
- Have clean and conveniently located toilet facilities.

Desirable Criteria

It would be desirable for the attraction to also:

- be open every day.
- be Quality Assured by Tourism Council Western Australia.

- provide a parking area for coaches and caravans.
- keep a record of visitor numbers (e.g. by way of a visitors book).

Other Considerations

Arts & crafts outlets, nurseries, garden centres and the like are generally not considered to be tourist attractions unless the premises are significantly large and they provide some kind of value added experience such as having a well known or established artist in residence, or they conduct interpretative tours of their premises.

Wineries must provide wine tastings and cellar door sales. Wineries, which are only 'open by appointment', are not considered to be a tourist attraction for road signage purposes. Historic sites, buildings, etc. must be classified by the Heritage Council of WA.

Natural Attractions-recognition Criteria

Natural attractions comprise geographic or other natural features of tourist interest:

- National Parks and Reserves.
- Waterfalls, lakes, dams and other water catchment areas.
- Beaches.
- Caves, rock formations.
- Scenic lookouts, viewing areas, vistas and areas of impressive natural beauty.

Essential Criteria

The natural attraction must:

- be managed by a recognised agency or body.
- be recognised by Tourism Western Australia as a significant feature of tourist interest.
- be accessible to the public at least 9 months of the year.
- clearly display when the attraction is closed (if not open year round).
    - at the turn-off to the attraction.

  - in brochures and all promotional mediums (advertisements, websites, etc.).
- have adequate designated parking areas at the site.
- be distinctly signed at the entrance point so that the natural attraction can be easily identified.
- have clean and well presented visitor facilities.
- have access roads, walking tracks and viewing platforms maintained in a safe and satisfactory condition all year-round by the management body responsible.

Desirable Criteria

It would be desirable for the natural attraction to also:

- have clean and conveniently located toilet facilities.
- provide a parking area for coaches.
- be interpreted.

The Economic Impacts of Tourism

Businesses and public organizations are increasingly interested in the economic impacts of tourism at additional, state, and local levels. One regularly hears claims that tourism supports X jobs in an area or that a festival or special event generated Y million dollars in sales or income in a community. "Multiplier effects" are often cited to capture secondary effects of tourism spending and show the wide range of sectors in a community that may benefit from tourism.

Tourism's economic benefits are touted by the industry for a variety of reasons. Claims of tourism's economic significance give the industry greater respect among the business community, public officials, and the public in general. This often translates into decisions or public policies that are favourable to tourism. Community support is important for tourism, as it is an activity that affects the entire community. Tourism businesses depend extensively on each other as well as on other businesses, government and residents of the local community.

Economic benefits and costs of tourism reach virtually everyone in the region in one way or another. Economic impact analyses provide tangible estimates of these economic interdependency and a better understanding of the role and importance of tourism in a region's economy.

Tourism activity also involves economic costs, including the direct costs incurred by tourism businesses, government costs for infrastructure to better serve tourists, as well as congestion and related costs borne by individuals in the community. Community decisions over tourism often involve debates between industry proponents touting tourism's economic impacts (benefits) and detractors emphasizing tourism's costs. Sound decisions rest on a balanced and objective assessment of both benefits and costs and an understanding of who benefits from tourism and who pays for it.

Tourism's economic impacts are therefore an important consideration in state, regional and community planning and economic development. Economic impacts are also important factors in marketing and management decisions. Communities therefore need to understand the relative importance of tourism to their region, including tourism's contribution to economic activity in the area.

A variety of methods, ranging from pure guesswork to complex mathematical models, are used to estimate tourism's economic impacts. Studies vary extensively in quality and accuracy, as well as which aspects of tourism are included. Technical reports often are filled with economic terms and methods that non-economists do not understand. On the other hand, media coverage of these studies tend to oversimplify and frequently misinterpret the results, leaving decision makers and the general public with a sometimes distorted and incomplete understanding of tourism's economic effects.

How can the average person understand these studies sufficiently to separate good studies from bad ones and make informed choices? The purpose of this bulletin is to present a systematic introduction to economic impact concepts and methods. The presentation is written for tourism industry analysts and public officials, who would like to better understand, evaluate, or possibly conduct an economic impact assessment. The bulletin is organized around ten basic questions that either are asked or should be asked about the economic impacts of tourism.

What is an Economic Impact Analysis?

A variety of economic analyses are carried out to support tourism decisions. As these different kinds of economic analysis are frequently confused, let's begin by positioning economic impact studies within the broader set of economic problems and techniques relevant to tourism. These same techniques may be applied to any policy or action, but we will define them here in the context of tourism. Each type of analysis is identified by the basic question(s) it answers and the types of methods and models that are appropriate.

Types of Economic Analysis

Economic impact analysis — What is the contribution of tourism activity to the economy of the region? An economic impact analysis traces the flows of spending associated with tourism activity in a region to identify changes in sales, tax revenues, income, and jobs due to tourism activity.

The principal methods here are visitor spending surveys, analysis of secondary data from government economic statistics, economic base models, input-output models and multipliers. (Frechtling 1994a) Fiscal impact analysis – Will government revenues from tourism activity from taxes, direct fees, and other sources cover the added costs for infrastructure and government services? Fiscal impact analysis identifies changes in demands for government utilities and services resulting from some action and estimates the revenues and costs to local government to provide these services.

Financial analysis – Can we make a profit from this activity? A financial analysis determines whether a business will generate sufficient revenues to cover its costs and make a reasonable profit. It generally includes a short-term analysis of the availability and costs of start-up capital as well as a longer-range analysis of debt service, operating costs and revenues. A financial analysis for a private business is analogous to a fiscal impact analysis for a local government unit.

Demand analysis – How will the number or types of tourists to the area change due to changes in prices, promotion, competition, quality and quantity of facilities, or other demand shifters? A demand analysis estimates or predicts the number and/or types of visitors to an area via a use estimation, forecasting or demand model. The number of visitors or sales is generally predicted based on judgement (Delphi method), historic trends (time series methods), or using a model that captures how visits or spending varies with key demand determinants (structural models) such as population size, distance to markets, income levels, and measures of quality & competition.

Benefit Cost analysis (B/C) – Which alternative policy will generate the highest net benefit to society over time? A B/C analysis estimates the relative economic efficiency of alternative policies by comparing benefits and costs over time. B/C analysis identifies the most efficient policies from the perspective of societal welfare, generally including both monetary and nonmonetary values. B/C analysis makes use of a wide range of methods for estimating values of non-market goods and services, such as the travel cost method and contingent valuation method.

Feasibility study – Can/should this project or policy be undertaken? A feasibility study determines the feasibility of undertaking a given action to include political, physical, social, and economic feasibility. The economic aspects of a feasibility study typically involve a financial analysis to determine financial feasibility and a market demand analysis to determine market feasibility. A feasibility study is the private sector analogue of benefit cost analysis. The feasibility study focuses largely on the benefits and costs to the individual business or organization, while B/C analysis looks at benefits and costs to society more generally.

Environmental Impact assessment – What are the impacts of an action on the surrounding environment? An environmental assessment determines the impacts of a proposed action on the environment, generally including changes in social, cultural, economic, biological, physical, and ecological systems. Economic impact assessment methods are often used along with corresponding measures and models for assessing social, cultural and environmental impacts. Methods range from simple checklists to elaborate simulation models. Benefit cost analysis and economic impact analysis are frequently confused as both discuss economic "benefits". There are two clear distinctions between the two techniques. B/C analysis addresses the benefits from economic efficiency while economic impact analysis focuses on the regional distribution of economic activity. The income received from tourism by a destination region is largely offset by corresponding losses in the origin regions, yielding only modest contributions to net social welfare and efficiency. B/C analysis includes both market and non-market values (consumer surplus), while economic impact analysis is restricted to actual flows of money from market transactions.

While each type of economic analysis is somewhat distinct, a given problem often calls for several different kinds of economic analysis. An economic impact study will frequently involve a demand analysis to project levels of tourism activity. In other cases demand is treated as exogenous and the analysis simply estimates impacts if a given number of visitors are attracted to the area. A comprehensive impact assessment will also examine fiscal impacts, as well as social and environmental impacts. Be aware that an economic impact analysis, by itself, provides a rather narrow and often one-sided perspective on the impacts of tourism. Studies of the economic impacts of tourism tend to emphasize the positive benefits of tourism.

On the other hand environmental, social, cultural and fiscal impact studies tend to focus more on negative impacts of tourism. This is in spite of the fact that there are negative economic impacts of tourism (e.g., seasonality and lower wage jobs) and in many cases positive environmental and social impacts (e.g., protection of natural & cultural resources in the area and education of both tourists and local residents). An economic impact assessment (EIA) traces changes in economic activity resulting from some action.

An EIA will identify which economic sectors benefit from tourism and estimate resulting changes in income and employment in the region. Economic impact assessment procedures do not assess economic efficiency and also do not generally produce estimates of the fiscal costs of an action. For many problems economic impact analysis will be part of a broader analysis.

Environmental, social, and fiscal impacts are often equally important concerns in a balanced assessment of impacts.

What Economic Impacts does Tourism have?

Tourism has a variety of economic impacts. Tourists contribute to sales, profits, jobs, tax revenues, and income in an area. The most direct effects occur within the primary tourism sectors – lodging, restaurants, transportation, amusements, and retail trade. Through secondary effects, tourism affects most sectors of the economy. An economic impact analysis of tourism activity normally focuses on changes in sales, income, and employment in a region resulting from tourism activity.

A simple tourism impact scenario illustrates. Let's say a region attracts an additional 100 tourists, each spending $100 per day. That's $10,000 in new spending per day in the area. If sustained over a 100 day season, the region would accumulate a million dollars in new sales.

The million dollars in spending would be distributed to lodging, restaurant, amusement and retail trade sectors in proportion to how the visitor spends the $100. Perhaps 30% of the million dollars would leak out of the region immediately to cover the costs of goods purchased by tourists that are not made in the local area (only the retail margins for such items should normally be included as direct sales effects). The remaining $700,000 in direct sales might yield $350,000 in income within tourism industries and support 20 direct tourism jobs. Tourism industries are labour and income intensive, translating a high proportion of sales into income and corresponding jobs.

The tourism industry, in turn, buys goods and services from other businesses in the area, and pays out most of the $350,000 in income as wages and salaries to its employees. This creates secondary economic effects in the region. The study might use a sales multiplier of 2.0 to indicate that each dollar of direct sales generates another dollar in secondary sales in this region.

Through multiplier effects, the $700,000 in direct sales produces $1.4 million in total sales. These secondary sales create additional income and employment, resulting in a total impact on the region of $1.4 million in sales, $650,000 in income and 35 jobs.

While hypothetical, the numbers used here are fairly typical of what one might find in a tourism economic impact study. A more complete study might identify which sectors receive the direct and secondary effects and possibly identify differences in spending and impacts of distinct subgroups of tourists (market segments). One can also estimate the tax effects of this spending by applying local tax rates to the appropriate changes in sales or income. Instead of focusing on visitor spending, one could also estimate impacts of construction or government activity associated with tourism. There are several other categories of economic impacts that are not typically covered in economic impact assessments, at least not directly. For example:

- *Changes in prices* — tourism can sometimes inflate the cost of housing and retail prices in the area, frequently on a seasonal basis.
- *Changes in the quality and quantity of goods and services* – tourism may lead to a wider array of goods and services available in an area (of either higher or lower quality than without tourism).
- *Changes in property and other taxes* – taxes to cover the cost of local services may be higher or lower in the presence of tourism activity. In some cases, taxes collected directly or indirectly from tourists may yield reduced local taxes for schools, roads, etc. In other cases, locals may be taxed more heavily to cover the added infrastructure and service costs. The impacts of tourism on local government costs and revenues are addressed more fully in a fiscal impact analysis.
- *Economic dimensions of "social" and "environmental" impacts-* There are also economic consequences of most social and environmental impacts that are not usually addressed in an economic impact analysis. These can be positive or negative. For example, traffic congestion will increase costs of moving around for both households and businesses. Improved amenities that attract tourists may also encourage retires or other kinds of businesses to locate in the area.

Direct, Indirect and Induced Effects

A standard economic impact analysis traces flows of money from tourism spending, first to businesses and government agencies where tourists spend their money and then to:

- *Other businesses* — supplying goods and services to tourist businesses,
- *Households* – earning income by working in tourism or supporting industries, and
- *Government* — through various taxes and charges on tourists, businesses and households Formally, regional economists distinguish direct, indirect, and induced economic effects.

Indirect and induced effects are sometimes collectively called secondary effects. The total economic impact of tourism is the sum of direct, indirect, and induced effects within a region. Any of these impacts may be measured as gross output or sales, income, employment, or value added.

Direct effects are production changes associated with the immediate effects of changes in tourism expenditures. For example, an increase in the number of tourists staying overnight in hotels would directly yield increased sales in the hotel sector. The additional hotel sales and associated changes in hotel payments for wages and salaries, taxes, and supplies and services are direct effects of the tourist spending.

Indirect effects are the production changes resulting from various rounds of re-spending of the hotel industry's receipts in other backward-linked industries (i.e., industries supplying products and services to hotels).

Changes in sales, jobs, and income in the linen supply industry, for example, represent indirect effects of changes in hotel sales. Businesses supplying products and services to the linen supply industry represent another round of indirect effects, eventually linking hotels to varying degrees to many other economic sectors in the region.

Induced effects are the changes in economic activity resulting from household spending of income earned directly or indirectly as a result of tourism spending. For example, hotel and linen supply employees, supported directly or indirectly by tourism, spend their income in the local region for housing, food, transportation, and the usual array of household product and service needs.

The sales, income, and jobs that result from household spending of added wage, salary, or proprietor's income are induced effects. By means of indirect and induced effects, changes in tourist spending can impact virtually every sector of the economy in one way or another.

The magnitude of secondary effects depends on the propensity of businesses and households in the region to purchase goods and services from local suppliers. Induced effects are particularly noticed when a large employer in a region closes a plant. Not only are supporting industries (indirect effects) hurt, but the entire local economy suffers due to the reduction in household income within the region. Retail stores close and leakages of money from the region increase as consumers go outside the region for more and more goods and services. Similar effects in the opposite direction are observed when there is a significant increase in jobs and household income.

Final demand is the term used by economists for sales to the final consumers of goods and services. In almost all cases, the final consumers of tourism goods and services are households. Government spending is also considered as final demand. The same methods for estimating impacts of visitor spending can be applied to estimate the economic impacts of government spending, for example, to operate and maintain a park or visitor centre.

Regional Economic Models

An input-output model (I-O model) is a mathematical model that describes the flows of money between sectors within a region's economy. Flows are predicted by knowing what each industry must buy from every other industry to produce a dollar's worth of output.

Using each industry's production function, I-O models also determine the proportions of sales that go to wage and salary income, proprietor's income, and taxes. Multipliers can be estimated from input-output models based on the estimated re-circulation of spending within the region. Exports and imports are determined based upon estimates of the propensity of households and firms within the region to purchase goods and services from local sources (often called RPC's or regional purchase coefficients). The more a region is self-sufficient and purchases goods and services from within the region, the higher the multipliers for the region.

Input-output models make a number of assumptions. The basic ones are that:

- All firms in a given industry employ the same production technology (usually assumed to be the national average for that industry), and produce identical products.
- There are no economies or diseconomies of scale in production or factor substitution. I-O models are essentially linear–double the level of tourism activity/production and you double all of the inputs, the number of jobs, etc.
- The model doesn't explicitly keep track of time, but analysts generally report the impact estimates as if they represent activity within a single year.
- One must assume that the various model parameters are accurate and represent the current year. I-O models are firmly grounded in the national system of accounts, which relies on a standard industrial classification system (SIC codes) and various federal government economic censuses, in which individual firms report sales, wage and salary payments and employment. I-O models will generally be at least a few years out-of-date, although this isn't usually a major problem unless the region's economy has changed significantly. An I-O model represents the region's economy at a particular point in time. Tourist spending estimates are generally price adjusted to the year of the model.
- Multiplier computations for induced effects generally assume that jobs created by additional spending are new jobs, involving new households in the area. Induced effects are computed assuming linear changes in household spending with changes in income. Estimates of induced effects may be inflated due to the violation of these

assumptions. Induced effects tend to account for the vast majority of the secondary effects of tourism, and therefore should be used with caution.

What are Multipliers and Multiplier Effects of Tourism?

Multipliers capture the secondary economic effects (indirect and induced) of tourism activity. Multipliers have been frequently misused and misinterpreted in tourism studies and are a considerable source of confusion among non-economists. Multipliers represent the economic interdependency between sectors within a particular region's economy.

They vary considerably from region to region and sector to sector. There are many different kinds of multipliers reflecting which secondary effects are included and which measure of economic activity is used (sales, income, or employment).

For example,

* The Type I sales multiplier = direct sales + indirect sales direct sales.
* The Type II or III sales multiplier 1 = direct sales + indirect sales + induced sales direct sales.

Multiplying a Type I sales multiplier times the direct sales gives direct plus indirect sales. Multiplying a Type II or III sales multiplier times the direct sales gives total sales impacts including direct, indirect and induced effects. The multipliers defined above are called ratio type multipliers as they measure the ratio of a total impact measure to the corresponding direct impact. Comparable income and employment ratio type multipliers may be defined by replacing sales with measures of income or employment in the above equations. Ratio multipliers should be used with caution.

A common error is to multiply a sales multiplier times tourist spending to get total sales effects. This will generate an inflated estimate of tourism impacts. The problem is that tourism spending or sales is not exactly the same as the "direct effects", appearing in the multiplier formula.

Tourist purchases of goods (vs. services) are the primary source of the problem. To properly apply tourist purchases of goods to an input-output model (or corresponding multipliers), various margins (retail, wholesale and transportation) must be deducted from the "purchaser price" of the good to separate out the "producer price". In an I-O model, retail margins accrue to the retail trade sector, wholesale margins to wholesale trade, transportation margins to transportation sectors and the producer prices of goods are assigned to the sector that produces the good.

In most cases the factory that produces the good bought by a tourist lies outside of the local region, creating an immediate "leakage" in the first round of spending and therefore no local impact from production of the good.

Before applying a multiplier to tourist spending, one must first deduct the producer prices of all imported goods that tourists buy (i.e. only include the local retail margins and possibly wholesale and transportation margins if these firms lie within the region). Generally, only 60 to 70% of tourist spending appears as final demand in a local region. While all tourist purchases of services will accrue to the local region as final demand, only the margins on goods purchased at retail stores should be counted as local final demand. The ratio of local final demand to tourist spending is called the capture rate.

Capture Rate = Local Final Demand / Tourism Spending in Local Area

The distinction between Type II and Type III multipliers involves a technical difference in how the induced effects are computed. Type II approaches include households as a sector of the economy and invert the technical coefficient matrix including the household sector, while Type III approaches treat households as exogenous.

Capture rates, like multipliers, will vary with the size and nature of the region as well as the kind of tourist spending included. One must therefore be cautious in taking a multiplier or capture rate cited in one study and using it in another.

Another way of calculating a multiplier (generally the preferred approach among economists) is as a ratio of income or employment to sales. This kind of multiplier is sometimes called a Keynesian multiplier or response coefficient.

Type III Income multiplier = Total direct, indirect, and induced income direct sales.

Type III Employment multiplier = Total direct, indirect, and induced employment direct sales.

This income (employment) multiplier produces total income (employment) impacts when multiplied by the direct sales. One must still be careful in distinguishing between tourism spending/ sales and direct sales effects. Some studies may embed the capture rate in the multiplier, expressing the ratio in terms of tourism spending rather than direct sales.

How are Tourism's Economic Impacts Measured?

The economic impacts of tourism are typically estimated by some variation of the following simple formula:

Economic Impact of Tourism = Number of Tourists.

* Average Spending per Visitor
* Multiplier.

The formula suggests three distinct steps and corresponding measurements or models: Estimate the change in the number and types of tourists to the region due to the proposed policy or action.

Estimates or projections of tourist activity generally come from a demand model or some system for measuring levels of tourism activity in an area. Economic impact estimates will rest heavily on good estimates of the numbers and types of visitors. These must come from carefully designed measurements of tourist activity, a good demand model, or good judgement. This step is usually the weakest link in most tourism impact studies, as few regions have accurate counts of tourists, let alone good models for predicting changes in tourism activity or separating local visitors from visitors from outside the region.

Estimate average levels of spending (often within specific market segments) of tourists in the local area.

Spending averages come from sample surveys or are sometimes borrowed or adapted from other studies. Spending estimates must be based on a representative sample of the population of tourists taking into account variations across seasons, types of tourists, and locations within the study area. As spending can vary widely across different kinds of tourists, we recommend estimating average spending for a set of key tourist segments based on samples of at least 50-100 visitors within each tourism segment.

Segments should be defined to capture differences in spending between local residents vs. tourists, day users vs. overnight visitors, type of accommodation (motel, campground, seasonal home, with friends and relatives), and type of transportation (car, RV, air, rail, etc.).

In broadly based tourism impact studies, it is useful to identify unique spending patterns of important activity segments such as downhill skiers, boaters, convention & business travellers. Multiplying the number of tourists by the average spending per visitor (be careful the units are consistent) gives an estimate of total tourist spending in the area.

Estimates of tourist spending will generally be more accurate if distinct spending profiles and use estimates are made for key tourism segments. The use and spending estimates are the two most important parts of an economic impact assessment. When combined, they capture the amount of money brought into the region by tourists. Multipliers are needed only if one is interested in the secondary effects of tourism spending.

Apply the change in spending to a regional economic model or set of multipliers to determine secondary effects. Secondary effects of tourism are estimated using multipliers or a model of the region's economy. Multipliers generally come from an economic base or input-output model of the region's economy. In many cases multipliers are borrowed (often improperly) or adjusted from published multipliers or other studies. One should not take a multiplier estimated for one region and apply it in a region with a quite different economic structure.

Generally, multipliers are higher for larger regions with more diversified economies and lower for smaller regions with more limited economic development. A common error is to apply a statewide multiplier (since these are more widely published) to a local region.

This will yield inflated estimates of local multiplier effects. Multipliers can also be used to convert estimates of spending or sales to income and employment. Simple ratios can be used to capture how much income or jobs are generated per dollar of sales.

These ratios will vary from region to region and across individual economic sectors due to the relative importance of labour inputs in each industry and different wage and salary rates in different regions of the country. Be aware that job estimates are generally not full time equivalents, making them difficult to compare across industries with different proportions of seasonal and part time jobs. Income or value added are generally the preferred measures of the contribution of tourism to a region's economy.

What are the Typical Approaches for an Economic Impact Assessment?

At the simple, "quick and dirty" end of the spectrum are highly aggregate approaches that rely mostly on judgement to determine tourism activity, spending and multipliers. Such estimates can be completed in a couple hours at little cost and rest largely on the expertise and judgement of the analyst. At the other extreme are studies that gather primary data from visitor spending studies and apply the spending estimates to formal regional economic models for the area in question. In between are a wide range of options that employ varying degrees of judgement, secondary data, primary data, and formal models.

Different levels of detail and corresponding expense (time and money) and accuracy are possible for each of the three steps — estimating tourist volume, spending, and multiplier effects. Four typical approaches illustrate the levels of detail that are possible and the associated methods.

1. Subjective estimates that rely mostly on expert opinion.
2. Secondary data in aggregate form, adapting existing estimates to suit the problem.
3. Secondary data in disaggregate form, permitting finer adjustment of data to fit the situation.

4. Primary data and/or formal models, usually involving visitor surveys and regional economic models.

The National Park Service's "Money Generation Model " is a simple fill-in-form for generating economic impacts. While an extremely simple approach, it captures the essential elements, of an economic impact analysis. The number of visits, average spending per visitor and an aggregate sales multiplier are entered on a simple work sheet to generate estimates of the direct and total sales effects of visitor spending. Sales effects are converted to income and jobs using simple ratios of income to sales and jobs to sales.

Tax effects of visitor spending can also be estimated by applying local tax rates In an engineering approach, one estimates the costs of producing a "trip" by itemizing typical costs for each input-e.g., a typical overnight visitor party of 4 staying two nights will incur $50 per night for motel room, $20 per person per day for meals, $10 for half tank of gas, and $50 for souvenirs = total of $320 per party per trip to sales estimates. With sound judgement in choosing the parameters, the MGM model can yield reasonable ballpark estimates of economic impacts at minimal cost.

This approach, however, provides little detail on spending categories or which sectors of the economy benefit from either direct or secondary effects. The aggregate nature of the approach also makes it difficult to adjust recommended spending rates or multipliers to different applications (USDI, National Park Service 1990.).

3

Advertisement of Motivations for Pleasure Vacation

Introduction

The travel market is often divided into four segments: personal business travel, government or corporate business travel, visiting friends and relatives, and pleasure vacation travel. This study focuses on the pleasure vacation travel segment.

The objectives of the research were to identify motives which directed respondents' selection of destination, and to develop a conceptual framework that would integrate such motives. It was anticipated that the motives might provide a basis for subdividing or segmenting those travelling for pleasure.

The concept of a stable equilibrium state is either stated or implied in most theories of motivation. Disequilibrium or tension in the motivational system occurs when some need arises. Disturbance of equilibrium drives the organism to elicit a course of action which is expected to satisfy the need and to restore equilibrium. The action ceases when equilibrium is restored as the result of the need being met. Hence, satisfactory resolution of the tension state is the criterion against which alternative actions are compared, contrasted,: and evaluated.

In the study reported here, the concern was to identify states of tension or causes of disequilibrium which provoked respondents' decisions to select particular vacation destinations. It is recognized that motivation is only one of many variables which may contribute to explaining tourist behaviour. To expect motivation to account for a large portion of the variance in tourist behaviour is probably asking too much since there may be many other interrelated influences operating. Nevertheless, motivation is considered a critical variable because it is the impelling and compelling force behind it all.

Just what motivates people What does Florence have over sitting in front of the television? Why the Fjords of Norway over Icing on a beach in the sun? Why Bali-or Acapulco? u — or wherever? Even more interestingly, why do some people choose not to take holidays at all? Are they just poor, or do they have ideological objections?

It has been suggested that it is possible to describe the who, when, where and how of tourism, together with the economic and social characteristics of tourists, but not to answer the question "why". Lundberg (1976) in the most recent edition of his basic text devotes a chapter to "Why Tourists Travel," but prefaces it with the comment:

Because research and established theory are lacking, the comments included here are necessarily impressionistic and made principally to stimulate investigation...the observations that follow make no claim to validity other than a validity based on observation and reflection.

Most discussions of tourist motivation have tended to revolve around the concepts of "pull" and "push." The push factors for a vacation are socio-psychological motives. The pull factors are motives aroused by the destination rather than emerging exclusively from within the traveller himself. In this study, this latter category of motives is termed "cultural". These motives reflected the influence of the destination in arousing them. Traditionally, push motives have been thought useful for explaining the desire to go on a vacation while pull motives have been thought useful for explaining the choice of destination. For example, Dann (1977) states: While a specific resort may hold a number of attractions for the potential tourist, his actual decision to visit such a destination is consequent on his prior need for travel. An examination of "push" factors is thus logically, and often temporally antecedent to that of "pull" factors. Prominent among the "pull" studies is the world reported by Williams and Zelinski (1970). They studied international tourism flows and partially explained these flows by the term "heliotropic." Gray (1970) suggested a synonymous term "sunlust" which may be a more descriptive term referring to the same phenomenon. Sunlust characterizes vacations which are motivated by the desire to experience different or better amenities for a specific purpose than are available in the environment in which one normally lives. It is prominent with particular activities such as sports, and literally occurs with the search for the sun. Williams and Zelinski (1970) effectively define this phenomenon when they state:

Specifically in those cases where Country B offers singly or in combination contrasting or desirable climatic characteristics, scenic attractions, cultural and historical features, sports, shopping facilities, night life, and so on, either missing or in short supply in Country A, one might expect a significantly high flow from A to B. Gray (1970) suggested that an alternate appeal to sunlust, that destinations may satisfy, is wanderlust. He defined wanderlust as: That basic trait in human nature that causes some individuals to want to experience different existing cultures and places, or the relics of past cultures in places famous for their historical associations, ruins and monuments.

Tourism researchers and writers have displayed a preference towards "cultural" motives in seeking to explain why tourists travel. Similarly, the tourist industry generally has focused on cultural factors in seeking to attract tourists. As a result, a review of the published literature reporting why people select one destination rather than another reveals that relatively little empirical research has been undertaken into socio-psychological motives. It is these motives which emerged as being of prime importance in the study reported here.

The most comprehensive empirical studies reported in the literature which are concerned with socio-psychological motives of tourists are those undertaken by Hill (1965), Plog (1976), and Dann (1977). The studies by Hill and Plog, like the study reported here, both used unstructured interviews to collect their data, focusing upon interpretation of individual responses in search of qualitative insights and understanding. Hill's (1965) study, which was commissioned by the Irish Tourist Board, identified some underlying motives for going on a vacation. These were used by the Irish Tourist Board as primary themes upon which to base its advertising and promotional efforts. Plog (1976) empirically derived typical vacationer profiles, which included motives, of each stage of the life cycle.

Dann (1977) confirmed his hypotheses that the answer to the question "What makes Tourists Travel" lies primarily in the socio-psychological concepts of "anomie" and "ego enhancement." In addition, both of these motives had a strong fantasy component. Underlying the anomie hypothesis is the need that man has for love and affection and the desire to communicate with his fellow man. Dann suggested that there is a desire to transcend the feeling of isolation obtained in everyday life, and that this need for social interaction can only be fulfilled by the individual getting away from it all on vacation. Similarly, Dann argued that man requires to be recognized, and that travel provides opportunity for ego-enhancement or self recognition.

Hill (1965) concluded:

> *A holiday is undertaken in response to a sense of internal damage or depletion and represents a period of replenishment and restoration. When he goes on holiday, the holiday maker is hoping to taller in and store "internal goods" with which he will return enriched, regenerated and recharged to his own environment.*

This appears to support the assumption of most writers in the field of tourism who generally express the primary motive for taking a pleasure vacation in terms of personal enrichment of one kind or another. However, personal enrichment may not be the exclusive prerogative of the pleasure vacation.

Howard and Sheth (1968) distinguish between specific and non-specific motivation. If motivation is specific, it is uniquely satisfied by the pleasure vacation experience. If it is non-specific it can also be satisfied by alternative opportunities available from other sources. For example, Hill reported that for those respondents who could easily give up the opportunity to go on a pleasure vacation, the same tension reliever or internal refreshment was sought in some other kind of activity:

> *It was noticeable that when alternatives to the holiday were mentioned, there existed a fundamental notion of repair and renovation to internal objects. However, for the majority of Hill's respondents, a pleasure vacation was regarded as a more or less essential period of refreshment. It was regarded as virtually priceless. If it has to be forfeited because of pragmatic constraints, this forfeiture was regarded as only temporary.*

The study explored the contention that socio-psychological motives may be useful not only in explaining the initial arousal, energizing, or "push" to take a vacation, but may also have directive potential to direct the tourist toward a particular destination. This differs from the traditional conceptual framework described earlier, in which the primary utility of socio-psychological motives lies in explaining the initial decision to go on a vacation, and the consequent decision, choice of destination, is conceived to be primarily a function of the cultural pulling power of the destination. Motives were a primary focus and typically recurred at a number of points throughout the interviews. The interviews were tape recorded, subsequently transcribed, classified and their content analysed to isolate all data which pertained to motives. The content analysis yielded patterns of responses which provided the basis for the conceptual framework formulated in this paper.

The respondents consisted of a sample of adults who were conveniently available. They resided either in College Station, Texas or in the Greater Boston area of Massachusetts. Nineteen respondents were female and twenty were male. Thirty were married, four were single, and the spouses of five were deceased. Only five respondents did not have children. The age and occupational profile of the sample. The occupational data suggests that the sample primarily was comprised of middle-class respondents.

It is important to note that the study reported here was essentially a qualitative study. Its objectives were limited to identifying, and obtaining insights into, tourists' motivations. Because of the research design, data collection technique, and the limited sample size, this study was not concerned with identifying the distributions of these motives in a population. An investigation into the distribution of these motives, which builds upon the basic work reported here, is currently being undertaken by the author as a subsequent project.

Analysis

A conceptualization of the role and relationships of respondents' underlying states of disequilibrium which emerged from patterns in the data. It identifies four main components.

First, a state of disequilibrium. Second, a break from routine, which was conceptualized as an initial overt manifestation of disequilibrium. Third, three behavioural alternatives: stay at home, go on a pleasure vacation, or travel for other purposes such as visiting friends and relatives or going on a business trip, each of which may provide a break from routine. Fourth, the particular motives which help determine the nature and destination of the pleasure vacation if that alternative is selected. These are aligned along a continuum as being primarily either socio-psychological or cultural.

The Nature of a Break From Routine

Almost every respondent described the essence of a vacation as being a break from routine. These breaks could generally be classified into two categories, short-term and long-term. These appeared to resolve different types of disequilibrium. Short-term disequilibrium seemed to reflect a particular set of circumstances or events which were temporal disruptions to homeostasis. Typically, these were expressed as "pressures." In this situation, a break from routine was perceived to be a necessary and sufficient condition to restore homeostasis. Long-term states of disequilibrium could not usually be satisfied by a single pleasure vacation. Instead these states of disequilibrium were satisfied through an ongoing program of pleasure vacations. A break from routine was perceived as necessary to facilitate the resolution of long-term disequilibrium states, but the break alone was not sufficiently inclusive to resolve the state of tension. Long-term disequilibrium was perceived by respondents as being ever present but postponable. In contrast, short-term disequilibrium demanded immediate attention. In other words, the data suggested that a two tier system of disequilibrium was operating.

This is hypothesized to have meant continuation of doing the same kinds of things but in a different physical, or social context. The essence of "break from routine" was, in most cases, either locating in a different place, or changing the dominant social context from the world milieu, usually to that of the family group, or doing both of these things. The kinds of activities in which people engaged were generally not different, although they were sometimes more concentrated. Respondents' life styles did not change. A break from routine often involved emphasizing particularly desired elements of the life style rather than changing the life style to incorporate different activities. The mundane elements in the routine were discarded, but the preferred discretionary elements of the normal life style were retained.

Motives Influencing Selection of Type of Pleasure Vacation and Destination

Once a desire to go on a pleasure vacation has been established, concern shifts from the impetus dimension of motivation to its directive dimension which serves to guide the tourist toward the selection of a particular type of vacation or destination in preference to all the alternatives of which the tourist is aware. In most decisions more than one motive is operative. Priorities between alternative destinations are a function of the intensity of the particular combination of motives which are dominant in a hierarchy of motives at a particular moment of time. This hierarchy of motives construct helps to explain divergent reaction at different points in time by the same respondent to the same stimuli.

The data suggested that respondents' motives usefully could be conceptualized as being located along a cultural — socio-psychological disequilibrium continuum. Much of the tourist industry's modus operandi is based upon the assumption that tourists are attracted to a destination by the particular cultural opportunities or special attributes that it offers. However, the findings of this study suggested that for some respondents, the destination itself was relatively unimportant.

Respondents did not go to particular locations to seek cultural insights or artifacts; rather they went for socio-psychological reasons unrelated to any specific destination. The destination served merely as a medium through which these motives could be satisfied. The following sections of the analysis briefly discuss each of the motives empirically identified in this study, and categorize them as being located either toward the socio-psychological or the cultural end of the continuum.

Socio-Psychological Motives

Socio-psychological motives were rarely overtly identified by respondents in early discussion of their pleasure vacation experiences. These motives were difficult for respondents to articulate.

However, as the interview proceeded, it often became apparent that while initial concern and effort had been with selecting a vacation destination, the value, benefits, and satisfactions derived from the vacation were neither related to, nor derived from, a particular destination's attributes. Rather the satisfactions were related to social or psychological factors unique to the particular individual or group involved. In effect, these motives represented a hidden agenda. This suggests that one of the reasons that some people do not take pleasure vacations is unknown. The data suggested seven socio-psychological motives which served to direct pleasure vacation behaviour. These motives were: escape from a perceived mundane environment; exploration and evaluation of self; relaxation; prestige; regression; enhancement of kinship relationships; and facilitation of social interaction.

Escape from a Perceived Mundane Environment

A temporary change of environment was a frequently expressed respondent motive. Even the most prized living environments sometimes became mundane to those living there. For example, one respondent who lived on Cape Cod indicated that when crowds of people descend upon the Cape in the summer, many of the local residents go to Maine, New Hampshire, or Vermont to avoid the crowds. Escape was sought not only from the general residential locale but also from the specific home and job environments. There did not appear to be any single optimum type of environment that facilitated escape.

The critical ingredient was only that the pleasure vacation context should be physically and socially different from the environment in which one normally lives. For some respondents, the escape offered by a pleasure vacation was for a much longer time period than the actual trip. As Clawson and Knetsch (1966) have suggested, anticipation of the trip was an important ingredient of the total experience. One respondent commented that "You are sustained a little through the winter, first by anticipation of Christmas, then by anticipation of the trip in February or March. It is something to which I look forward in the long winter."

Exploration and Evaluation of Self

The data suggested that a pleasure vacation may be viewed by some people as an opportunity for re-evaluating and discovering more about themselves or for acting out self-images and in so doing refining or modifying them. For example, one respondent commented:

> *This trip put a lot of things in perspective for me. It helped me to get a clearer picture of myself because I put myself in different situations. I saw how I interacted with other people in other conditions. I had some constraints come up, some hardships, and I had to deal with that. It gave me a chance to see what is inside of me and how that would come out, without any outside pressures. You don't find this out when you go to the office from eight to five.*

Self-discovery emerged as a result of transposition into a new situation. The novelty of the physical and social context appeared to be an essential ingredient in the process. These insights into the person's self could not be achieved by staying at home or visiting friends and relatives. In the case of the latter there would be outside pressure serving to ameliorate hardship, and hence dilute the value of the experience, because of the accessibility of friendly other people. In the case of the former, there would be less likelihood of finding different situations or conditions. Exposure to a different milieu sometimes caused a revision of existing perceptions of self-status and enhanced feelings of self-worth. A respondent who was a boat be of low status in that community, but on pleasure vacations, " I see people who are a lot worse off than I am, and I sort of appreciate what we do have." Other respondents stressed that exposure to a different milieu for a period of time served as a reference point re-evaluation of their own life style.

Self-discovery was not confined only to those respondents who went camping or sought inexpensive pleasure vacations. The wealthiest and most widely travelled respondent in the sample expressed similar sentiments. After a cruise vacation in which she found that she was not disposed to the socializing and organized activities which characterized the experience she commented, "I learned a lot about myself on that cruise."

Relaxation

The term relaxation was a constant respondent theme, but its use was often ambivalent. Generally, there was a reluctance on the part of respondents to relax physically. Respondents would say they felt relaxed and then admit that they came home physically exhausted. It was apparent that the term relaxation referred to a mental state rather than a physical relaxation. Given this interpretation it was possible to reconcile physical exhaustion or fatigue as being mentally refreshing and relaxing.

Relaxation meant talking the time to pursue activities of interest. The activities selected were often a reflection of the increased time available at the vacation destination. In the rhythm of the normal routine, the mind was not directed toward these hobbies or interests. These interests were not selectively perceived because they were not pertinent to the prevailing train of thought or dominant motive.

Most respondents indicated that they were fatigued upon their return home from the exertions expended on the vacation and on associated travel. This fatigue factor together with the contribution the vacation has made to ameliorating tension states possibly accounted for the sentiment that respondents frequently expressed, "I am always delighted to go on a vacation, but I am just as delighted to return home again."

Prestige

Although some respondents suggested prestige was a primary motivating factor in other people's trips, few of them accepted that there was any prestige motive involved in their own pleasure vacation decisions. It may be that as travel has become more frequent, it is perceived to be less prestigious. Travel may have become part of the indigenous life style rather than symbolic of a higher life style. Prestige potential disappears with frequency of exposure.

Regression

Some respondents suggested that a pleasure vacation provided an opportunity to do thingswhich were inconceivable within the context of their usual life styles. The things respondents' cited were often puerile, irrational, and more reminiscent of adolescent or child behaviour than mature adult behaviour. The opportunity to engage in this behaviour was facilitated by withdrawal from usual role obligations. On vacation, respondents were freed of the mores that inhibit capacity for this type of enjoyment. One respondent stated, "My life style is free and more relaxed when I go away from home. I let my guard down more than I would at home." While puerility was the prevailing form of regressive behaviour, another form was identified by some respondents. This was the search for the life style of a previous era. This is sometimes referred to as the "nostalgia factor." In essence, the desire was to regress to a less complex, less changeable, less technologically advanced environment. For example, a respondent stated that she and her friends were:

> *Looking for the simple life. We are not looking for big cities, but are looking for peasants of the soil. A lot of us are very romantic. We want to go out and see the fields; to escape Americanism.*

Like the puerile regression state, this search for the life style of a previous era is a transitory, ephemeral tension state, and when homeostasis is restored, return to the routine of life is accepted.

The actuality frequently is not congruent with the image, for as the same respondent commented, "It depends where they go, but a lot of people come back not always totally satisfied."

Enhancement of Kinship Relationships

Many respondents perceived the pleasure vacation as a time when family members were brought close together. Hence, the pleasure vacation served as a medium through which family relationships could be enhanced or enriched. This enhancement is often facilitated by long drives in an automobile because family members are physically juxtaposed for long periods and forced to interact with each other. It is inevitable that a much greater exchange and understanding of each other is likely to occur than in the normal routine situation in which family members go in different directions interacting only spasmodically. The essence of this tension state was well expressed by a respondent who stated:

The important notion is being out of routine. It isn't that you are away from a place anymore than you are at a place. What is different is the act that you are together as a family. You are able to put aside the other kinds of responsibilities that each of you may have that would otherwise be impinging themselves upon that notion of focusing inwards and putting things together.

Facilitation of Social Interaction

It was evident that an important motive for some respondents going on a pleasure vacation was to meet new people in different locations. These trips were people oriented rather than place oriented. Like several of the other motives which were located towards the socio-psychological end of the disequilibrium continuum, respondents often became aware of this motive only after the trip was completed.

A variety of dimensions of this motive emerged from the data. For some respondents, an opportunity for transitory meetings with others from outside familiar reference groups to exchange views, was all that was sought. Others were seeking more permanent relationships that would serve to extend their range of social contacts. Several observed that interaction with non-familiar people was more likely. In some cases, social contact was initiated by children, who were a common ingredient shared by some parties. The physical planning of accommodations was also perceived to be an ameliorating factor, for if the accommodations were closely juxtaposed they facilitated interaction.

Although several respondents expressed a desire to interact with local people in the destination area, they reported that this was frequently difficult to achieve. Most interaction was with other tourists in the area. There was little common identity with local people who were serving as waitresses, and much more with other tourists who were also waiting in line or visiting a particular attraction for the first time. Some respondents suggested that travelling with others may inhibit opportunities for interacting with local people at the destination. The availability of companions provided built-in entertainment and removed the urge to visit with others outside of the group; the natural tendency was to turn inward rather than outward.

The organized tour was a preferred type of vacation for some respondents because it served as a vehicle for facilitating social intercourse as well as being financially expedient. The prime ingredients inducing the camaraderie which respondents reported from tour experiences appeared to be the sharing of many dimensions of the experience and close physical juxtaposition with others. Some participated regularly in group tours which were arranged locally and were comprised of people who knew others in the group from the outset. In essence, these people were taking some of their home social environment with them to a different location. The existence of a nucleus of known people provided a good foundation upon which to establish new social relationships through introductions. In addition, the group often had a common interest which facilitated social interaction. For example, it may be comprised of lawyers, teachers, doctors, rose growers, or home builders.

Cultural Motives

Motives located towards this end of the continuum were concerned with the destination rather than with the social and psychological status of the individual. Most respondents explained their reasons for going on pleasure vacations in terms of cultural motives. In many cases, cultural motives were more apparent than real. In other cases, the data suggested that many respondents did not receive socio-psychological satisfactions, but received almost exclusively cultural benefits.

Two primary cultural motives were expressed. They were novelty and education. These may be related since exposure to new destinations, sights, and experiences is presumably educational. However, respondents did not always perceive this relation ship and hence they are discussed separately.

Novelty

Novelty was defined by respondents in a variety of ways. Synonyms included curiosity, adventure, new and different. Novel meant new experience but it did not necessarily mean entirely new knowledge. Often respondents knew a lot about a place. The novelty resulted from actually seeing something rather than simply knowing of it vicariously.

A prefe*rence for going to a previously unvisited destination was a consistent factor. This* aspect had previously proved satisfactory, rather than to purchase a brand with which they have had no previous experience. Generally, this does not appear to apply to pleasure vacations. Cultural disequilibrium appears to be an on-going state which requires a supply of fresh cultural stimuli to restore homeostasis. In most cases, respondents anticipated that re-experiencing known cultural stimuli would not contribute as much as experiencing new stimuli to reducing the tension state. Hence, when the pleasure vacation product was purchased, a different destination brand was selected by respondents.

At the same time, there were some respondents who returned to a previously visited vacation destination. In some cases, the same destination was selected each year. While the data did not enable the reasons for this to be identified, it may be speculated that three factors account for this phenomenon.

First, habitual destination respondents may be motivated primarily by socio-psychological rather than cultural motives. Second, they may have restricted knowledge of the want satisfying attributes of other places. Returning to a proven destination reduces the risk that an unfamiliar alternative may not be as satisfying as those previously experienced. The third factor may be fear, or anxiety of the unknown, which is removed by revisiting a destination.

The urge for new and adventurous experiences was frequently compromised by the felt need to minimize rises of exposure to novelty which may be threatening. One respondent, who was a travel agent, pointed out that for some people, it was a fearful experience to go into an unknown situation in a country where the people did not speak your language. These people "would like to go away from home but they also have the desire to be taken care of. That is why you get tours and tour conductors, because it is a security blanket." People used organized tours to introduce themselves to travel, its problems and associated fears. Organized tours served to remove any anxiety or exposure to unfamiliar situations that may have been threatening.

An alternative strategy to the organized tour for reducing anxiety and fear was to experience the unknown by starting with the known and using that as a base. For example, a number of respondents indicated that they had visited the Mexican border towns, but had no intention of going further into Mexico. The border towns were close to the perceived safety of the known United States and could thus be experienced relatively quickly with minimal anxiety. Similarly, some of the respondents who had visited Europe indicated that they started in the United Kingdom where they knew the language, or in a country that they had previously visited, so that there was some familiarity. From this relatively familiar base, sorties were made into new areas. When they felt comfortable there, the process was repeated and exploration extended to their new destinations.

Education

The positive influence of pleasure vacations on children's' education was exhorted by most respondents and in some cases was the primary consideration in the selection of a destination. Education was perceived as a means of developing a rounded individual. One respondent suggested, "As a generalization, those who have been on vacation, and have travelled, are usually more interesting to talk with than those who have not." It was perceived as almost a moral obligation to take the opportunity to visit a distinctive phenomenon, particularly if it was reasonably accessible. The sense of "ought" to see and experience a particular place frequently meant that circumstances, especially present location, had been the trigger which initiated selection of a destination. Cultural disequilibrium was not site or destination specific. It did not relate to one particular place, but it was generally applicable to all places. Hence, there was a feeling expressed by several respondents that, "I ought to go because I am here," particularly if it was anticipated that the present residential location was transitory. In this situation, it may have been perceived as the one opportunity in a lifetime to see particular cultural phenomena. If the opportunity was not grasped then educational benefits were lost.

Conclusions and Implications

Delineation of underlying motives offers useful insights into understanding the destination selection decision process. All else equal, preference is likely to be given to a destination which is perceived as most likely to service the dominant motive. Nine motives were identified. Seven of these were located towards the socio-psychological end of the disequilibrium continuum and two towards the cultural end. For ease of exposition, the motives were discussed as separate entities. However, they should not be considered as mutually exclusive, nor should any single tension state be selected as the determinant of behaviour. They operate in tandem or combination, for motives are multidimensional.

Thus, destination decisions were usually energized by several motives acting in tandem. The study suggested that any given destination can in principle attract customers whose motivations are neither homogeneous nor necessarily compatible. While the study gave no indication of the distribution of the two disequilibrium states in the population, it suggested that more attention usefully could be given by the tourist industry to socio-psychological disequilibrium in developing its product and promotion strategies than is presenting the case. The tourist industry's modus operandi is based upon the assumption that people go on vacation to do and see things. The data suggested that, for many respondents, this assumption is challengeable. They have been conditioned to thinking in terms of destination, but a number of motives emerged from the data which were not place specific. Consumers motivated by socio-psychological motives were not looking for uniqueness in the product. That is, some specific attribute it possessed which other destinations did not have. The pleasure vacation destination was not perceived by most respondents as a "speciality good."

There appear to be two directions which could usefully be pursued profitably by the tourist industry if it accepts the significance and role of socio-psychological tension states in pleasure vacation decisions suggested in this study. First, efforts are required to arouse people's awareness of their own real motives. The in-depth interviews caused many respondents to confront for the first time their real motives for going on a pleasure vacation. Several commented similarly to the respondent who stated, "This is interesting, I am learning all these things about myself." They expressed surprise at what they revealed, for the motives which ultimately emerged were often radically different from the reasons they were accustomed to giving for going on a vacation. The interviews proved to be an exercise in self-discovery. The role of the travel agent may be a factor. These details were discovered through interviews, then the counsellor would be in a much better position to recommend the most appropriate type of pleasure vacation and destination. The second direction lies in the development of the destination product and its promotion.

The motives may be used as a basis for market segmentation. They provide cues and insights around which destinations can develop and promote their product to target segments. Supplier efforts have generally focused on unique amenities and facilities of the destination. Socio-psychological tension states suggest that this may not be the most appropriate strategy. For example, the escape from a mundane environment, exploration of self, and regression motives, require only a destination which is physically and socially different from the residential environment. Literally thousands of destinations could meet these criteria and thus serve as direct substitutes. The detailed cultural attractions of a destination are not important in this context. The best promotion strategies for this market segment may be to stress the contribution the destination can make to reducing these disequilibrium states and to stress price advantages.

Those destinations seeking to cater to the relaxation motive may stress familiarity and the availability of facilities to enjoy preferred activities rather than a radically different environment or new activities. Destinations targeting at the prestige market segment may emphasize their unique qualities as a destination, rather than the activities or facilities available. This uniqueness must be fairly widely disseminated so that it is known to peer groups in order that they are able to confer upon members appropriate prestige for visiting it. At the same time it should not be promoted as a popular mass destination. The social interaction motive may be accommodated by physical juxtaposition of parties and organized programming, while enhancement of kinship relationships may be a useful theme for promoting family pleasure vacations.

Cultural disequilibrium referred to the desire to see new places or do things in a different environment. It is this motive to which most tourist supplier effort is presently directed. Two culturally oriented motives were identified. These were novelty and education.

Novelty implied that there was no desire to return to a previously visited destination no matter how successful the vacation. This lack of "brand loyalty" may be ameliorated by establishing a network of cross recommendations. That is, agreement between destinations to recommend satisfied consumers to a destination with similar characteristics in a different location. Chain and franchise organizations offer illustration of this at the individual motel or fast-food facility level. For example, if the vacationer enjoyed Dade County, Florida, they may be recommended to try the Rio Grande Valley region of Texas, or Orange County, California. This offers the credibility accrued by the proven destination that there is a good probability of the vacationer enjoying a similarly satisfying experience in a different cultural context.

To remove the fear inhibition present for some in contemplating a novel pleasure vacation, the organized tour may more prominently promote its anxiety reducing potential, rather than concentrating exclusively on price advantage which is its present tendency. Similarly destinations may stress the attributes with which vacationers were likely to feel familiar, that is their recognizable cultural ties, before pointing out cultural differences. Establishing the known before proceeding to the unknown.

Educational prowess may be useful in attracting vacationers for whom the education motive is dominant. Finally, many respondents changed residential location frequently. Location appeared to be an important ingredient in bringing the education motive state to the head of the hierarchy of motives.

This suggests that people are likely to be susceptible to promotions reminding them that the opportunity to visit a destination in reasonable proximity may not arise again. People went on pleasure vacation to satisfy a variety of different motives. As a result, the attributes which might attract them to a destination differed. The implications suggested in the above paragraphs are intended to be illustrative of how these data may be applied rather than exhaustive. Specific implications appropriate to a particular destination will according to its attributes, environmental niche and goals.

Theoretical Aspects of the Sustainable Tourism Strategies

In order to identify the importance and appropriateness of the sustainable tourism strategy in the growth and development of the industry, it has to identify the theoretical support. The major tourism theories are discussed here for identifying how the CSR concept is relevant in the tourism development and growth.

Tourism theories: Travel and tourism theories are mostly based on travel motivation. The basic factors that influence the travelling decisions are tourist need satisfaction, customer satisfaction and destination loyalty. Tourist motivation factors have higher influence on the tourist behaviour of travellers with regard to their destination choice, needs, goals and preferences. In case of ecotourism, social psychological desire to break out from the habitual ordinary life is the primary push factor. The major pull factors which force travellers to take travel decisions are destination attributes such as natural attractions like wild life and immaculate environment.

As per the theory of Iso-Ahola interpersonal escape and interpersonal seeking motivate tourism and recreation among the individuals. In case of personal seeking and personal escape dimensions, tourism experiences have great role in motivation. Sporting events, beaches, amusement parks, and natural parks improves the motivational levels of tourism and recreational activities to a greater extent. Tourism motivation in holiday trips is the desire to travel for satisfying the internal needs and wants. Incentive tourism is a motivational tool among the employees as well as other organizational personnel.

Most of the weekend travel decisions are related to the intention to take rest and spend the weekend for relaxation. Travel behaviour among individuals can be described as a function of quantifiable aspects such as socio-demographic characteristics and physical characteristics of the region. Most of the travelling decisions are situational in nature.

Travel behaviour of individuals is influenced by individual personality, attitudes and perceptions. Attitude of travellers has influence on beliefs and behaviour in travel decision such as the frequency of use. Novelty seeking is the prime motivating factor that affects the travelling of most of the individuals. The positive and negative feed back from the travel affect their future decision to travel a particular destination.

The motivational factors have a key role in the tourist decision making behaviour. In the motivational factors, push and pull concept was introduced by Crompton and Chon in 1979.

Push factors affect the desire for travel whereas pull factors affect the actual destination choice. In the concept of Crompton 1979, there are nine motive factors influencing the leisure travellers. Seven of them are socio psychological factors and two are cultural motives. Push factors are internal factors whereas pull factors are external The seven push factors include, making a change in the routine life environment, meeting self needs, relaxation, establishing social relationships, prestige and social interaction.

Novelty and education are the pull factors. According to Iso-Ahola, 1980, there are mainly two motivational factors in tourist behaviour. The first feature is approach, focusing on recreational opportunities for intrinsic rewards, and the second feature is avoidance which is escape oriented. The increasing trend of shorter holiday breaks is a signal of escape dimension among the tourists behaviour.

The study by Teare (1994) on peoples' motives for selecting hotel leisure breaks in the UK states that there are six factors such as attending a pre arranged event, as a break from personal commitments, as well as employment pressures, to fulfil the desire of relaxation or visit a particular destination and to exploit the seasonal benefits of short breaks. The personal motivation factor may differ as per individual behaviour. When considering the theoretical concepts it revealed that protection of the natural environment is an essential factor for motivating the travellers to visit the destinations.

Through the keeping of novelty of the destination environment, its attraction can be sustained over a longer period of time. Thus the tourism theories better support the appropriateness of sustainable tourism strategy for the sustainable growth of the industry. Motivation for travel is a complex area of tourism research. Sharpley (1994) identifies many factors which motivate people to travel. These include a personal need to escape from daily routines, to visit friends and relatives or to learn about other cultures. To understand an individual's motivation to travel, it is necessary to examine their desires, needs, experience and preferences and social, economic and demographic circumstances as well as prevailing social norms and customs.

Although there is a large amount of literature on what motivates people to undertake travel and tourism, the quantity of research into cultural tourist motivation is limited. In particular, there are few studies or surveys of international visitors' motivations and attitudes to Australia's cultural attractions, events and products, despite considerable interest in the Australian cultural tourism industry. Some people, like the English elite who undertook the Grand Tour in the sixteenth and seventeenth centuries, are motivated to travel because of culture.

Such visitors, therefore, can be termed 'specific' cultural or culturally motivated visitors. However, for most people, culture is not a sole motive for travel. Rather, participation in cultural activities is one potential component of a travel itinerary and may occur if opportunities arise. Visitors for whom this is the case can be called 'general' cultural visitors.

Studies of the Motivations of Cultural Visitors

According to some tourist motivation theories, motivations are developed as a result of 'pull' and 'push' factors. Pull factors relate to the characteristics or attractions of a travel destination. For cultural tourists visiting Australia, they include attractions such as the Sydney Opera House and Aboriginal sites. Push factors relate to the needs and wants of individuals that lead them to 'buy' particular holidays. For cultural tourism and tourism as a whole, they include the desire for social interaction and relaxation, to experience something different and to learn about themselves and the places they visit for participating in cultural activities. Other researchers have identified more specific motivations.

Motivation Theory

"Crompton (1979) notes it is possible to describe the who, when, where, and how of tourism, together with the social and economic characteristics of tourist, but not to answer the question "why," the most interesting question of all tourist behaviour."

While motivation is only one of many variables in explaining tourist behaviour, it is nonetheless a very critical one, as it constitutes the driving force behind all behaviour. Motivation sets the stage for forming people's goals and is reflected in both travel choice and behaviour; as such it influences people's expectations, which in turn determine the perception of experiences. Motivation is therefore a factor in satisfaction formation.

Basic motivation theory suggests a dynamic process of internal psychological factors (needs, wants and goals), causing an uncomfortable level of tension within individuals' minds and bodies, resulting in actions aimed at releasing that tension and satisfying these needs. Motives, implying such an action, require the awareness of needs, as well as objectives, promising to satisfy these now conscious needs in order to create wants and move people to buy. Objectives or goals are presented in the form of products and services, it is therefore the role of marketing to create awareness of needs and suggest appropriate objectives, promising the satisfaction of these.

Several authors suggest that in the Western World free time and holidays are connected to the concept of self-actualisation or self-realisation. The latter defined by Grunow-Lutter (1983.) as *"a person's dynamic relationship between the real and the ideal self, constituting a process of decreasing the distance between these two cognitive systems, themselves subject to continuous change."* It is the individual's aim to achieve a state of stability, or homeostasis, which is disrupted when the person becomes aware of the gap between real and ideal self, or as Goosens calls it a need deficiency. The resulting need to self-actualise represents the motive, which under the constraints of the situation sets the stage for the process of motivation. But to what extent does tourism satisfy the intrinsic need for self-actualisation? Tinsley and Eldredge (1995) summarise 15 years of research into psychological needs, satisfied by leisure activities, and proposed leisure activities clusters such as novelty, sensual enjoyment, cognitive stimulation, self-expression, creativity, vicarious competition, relaxation, agency, belongingness and service. It is questioned however; whether these superficial needs are intrinsically motivated, suggesting that these motivations are merely culturally learned stereotypes or explanations for leisure behaviour. As Fodness (1994) states, a widely accepted integrated theory for needs and goals behind motivation is lacking. The question is of course why this is the case.

Research into motivation can be distinguished into two categories, the behaviourist and the cognivist approach. The discussion has therefore traditionally revolved around either push or pull factors influencing tourist behaviour. Push factors represent lasting dispositions, as they are internally generated drives. The individual, energised by such drives, will then search objects for the promise of drive reduction and develop a motive. The behaviourist view thus emphasises the emotional parameter of decision-making, while the cognivist approach focuses on situational parameters in which motives are expressed, consequently encompassing a certain knowledge which the tourist holds about goal attributes as well as a rational weighing up of situational constraints. This cognitive process results in motivations, which are more object specific than motives, as these only imply a class of objects and may result in a range of different behaviours, depending on the situation.

This unidimensional approach has been criticised however, as push and pull factors influence the consumer simultaneously, integrated by the concept of involvement, an unobservable state of motivation, arousal, or interest, which is evoked by stimulus or situations. This is the case, since pull factors such as marketing stimuli as well as the destination's and service's attributes respond to and reinforce push factors. Consequently research increasingly seeks to integrate emotions and cognition in the individual's decision-making process, indicating a more holistic approach.

As a result it became evident that people's intrinsic needs are influenced by external factors. Rojek (1990) asserts that in post-modern society the superstructure of advertising, television, fashion, lifestyle magazines and designer values increasingly take the role of forming knowledge and beliefs. People's needs are neutral, as motives however, they require an object towards which the need is directed, and when linked to actual situations, cultural and social impacts are also applied. Situations raise motives to the level of values, as such they are evaluations based on learned behaviour and perception.

If a drive is reduced satisfactorily the individual is likely to remember the behaviour and employ the same behaviour again, thus acquiring habits. Tourism experiences may therefore become learned behaviour and acquire the role of habit enforcers. Cognivists argue that knowledge and beliefs in future rewards, anticipatory in nature, are equally a product of formerly encountered situations, and external formation.

It may be concluded that motives merely represent learned behaviour, which are influenced by offered objects or tourism activities, while motivations represent knowledge and beliefs formed by society and culture or tourism marketers. The psychogenic need for self-actualisation, abstract in nature, is therefore operationalised in a learned and practical manner and expressed in values, which are learned strategies to either adapt one's environment to one's needs or adapt one's self to a given environment. Such values equally include effects of enculturation and socialisation. Furthermore the perceived gap between real and ideal self, may indicate both externally and internally controlled evaluations. McCabe therefore asks what researchers can expect to know about individuals' drives, by asking them about their motivations and needs as these may not be available to individuals as part of their consciousness (2000a,). Iso-Ahola (1982) states that *"people do not walk around with numerous leisure needs in their minds and do not rationalise specific causes of participation if their involvement is intrinsically motivated"* (cited in Goosens 2000). Hence it may be assumed that needs are suggested by immediate social peers, and the wider context of particular social realities as well as the influence of the media. Yet as Weissinger and Bandalos (1995) stress, intrinsic leisure motivation, which is a global disposition and describes a tendency to seek intrinsic rewards, is characterised by self-determination, an awareness of internal needs and a strong desire to make free choices based on these needs.

While self-actualisation may be accepted as a need intrinsic to all individuals, society exercises a great deal of influence on the formation of the ideal self and thus perceived needs. However the notion of authentic or true self, determined by way of experience, offers a solution to the predicament. According to Waterman (1984), individualism symbolises four psychological qualities, the first one is a sense of individual identity, based on the knowledge of who one is and what one's goals and values are, as such it is related to the philosophical concept of true self, which indicates what an individual reckons personally expressive and what it is to be actualised. The second is Maslow's self-actualisation, which is the driving to be one's true self. The third quality is Rotter's (1966) internal locus of control, which reflects a willingness to accept personal responsibility for one's life, and finally principles (postconventional), moral reasoning, which involves consistency with general abstract principles.

Consequently, only if tourists become more autonomous and thus aware of intrinsic needs and motives are they able to self-actualise. As McIntosh and Goeldner (1990) explained, order is becoming less important in Western society and a desire for disorder in the tourism experience is becoming more important. Kim and Lee point out that *"opportunities for unplanned action and freedom from institutionalised regulations are distinctive of Western tourists"* (2000). This indicates that tourists exhibit a certain desire to liberate their identities. According to Krippendorf (1984), in order for tourists to cease being just users of holidays, they must come to know themselves, their motives and other cultures. It may therefore be assumed that self-actualisation is an intrinsic need, characteristic of any tourist, but must be understood in terms of true self as opposed to ideal self and as such is independent of societal pressures and involves the transcendence of habitual behaviours and mindstates. This proposition requires further elaboration and must be viewed in the context of modernity, which hinders this process but at the same time brought about its awareness.

The Escape Motivation

Recently, means-end theory has been applied to recreation and leisure settings by using the laddering method to investigate activities such as ski destination selection, spring break destination choice, nature park interpretation and marketing for urban tourism what a product is, what it does and what people get from it.

These form the three main elements of focus in means-end theory, starting with the physical, observable *attributes* (the "means"), *consequences* (benefits or costs) that follow from the attributes, which further lead to personal *values* (the "ends"). Means-end theory focuses on why and how product attributes are important. Attributes! Consequence (benefits or costs)! Value different) at either end based on personal values.

Individuals are attracted to a particular destination based on a variety of factors such as one's personal traits and leisure and travel motivation grounded within a broad conceptual push-pull scenario. Leisure and recreation are important motives for amenity migrants. This model contends that motivation to reside specific to the Bow Valley include a desire to balance a mountain recreation lifestyle with work, to be with a friend or partner, to escape, to purchase a second home, to be in a place suits one's values, to be next to the (aesthetic lifestyle) mountains and to pursue a career in tourism or parks. Factor analysis results revealed two factor components labelled To Live and To Escape. The former included to pursue a career in tourism, hospitality or parks, to start a business, to balance work with a mountain recreation lifestyle and just to be with a friend or partner while the former included to own a second home and to escape.

Lived Experience of Negotiated Leisure. The leisure negotiation process is framed by the human-environment relationship and remains dynamic due to constant evaluations of the one's ability to negotiate aspects of a changing environment with one's personal resources. The lived experience component of the model includes the element of leisure and recreation behaviour.

Behaviour is important as it is postulated here that leisure/ recreation behaviour imprints the destination through the expression of demand. For example, the persistent behaviour of mountain biking may result in the development of additional mountain trails, a built mountain bike park, or even the banning of mountain biking from certain or all trails. Likewise, the presence of upper middle class urban dwellers may bring about a perceived demand for up-scale restaurants and cafes. Or the presence of families with children may bring increased demand for traditional recreation facilities such as pools and ice arenas. Recreation behaviour is an expression of demand which is likely to impact supply thereby altering the environment.

Environment: The environment within a high recreation amenity destination can be characterized as having significant natural and cultural resources. It involves a strong social component of community and reference groups. The social element can also include detractions such as crowding, congestion and other forms of conflict such as with recent and long time residents. It also includes structural components such as the economy, housing, roads and health and educational infrastructure which all contribute to the negotiation. Physical, social and structural aspects of the environment are assumed to act both as a facilitator to one's leisure goals, and constraint or stressor at different times. It is also assumed that over time the nature and character of the Environment evolves (dotted line) as the physical and social aspects of the destination evolve.

Negotiation and Coping Strategies: From a leisure and recreation perspective negotiation with one's internal and external constraints is widely understood within the Leisure Constraints model which includes three basic levels of leisure constraint of intra-personal, interpersonal and structural. The Leisure Constraints model is perhaps best suited to understanding what aspect of the internal (personal traits and motivation) and external (physical, social and structural) environments are being negotiated and how. The Recreation Coping model is used to understand the way in which people respond to stressors within a recreation setting.

The Recreation Coping model posits that individuals will respond using one of more of four possible responses to stress within a recreation environment they include two cognitive based responses of rationalization and product shift and two behavioural based responses of displacement and direct action. It is postulated that an individual will begin leisure and recreation negotiations relying on typical leisure constraint negotiations for the selection and pursuit of activities and behaviours. With increased time at the site it is believed that an individual will rely more heavily on recreation coping strategies as various types of stressors persist and complimentary strategies are found. However, it is assumed that despite the shift in emphasis over time both leisure constraint and recreation coping negotiation strategies may be present at any one time.

Amenity Migrant Typology: Resulting from Motivation and the dynamic of the leisure centred human-environment negotiation is a typology of amenity migrants based on the findings of this investigation. The typology is primarily based on the qualitative data analysis and appears in Box A. The typology is a result of different types (what is being negotiated) and levels (intensity) of negotiation within the human environment. Various amenity migrant typologies appear in the literature. Factor analysis results revealed four distinct factor components based on importance of recreation amenities they include; back country, culture, recreation and entertainment.

Amenity Migrant Typology

1. Those who wish to pursue a mountain recreation lifestyle in the Bow Valley rely on it for their livelihood but can not negotiate the costs over the benefits and decide to leave;
2. Those who wish to pursue a mountain recreation lifestyle in the Bow Valley and rely on it for their livelihood but negotiate to overcome the costs for the benefit;
3. Those who live in the Bow Valley to pursue more urban recreation and hospitality & tourism careers within the area;
4. Those who wish to pursue a mountain recreation lifestyle but do not rely on the Bow Valley for their livelihood directly (commute or remote work situations); and
5. Those who wish to escape to the Bow Valley part-time (second home) and do not rely on the valley for their livelihood.

Place Attachment, Dependence, and Identity. The relationship the individual recreationist develops with the place over time can be understood using the concept of place attachment including underlying concepts of place dependence and identity.

Together, as place attachment, it is used to characterize the continuous manifestation of the human-environment negotiation as a relationship with the place. Place attachment, dependence and identity are assumed to be strong predictors of whether an individual will stay or leave a destination. Some will leave and others will remain. Even those who leave the site impact the evolution of the destination as was their behaviour an expression of demand for the tenure of their residency. Those who leave may be seeking other destinations more supportive of their identity, goals and personal resources. Those who remain impact the destination through their behaviour, and in other ways such as policy development, and through on-going, shared discourse that creates a collective understanding of place. Place attachment loops back (dotted line) to motivation as the individual's relationship with the place will be affected by the continuous negotiation process which is assumed to influence one's motivation to engage in future negotiations and in what manner. Place attachment loops back as an antecedent to the continuous negotiation process.

Affect on Destination and Recreation Supply. The final component of the models seeks to provide insight into how the leisure based human-environment relationship physically affects a high recreation amenity destination. It is postulated here that as population increases urban-type recreation supply increases and backcountry (outside of the townsite) generally remains stagnant or decreases. This general pattern has been previously observed. For example Glorioso & Moss (2006) discuss the rapid increase of urban amenities in the Santa Fe region during the 1980s to present in association with amenity migration. Moore, Williams & Gill (2006) report loss of recreation land adjacent to Whistler BC townsite as a result of residential and golf course development coupled with increased urbanization. As the destination evolves including the quantity and quality of urban and recreation supply this will result in an equally evolving image of the destination that will serve to attract different types of individuals. This is a simple displacement process similar the Plog's (2002) model, however based on tourists, whereby a destination evolves and as it does it attracts 'venturerers' at first then 'dependables' later on. Similarly, early, density-crowding-satisfaction models realized that within any one site varying conditions would attract different groups of people more or less comfortable with crowding conditions. The quantitative survey included a 27-item scale to assess whether residents perceived change in their recreation and structural environment in the form of increases or decreases in urban-type recreation, backcountry recreation, tourism activity, and structural elements such as jobs, housing and cost of living.

Factor analysis on the scale revealed seven factor components in accordance to where most change has been perceived (no particular direction of change) they were labelled as crowding, backcountry, urbane, town, outdoor recreation, and urban. A five-cluster solution revealed that overall some factor components were perceived to have increased and others decreased. More specifically, overall factor components 'crowding' (seven crowding related items) and 'urbane' (four items related to cafes, restaurants, and bars) were perceived to have increased while 'outdoor' (four items related to trails, ski areas, festivals), 'backcountry' (four items related to more remote outdoor activity), was perceived to have decreased while 'town' (five items related to structural aspects and public recreation) has remained about the same. The quantitative results generally support the final component of the model whereby in-town recreation supply increases while backcountry recreation increases. The results of cluster analysis on one of the four measures contained within the questionnaire. The sub-scale means for each of the clusters, the composite mean for each cluster, a cluster label and the results of the Scheffe test. The scale for Q8 was a six point scale with the final scale item of 'don't know' recoded as missing therefore it is based on a five point scale whereby 1 has increased greatly 3 is has not changed and 5 is has decreased greatly.

An ANOVA was conducted to determine if there were differences among the means of the clusters which yielded value of for each of the subscale items. A post hoc analysis of a Scheffe Test was conducted to determine which clusters are significantly different from which and in what direction. Numerous significant tests (p=.05) were reported with the direcion of difference indicated by the arrow. Additionally Classification Results(a) test reported that 97.2% of the originally grouped cases were classified correctly.

Indicate that overall some factor components are perceived to be increasing and others are perceived to be decreasing for example if a cut off point of 2.5 within the scale is adopted whereby that which is less than 2.5 is perceived to be increasing and that which is over 2.5 is perceived to be decreasing than overall respondents report that 'crowding' and 'urbane' components are perceived to be increasing while 'town' has generally remained the same and 'outdoor', 'backcountry' and 'urban' (only one item) have all decreased. Also, that the five clusters are different however some basic patterns emerge. With respect to the 'crowding' subscale, cluster 1 (nothing is different) is different from the others. Cluster 2 (crowded out) generally differs from the others with respect to the 'urbane', 'outdoor', 'backcountry' and 'urban' subscales.

Overall, cluster 2 (crowded out, N=65) is different from others with respect to perception of change in the Bow Valley. In general, the exploratory findings support the assertion that change is occurring the direction of increased crowding and urban-type recreation amenities and opportunities with a perceived decrease in backcountry-type recreation amenities and opportunities

Relaxation

How Motivations, Constraints, and Demographic Factors Predict Seniors' Overseas Travel Propensity

As the trend in aging societies is growing all over the world, the travel and tourism market for senior citizens has attracted much attention recently from both practitioners and academics. The market shows great potential, not only because of its considerable population proportion, but also because of senior citizens' great contribution to a tourism economy. It is generally accepted that seniors in developed countries on average possess a relatively large share of discretionary income and time and are still in good health. These characteristics enable them to travel more, and many seniors have the time to travel and are willing to spend a significant amount of their savings on travel. In addition, the travel behaviour of seniors is characterized as travelling more frequently, going longer distances, staying away longer, spending more money, and relying more on travel agents. Hence, senior travellers are important to the tourism industry and will grow in importance as their segment grows in size and wealth. Understanding seniors' travel decision behaviour is a crucial issue to travel marketers who compete for this important market.

The theory of tourism demand states that it is influenced by three major determinants: economic factors, socio-psychological factors, and exogenous factors. The economic factors include per capita income, cost of living, exchange rate, tourism prices, and transportation costs, among others. The social-psychological factors are associated with the decision-making of travellers such as demographic factors, travel motivations, constraints, images of destinations, and travel preferences, among others. The exogenous factors are associated with the business environment. The psychological determinants of demand in explaining some reasons why tourists travel and select particular destinations. Motivation is defined as the 'driving force behind all behaviour'. From the perspective of the traveller's decision-making process, travel motivations are seen as the energizers of demand that promote an individual to decide on a holiday. Travel behaviour can be predicted by underlying motivations.

Hence, those who are highly motivated might be those who are most likely to overcome constraints and participate in more leisure activities. The concept of travel motivations is based on the existence of "push" and "pull" factors. This has been extensively discussed and is a generally accepted concept. Push motivation refers to an individual's internal energy and an increase in the desire for people to travel, while pull motivation refers to a force external to an individual that influences where people travel, given the initial desire to travel.

Ryan (1991) finds that tourist travel motivations could be identified as wish fulfilment, shopping, escaping from a mundane environment, rest and relaxation, an opportunity for play, strengthening family bonds, prestige, social interaction, and educational opportunities. The most common motivations identified by related research regarding seniors' travel motivation are rest and relaxation, escaping from a mundane environment, social interaction, physical exercise, learning, nostalgia, visiting friends and relatives, and excitement. Shoemaker (1989) notes that among fourteen motivations, rest and relaxation as well as escaping from a mundane environment are the most salient two motivations, while knowing friends of a different gender and playing golf are the least important two motivations for senior travellers in Pennsylvania.

Interestingly, after ten years, Shoemaker (2000) finds that the main motivations of senior travellers shifted to visiting new places and experiencing new things. Regarding seniors' travel motivation, some main classifications can be identified in the literature such as rest/relaxation, social interaction, health, learning, seeking, escaping, attracting, cost, nostalgia and visiting historical sites.

Huang and Tsai (2003) reported that 'Get rest and relaxation' (35.6%) and 'Meet people and socialization' (20.1%) are found as the main travel motivation of Taiwanese seniors. In addition, considering both push and pull dimensions of Taiwanese senior travel motivations, Jang and Wu (2006) found the push motivations include 'ego-enhancement', 'self-esteem', 'knowledge seeking', 'relaxation', and 'socialization' while the pull motivations encompass 'cleanliness and safety', 'facility, event and cost', and 'natural and historical sites'.

Travel Constraints

Unlike motivations that serve as energizers, constraints towards travelling function as filters for tourism demand, preventing the decision makers from engaging in travel even though the motivation may exist.

Leisure constraints can provide a conceptual framework that may help understand why individuals do not participate in specific tourism activities. The hierarchical model proposed by Crawford and Godbey (1987) and Crawford et al. (1991), is the most accepted theoretical framework of leisure constraints.

Their studies categorize leisure constraints into three hierarchically organized levels: intrapersonal, interpersonal, and structural constraints. Furthermore, participation in leisure activities is seen as a process of overcoming the various constraints. The intrapersonal constraints are defined as individual psychological states and attributes, such as stress, anxiety, attitudes, and perceived self skill, that might inhibit one from participating in leisure activities. They exist when people fail to develop leisure preferences due to problems or misconceptions associated with personality needs, prior socialization, personal ability, and perceptions of reference group attitudes. The interpersonal barriers result from social interactions with friends, family, and others. The structural constraints include factors that block people's intentions from taking actions such as economic resources, availability of time, and accessibility. The most often cited constraints to travel in related research are a lack of time, financial considerations, physical and emotional costs, health status (objective and self-reported), perceived disability, age, security concerns, lack of information, family approval, and family responsibilities.

Regarding the dimensionality of leisure constraint measurement, Jackson (1993) identifies six dimensions of leisure constraints from eight studies: social isolation, accessibility, personal reasons, costs, time commitments, and facilities. The social isolation dimension can be deemed as an interpersonal dimension that is based on characteristics involving interaction between/among people. The accessibility dimension includes factors such as a lack of or limited access to transportation or 'getting there'.

The personal reasons dimension is an intrapersonal dimension that includes items pertaining directly to an individual's abilities or motivations. The cost dimension covers items related to the outlay of money. The time dimension represents a collection of items referred to as reasons that affect levels and intensity of participation among adults. Finally, the facility dimension relates specifically toleisure settings and individuals' perception. Although the theoretical hypothesis assumes a positive impact of travel motivation on travel propensity, it is acceptable to see a negative impact of *socialization* motivation on travel intention in this study.

The decision of whether to travel overseas or to travel domestically involves different decision-making considerations. The push power of travel motivation, such as socialization in general, can motivate seniors to travel in the domestic context due to familiar cultural and/or social customs, languages, etc. However, travelling overseas might be a barrier for seniors due to an unfamiliar or foreign environment. This is indirectly supported by about 70% of retirees choosing group package tours as their overseas travel mode in Taiwan.

The Psychology of Relaxation

The Gospel of Relaxation was the subject of a speech made by Mr. Herbert Spencer at a dinner given in his honour in New York City in 1882. Mr. Spencer called attention to the extreme form of "persistent activity' 3 which characterizes the American people. The energy of the savage, he said, was spasmodic. He could not apply himself persistently to work. He lived in the present and did not worry about the future. Civilized man more and more pursues a future goal and applies himself to work until it becomes a passion.

In America, said Mr. Spencer, this strenuous and high-pressure life has become extreme, and a counterchange a reaction must be imminent. We take our multitudinous responsibilities too seriously. There are too many lines in our faces, our gray hairs appear too early, our nervous breakdowns are too frequent. Damaged constitutions and a damaged posterity are among the results. Emerson, with his saying that the first requisite of a gentleman is to be a perfect animal, is a safer guide for us than Carlyle with his gospel of work.

More recently, Professor James, Annie Payson Call, and other writers 1 have eloquently preached this same gospel of relaxation. We are told that we are too breathless; that we live under too much stress and tension; that we are too intense and carry too much expression in our faces; that we must relax, let go, breathe deeply, and unburden ourselves of many useless contractions.

There seems to be a good deal of truth in this. Some of us manage to escape neu-rasthenia, but few of us are free from fatigue, chronic or acute. We hear with amazement now and again some one say, "I was never tired in my life." Surely under normal conditions we ought not to be so tired as we are, nor tired so often.

Impressed with the strenuous character of American life and the need of more rest and recreation, practical common sense, not waiting upon theory, has turned to discover means for relieving the excessive tension incident to our present habits of living. Some, as we have said, preach the gospel of relaxation, content to tell us that we are too intense. Others have established schools with practical and helpful rules and methods for relaxation and have brought comfort and relief to many. Again, a new and unique interest has suddenly arisen in play. Men and animals have always played; but now we have first become conscious of play and curious about it. We insist on play. If children do not play, we teach them to play. And we are anxious to know about the theory of play.

Finally, a score of movements, perhaps many score, have sprung into notice, whose purpose is to encourage or provide some form of relaxation. We recall the recreation movement; the physical-culture movement; the playground movement; the Boy Scouts; the Camp-Fire girls; the ever-increasing interest in athletics, not only in our colleges, but also in our high schools and grammar schools; the radical change in Young Men's Christian Associations from devotional to hygienic and athletic religion; the renaissance of the gymnasium and the Olympic games; the increased interest in outdoor life of all kinds; the renewed devotion to outdoor sports, like tennis, golf, baseball, and football; the rapid extension of the play motive into almost every branch of education; the new vacation schools and school excursions; finally the supervised playgrounds, supervised folk-dancing, supervised swimming, wading, tramping, gardening, singing, and storytelling. Even with very young children the Montessori system seeks to relieve the tension of the old task methods by making the child's activities natural and interesting as well as useful.

More than twenty-five hundred regularly supervised playgrounds and recreation centres are now maintained in about six hundred and fifty cities in this country. A brand new profession has appeared, that of play leader, employing nearly seven thousand professional workers.

The legislatures of some States have passed laws requiring every city of a certain size to vote on the proposition of maintaining playgrounds. New York City expended more than $15,000,000 on playgrounds previous to 1908.

The city paid $1,811,000 for one playground having about three acres. Chicago spent $11,000,000 on playgrounds and field houses in two years. Formerly the boy could play on the street, in the back alley, in the back yard. Now, the alley and back yard have disappeared, the street is crowded with automobiles, and the few remaining open spaces are given over to the lawn-mower and keep-off-the-grass signs, while more and more the school has encroached on the boy's precious period of growth, filling at least nine of the twelve months of the year and adding the evils of evening study and the dread of examinations.

For reasons which will be shown presently, boys must play. Take away the opportunity for legitimate play, and the play instinct, the instinct of rivalry, of adventure, of initiation, will manifest itself in antisocial ways. Hence the juvenile court and the reform school. "Better, playgrounds without schools," says one writer, "than schools without playgrounds." Up to the present time this is about as far as we have gone into the subject of relaxation. Its psychology has not really been studied at all. We have simply been impressed by the tense and strenuous character of our manner of life and have connected this with the increase of nervous disorders and nervous breakdowns and perhaps with the increase of insanity, and have felt the need, accordingly, of more recreation and play, and more harmony and poise in our way of living, and have taken, there fore, a few practical steps in this direction. But suddenly within the most recent days things have happened which have caused some of us to begin to think more deeply on the whole subject of work and play, and have suggested that it is not a local American problem at all, but a world problem of the present age, and that perhaps great social questions may be involved. The outbreak of recreation crazes in America was the first of these events, but it was the calamity of the European war which most distinctly called our attention to the need of a more careful study of the psychological conditions of our modern life.

Just as we thought the world to be getting very serious, and settling down to work and to problems of social and individual welfare and to political and moral reform, it has suddenly gone amusement-mad in America and reverted with unparalleled ferocity to primeval bloodshed in Europe. These amusement crazes have taken many forms, but the most virulent form was seen in the dancing mania, which has passed through various stages in North and South America and has been so widespread and so compelling that it has reminded us of the epidemics of the Middle Ages. At its height, according to the newspaper reports, a tribe of Indians in Nevada built a great dance-hall in the midst of their village, and imported a teacher of the tango.

Then came the moving-picture craze, which has seized the world like an obsession. No one can suppose that this colossal social phenomenon is to be explained by the mere fact of the discovery of the cinematograph, and that the people were merely waiting upon the invention in order to flock to the spectacles. The invention was an incident. The real significant fact was the psychological situation. Consider the following editorial from a recent number of the "Nation":

The historian will come to grief if he attempts to describe the cause of frivolity in the New York of 1915 A.D. as historians have depicted the frivolity of Rome under the early emperors, and to compare bread and the circus with lobster a la Newburgh and the cabaret. Going back to Rome, and assuming the grand manner, he will speak of a city that drew to itself the booty of the civilized world, of a population enervated by the largess of politicians doling out the plunder of three continents, of a citizenship lulled into civic indifference by gifts and amusements in other words, an imperial city gone rotten with prosperity.

If the parallel holds for New York, the historian would have to describe a city that went mad over cabarets because it had more money than it could spend wisely, because it had no serious interest in the problems of the civic and social life, because its serenity was undisturbed by wars or the fear of wars, because there was no unemployment problem, no city-budget problem, no workmen's compensation problem, no widows' pension problem, no Mexican problem, no German problem. Else how account for a city gone mad over the fox trot and the white lights? Life was much simpler in imperial Rome than it is in New York today, though even under the early Caesars the picture was not so uniform as the average historian has painted it.

At least we know today that the fact of 400,000 unemployed in New York City does not militate against the prosperity of the "movies," which are the circenses of the masses; and the fact of Wall Street's unemployed has not interfered with the prosperity of the cabarets. Quite the contrary. There is good reason for believing that not all the young men at the afternoon teas are professional idlers and parasites, but that a good many business men and brokers have taken to dancing in the afternoon because there was nothing to do downtown. Perhaps the grasshopper in La Fontaine's fable, who sang all summer, did so because business was rotten, and when the ant told him to go and dance in winter, he was only advising him to do the best possible thing under the circumstances.

To be sure it is no longer possible to dispose of such things as these by referring them to "frivolity" or to "luxury," but neither is it possible to say that they are due to idleness. For instance, a correspondent in a small mining-camp near the Mexican border writes that the Mexican labourers, who comprise six-sevenths of the population, are strictly amusement-mad, spending their last pennies at the "movies" or the merry-go-round or for intoxicants. May it not be that these amusement crazes are a form of reaction against a manner of life that is too serious and tense. May they not be indications of a lack of physiological adjustment. We are making great efforts in these days to secure better social adjustment through the study of social and economic conditions; but is it not possible that the trouble is not in the lack of social adjustment, but in the lack of physiological adjustment in the individual, so that what we have to strive for is not so much improved social conditions, as improved health and improved physical constitutions, to be gained by a different manner of life, a different kind of education, and a different proportion of work and play.

Then there is another cloud which has recently appeared on the social horizon leading us to think that the problem of work and play needs further study. We refer to the remarkable increase in the number of deaths from diseases of degeneration. A few years ago, rejoicing over the discoveries of Pasteur and his followers, we had great hope of increasing the span of human life by the conquest of the devastating parasitic diseases. These diseases have, indeed, to some extent been conquered. We have now less dread of typhoid, tuberculosis, pneumonia, and diseases of this class due to microscopic enemies, but the expected increase in racial stability has not come. Some, therefore, are beginning to ask whether the better way to lengthen human life is to remove the enemies which threaten it, or to increase our power of resistance to these enemies.

According to Mr. E. E. Rittenhouse, president of the Life Extension Institute, there is a marked decline in the power of American workers to withstand the strain of modern life. They wear out sooner than they did a few years ago. The chances of death after reaching the prime of life have increased because of the extraordinary increase in the death-rate from the breaking-down of the heart, arteries, kidneys, and of the nervous and digestive systems. Mr. Rittenhouse's conclusions as to the serious inroads of these diseases in modern life are based not on mortality records of the idle rich and such classes, but upon actual physical examination of a large number of male workers, including officials, clerks, and employees of banks and commercial houses, averaging about thirty years of age. The results show that these diseases of degeneration, so-called diseases of old age, are " reaching down into middle life and below, and increasing there, and apparently at all ages." These diseases, not being so quickly fatal as the parasitic diseases, produce decreased efficiency and increased misery, oftentimes through many working years.

The lesson which investigations such as this teach is that the problem of public health and longevity is not altogether a problem of hygiene in the narrower sense in which this word is commonly used. It is rather the deeper question of vitality, of biological adjustment, of racial stability; and it involves questions of heredity, of mental and physical balance, of manner of life, of physical education, of work and play.

Sociologists are becoming acutely conscious of the fact that our cultured classes are not self-perpetuating. The increasing number of childless marriages and small families in these classes indicates that a process of displacement is taking place in favour of peoples of hardier stock and simpler habits, depriving us at once of the advantages of physical heredity and making progress depend very largely upon social heredity alone. A given stock of people may cultivate its brains to the highest point of intellectual and moral efficiency, but, if it neglect the corresponding development of somatic vitality, if it neglect strength and vigour of muscles, heart, lungs, stomach, and reproductive system, it is doomed to extinction and cannot pass on to posterity the intellectual and moral power which it has itself inherited.

Finally, the increased desire for narcotics in the form of drugs, tobacco, and alcohol, prevalent in all civilized countries, is a further indication of some serious lack of balance between body and brain. There is a lack of adjustment somewhere, and the problem of the day is to find out where it is and how it may be remedied. It is not our purpose in this book to study this great problem, but rather a single phase of it, namely, the relation of work and play and the results both to the individual and to society of excessive work and insufficient relaxation. It is very probable that our modern strenuous life is bringing too heavy a strain upon the brain, particularly those parts of the brain immediately connected with the mental powers which condition that peculiar kind of progress which the world is now making. The tendency of the times is toward a very swift industrial, commercial, professional, and intellectual activity.

It is an age of great effort and endeavour, of stress and tension, of labour and strain, of scientific and inventive ability; an age of great efficiency and striving for efficiency; an age of variegation; a centrifugal age. It is not an age of peace, of calm, of poise, of relaxation, of repose, of measure, of harmony, of conservation. It is not a centripetal age. The spirit of the age is that of Francis Bacon. It is not the spirit of such greater minds as Buddha and Jesus and Sophocles and Plato and St. Francis.

What is likely to be the outcome of such tendencies as these? Our current sociology speaks almost exclusively of the proximate social results. What is perhaps more important is to speak of the immediate physiological and psychological results, because they throw light upon certain ultimate and still more important social consequences.

The immediate social results of an age of such great activity and great expenditure are clearly pointed out, for instance, by Professor Giddings in his "Democracy and Empire." These are, in brief, (i) an increase of wealth, culture, and refinement, followed by a marked increase of population; (2) a movement of the people toward the large cities; and (3) a displacement of the higher types of people by the lower, followed by an increase of crime, vagabondage, suicide, and feeble-mindedness.

These social results we may leave to the sociologist. But what is the effect of such an age of great activity and great expenditure upon the individual? This we believe to be just now the important question, and it is to the answer to this question that we hope the studies in this book may be a contribution.

The result, in a word, is a rapid and extreme fatigue of the higher brain and an unusual and imperative demand for rest and relaxation. Nature has provided various means for rest and relaxation, in sleep, play, sport, laughter, etc. But what will happen when the claims made upon the working brain are in excess of the powers of repair provided by these natural means of relaxation, or when these means themselves are neglected ? There will be increasing irritability and probably reactions more or less violent and spasmodic, and if there are any artificial means of relieving the strain and temporarily restoring the balance, there will be recourse to such aids.

The craving for narcotic drugs, tobacco, and alcohol, will be an example of the latter, and the recurrence of recreation crazes will be an illustration of the former. Finally, it is altogether possible that society as a whole may suffer from such excessive mental activity and such excessive tension, and that great social upheavals may follow, such, for instance, as war. Thus we may understand why the psychologist in treating the laws of relaxation may bring together in one volume subjects apparently so unlike as play, sport, laughter, profanity, alcohol, and war.

The principle involved in all the forms of relaxation here studied is relief from tension or release from some form of restraint. Although this tension and restraint on the part of the individual are necessary conditions of all social evolution, they have been greatly intensified by the manner of life which characterizes the nineteenth and twentieth centuries. The repression of primitive impulses to the end of growing social needs is the fundamental law of human progress. Such continual repression necessitates constant effort, constant strain, and constant exercise of voluntary attention. It involves those higher brain centres whose development has conditioned human progress, and brings upon them a severe and constant strain, making rest and relaxation imperative.

When this everlasting urge of progress is excessive, as it has been in recent times, we may say that there is in a way a constant subconscious rebellion against it and a constant disposition to escape from it, and the method of escape is always the temporary reversion to simpler and more primitive forms of behaviour, a return to nature, so to speak. Sudden momentary and unexpected release from this tension, with instinctive reinstatement of primitive forms of expression, is laughter. Daily or periodic systematic return to primitive forms of activity is sport or play. War is a violent social reversion to elemental and natural in-tertribal relations. Profanity is a resort to primitive forms of vocal expression to relieve a situation which threatens one's wellbeing. Alcohol is an artificial means of relieving mental tension by the narcotizing of the higher brain centres.

Thus the reader may understand why we have associated in a single volume these seemingly diverse kinds of human behaviour they are all forms of relaxation. That which is common to all these phenomena is the relief from the tension of our modern strenuous life by means of a return to nature, or a return to early and elemental forms of behaviour which offer rest or release from the burdens of life. All therefore appear as forms of relaxation, some helpful and normal, others abnormal and brutalizing.

If we should succeed in tracing all of these modes of human behaviour to their psychological sources, we may contribute something to the clearing-up of certain difficult social problems of the day. We may, for instance, be enabled to see very clearly that evil and destructive forms of relaxation cannot be banished except by substituting normal and healthful forms.

The growing worldwide craving for alcohol, tobacco, and other narcotic drugs and the fatal and inevitable recurrence of war, with its fearful toll of human life and its still more fearful toll of hard-earned human savings, perplexing though they are as social problems, nevertheless might become much clearer in the light thrown upon them by the study of the laws of mental relaxation.

In the present stage of human culture, war seems like a species of insanity. It is no longer taken for granted. It no longer fits in as a part of the natural order of events. It seems anomalous and grotesque. It has lost its glory and seems now barbaric. We have been so long accustomed to have our disputes settled by courts of law, whose decisions are based upon principles of justice, that an appeal to mere brute force in the settlement of international disputes appears to us more and more absurd.

Recently the reversionary character of war has been startlingly revealed to us by the reversionary logic and the reversionary morals which accompany it. And yet wars one after another, each more terrible than the last, are flaunted in the face of nineteenth and twentieth century civilization, are flaunted directly in the face of worldwide movements for international conciliation.

In like manner the use of alcohol, from the standpoint of modern science, appears as a kind of insanity. Scientific study has now shown that alcohol has none of the good effects upon the body or mind which formerly it was supposed to have, and that it is not even a stimulant. Yet the consumption of alcohol steadily increases.

Under these circumstances we should welcome any light, however small, which psychology can throw upon these subjects. The desire for alcohol and the instinct for war are phenomena which lie in the field of psychology, and reformers will make little headway against these evils unless they take into account the psychological motives.

We may, if we choose, redouble again our efforts against alcohol, but it would be the part of reason to find out, if we can, the causes of this growing desire in order that they may, if possible, be removed. So we may, if we choose, redouble our efforts toward universal peace, but a more rational method would seem to be to find out the deep-lying causes of war and see whether anything can be done to remove them.

In the chapters which follow, an attempt is made to treat these subjects psychologically and in particular to consider them from the standpoint of phylogenetic experience. We must call to mind not only the animal and savage past from which man has emerged, but also the forces or tendencies which are manifest in his development. It is not sufficient to explain war by recalling that man is a fighting animal, that he has literally fought his way up to manhood. It is far more important to understand that his constant advance has been attended by conditions of tension and stress which have made his periodic and temporary reversion to primitive habits an actual condition of renewed progress. It is still more important to learn how the supreme intelligence with which evolution has finally crowned mankind may be used to devise some means by which these periodic reversions to savagery may be made unnecessary.

Lately we have seemed to forget that human progress is rhythmical, that mankind advances by a series of relapses and recoveries, and that after each recovery there is new ground gained, sometimes very much new ground.

It may be that we have here the explanation of war, and it may be that there are conditions present in the social life of our times which intensify these rhythmical reversionary tendencies, so that no manner of humanitarian effort can withstand the periodic demand for war, just as no manner of prohibitive legislation and no manner of science sermons can stem the desire for alcohol. Especially in the last century has "progress," as it is called, been very rapid, progress in science, in industry, in invention, in everything, and the tension and rapidity of our lives have become correspondingly great. After great tension there must be great relaxation. There is a limit to the strain which the social mind can stand. It is imperative that we study the laws of mental tension and mental relaxation. The psychology of play may throw much light on the psychology of war.

No engineer or architect undertakes to build a bridge or skyscraper without an accurate knowledge of the strength of material. Modern life is a kind of social skyscraper. The minds of the individuals who constitute society are the material. This material is put under too much tension. A collapse necessarily follows. In our social life these collapses appear as reactions or reversions, sometimes cataclysmic, as in the case of the war in Europe, sometimes sporadic, as in the dancing crazes and the amusement crazes in America.

In the following pages an attempt has been made to study the strength of this human material, to study the causes of the social strains and the forms and directions taken by the social reactions. If these studies teach us nothing more, they will at least show that the folly of explaining war by referring it to mere political rivalries is no less than that of referring amusement crazes to "frivolity" and the desire for alcohol to "depravity."

The Psychology of Play

When we think of play, we usually have in mind the play of children. But grown-ups likewise play, and to their plays we sometimes apply the word "sport." Since it is our purpose in this book to study relaxation in its various forms, evidently it is sport, rather than play in its narrower sense, that we are especially interested in, for one could hardly speak of the play of children as a form of relaxation. Many books have been written about play, and it is the play of children that they usually deal with, a subject indeed of the greatest interest and the most vital importance. Little or no study has been made of the psychology of the play of adults, and this is unfortunate for two reasons: first, because of the importance of the subject itself in its relation to certain fundamental problems of our social life, and, second, because the play of children receives new and valuable light when it is studied in its relation to the play of man in the wider sense.

While our interest, then, in this chapter is primarily in the play of adults considered as a form of relaxation, nevertheless it is very evident that we could make no progress in this study without first examining the nature of play in general and without first considering the theories of play which other writers have proposed. It will be interesting, then, to follow this plan and see whether the old theories of play are satisfactory, and if not, whether it is possible to propose a new theory which shall bring the plays of children and the plays of men into harmony with each other, and at the same time into harmony with the laws of recreation and relaxation in general.

Many theories of play have been offered, but they may all be referred to three principal ones, which have been named the Schiller-Spencer theory, the Groos theory, and the Recapitulation theory. An examination of these theories will no doubt show that none of them are wholly incorrect.

They are rather partial views, not necessarily inconsistent with one another, but in need of more careful definition and limitation. Herbert Spencer's theory is that play activities are those which do not directly subserve life processes, but are due to an inner need of using those bodily organs which are over-rested and under-worked. In the lower animals, therefore, the occasion for play would not arise, since all their energies are constantly expended in the maintenance of life; but in the higher animals and in man, time and strength are not wholly absorbed in providing for immediate needs. There is thus a surplus of vigour and this surplus is expended through the usual channels; not, however, in real activities, that is, in work, but in simulations of real activities, that is, in play. Play is thus the dramatizing of real life. Kittens chasing balls and children nursing dolls are illustrations. Although modern writers might state this in somewhat different form, the theory is essentially sound so far as it goes. The rather hypercritical objection which has often been urged, namely, that we sometimes play when we are tired, is easily answered and need not be considered here. The real weakness of the theory is that it is incomplete. It explains why people that is, grown people--tend to be active all the time when they are not sleeping.

It explains nothing more than this and this needs no explanation, since it is characteristic of all animal life to be active. To explain how processes of nutrition lead to the accumulation of energy, which results in muscular activity, and that when there is no work to do this takes the form of play, is only a longer way of saying that an animal is alive and necessarily active. To speak of that energy which is not expended in life-serving processes as "surplus energy" is to assume that man exists to work, and that play is something extra, a kind of afterthought, to fill up the time.

A further difficulty with Spencer's theory is that it does not apply to the play of children at all, for the reason that the child is not a working animal, and does not provide his own sustenance. Hence there could be no "surplus energy." His whole life is a play life. Of course, if the theory had been stated a little differently, it would apply perfectly to the play of children. Children are alive and active, and their activity, not being directed to immediate life-serving ends, we call play.

But the most serious difficulty with Spencer's theory is that it does not explain the form taken either by the plays of children or of adults. His view is that men and animals in their surplus-energy moods that is, in their play would simply go on doing in a dramatizing way what they are accustomed seriously to do in their working moods. The horse would run, the tiger would jump, the cat would chase imaginary mice, and the man presumably would plough and reap and dig and write books and give lectures. But this is precisely what the man does not do. He goes fishing, plays golf and baseball, goes to horse-races, and rides in automobiles. The Spencer theory, therefore, misses the whole point. It is true because it is a truism.

The Groos theory of play attempts to supply what the Spencer theory lacks, that is, to account for the actual form taken by the plays of children and young animals. Unfortunately, it gives little attention to the plays of adults.

According to the Groos theory of play, the plays of animals and children are instincts which have arisen through the action of natural selection because of their usefulness as a practice and preparation for life's later serious duties. Professor Groos has written two volumincus books on the play of animals and the play of man containing a wealth of material on these subjects, but the reader cannot fail to be impressed by the lack of connection between the facts and the theory. The author seems, indeed, to have arrived at his theory of play through a purely deductive process. Since play is an instinct, and since, as we cannot admit the inheritance of acquired characters, every instinct has arisen in response to some definite practical need, and since it is evident that play has no immediate life-serving function, it must serve as a practice and preparation for life's serious pursuits.

In this argument the premises may be sound, but the conclusion has no necessary connection with them. Plays, indeed, are instinctive, and no doubt all instinctive reactions have had at some time in our racial history some life-serving meaning. But the fact that natural selection has not yet eliminated the great multitude of old racial habits with which the young child's nervous system teems does not prove that they have been retained because of their usefulness as a practice and preparation for future life. In any animal species, such as man, that lives in a changing environment and has a long period of youth followed by a period of great rational power of transformation, we may expect behaviour to be largely determined by inherited habit.

As Professor Thorndike says: "We fear, not the carriers of malaria and yellow fever, but thunder and the dark; we pity, not the gifted youth debarred from education, but the beggar's bloody sore; we are less excited by a great injustice than by a little blood." We are no longer so impressed by the infallible powers of natural selection as when Professor Groos wrote.

Man's original nature is not so perfect as we once thought. We are more impressed by its "archaic unreason." And even in the case of instincts which are now useful, it does not follow that, if they appear before the time of their life-serving usefulness, they must serve as a practice and preparation for such later use. Nature is not so parsimonious and calculating as that would indicate. It is not necessary to explain the doll plays of little girls as a practice and preparation for their future maternal duties. They may be simply exhibitions of a maternal instinct which sometime in the life of the individual may be useful, as when a tree showers down ten thousand seeds, of which one only may germinate. So the fighting plays of boys may be simply old racial habits, the line of least resistance for boyish activities. In one sense, to be sure, if one should wish to look at the matter ideologically, play, like food or sleep, or like growth itself, is a preparation for manhood. But it is better to regard the child as a playing animal, realizing in himself his own end. Play, like growth or life itself, belongs to the concept of childhood. Play is just the name we give to the child's activities. In the Groos theory, as in that of Spencer, there seems to lurk the belief that the child is naturally quiescent, and that if he plays, his play must look forward to that particular aspect of life which we call his serious or bread-winning activity.

When we consider what the plays of children actually are, we discover, except in a limited number of imitative plays, but faint resemblance between them and the serious pursuits of adult man. They resemble rather the pursuits of primitive and prehistoric man, and many of them are like the sports of adults of the present day. The plays most dear to the hearts of boys are running, jumping, climbing, coasting, skating, wrestling, wading, swimming, boating, fishing, hunting, shooting with darts, spears, arrows, or guns, building bonfires, robbing birds' nests, gathering nuts, collecting stamps, eggs, beetles or other things, flying kites, digging caves, making tree houses, spinning tops, playing horse, playing marbles, jackstones, numbers, hide-and-seek, tag, blackman, prisoner's base, leap-frog, baseball, football, tennis, cricket, golf, etc.

Children of all ages have the greatest interest in pet animals, dogs, cats, rabbits, birds, horses, etc. No small part of the child's life is occupied with playing with these pets and in earlier years with toy animals of all kinds. To these plays should be added, of course, the countless indoor games, such as checkers, chess, cards, dominoes, etc.

These children's plays have so little in common with the later pursuits of adult life that it is evident that some quite other theory is needed to explain them than the practice and preparation theory. When the boy is grown to manhood he will not be found doing these things, except in his hours of relaxation. His serious pursuits will take other forms. He will be found cultivating the soil, harvesting his crops, shoveling dirt, sand, or coal, blasting rocks from quarries and minerals from mines, building houses, buying, selling, manufacturing or transporting goods, teaching school, healing diseases, preaching sermons, practising law, engaging in politics or commercial transactions, giving lectures or conducting scientific research. This is the "serious" life of today and the life of the ancient Greeks and Romans was much the same, and it is all far removed from the play life of the child, which likewise is much the same in ancient and modern times, and involves altogether simpler forms of response. If the serious life of today consisted in escaping from enemies by foot, horse, or paddle, in living in close proximity to domestic animals, in pursuit of game with bow or gun, in subsisting on fish caught singly by hand, in personal combat with fist or sword, in throwing missiles, striking with a club or pursuing an enemy, in seeking safety in trees or caves, in living in tents or tree houses, and in sleeping and cooking by a campfire, then we might venture to explain the play life of the child as "an instinctive activity existing for purposes of practice or exercise and without serious intent." But these are not the pursuits of adult men, except in their hours of sport. Most of the plays of children find their significance, not in their likeness, but in their unlikeness to man's laborious duties. In fact, the plays of children bear a striking resemblance to the sports of men, and the latter would not be sports if they did not stand in direct contrast to work.

As regards the imitative plays of children, their resemblance to the serious activities of adult life is, of course, closer, and to them the Groos theory of play would seem to be less strained in its application. But the imitative plays themselves are not instinctive for the reason that they are imitative. If it is meant merely that imitation itself is an impulse which has been perpetuated by natural selection owing to its usefulness in preparing children for mature life, this view might be maintained, of course, if one still wished to put so much emphasis upon natural selection.

Other objections to the Groos theory may be passed with a mere reference. Perhaps the most serious of them is the failure of this theory to explain adult sports and to correlate them with the plays of children. Again, one is troubled by the frequent use of the word "serious" as applied to the activities of the adult, while the plays of children are spoken of as "sham," "make-believe," or "selfillusory." This distinction can no longer be made.

Child life and its plays are quite as serious and quite as real as the life of the man. If we are to speak of "ends," it would be difficult indeed to show that the life of the grownup is any more final or purposeful than the life of the child. Would it not be just as appropriate to say that the man's toil and sweat are a preparation for the radiant childhood of the son and daughter whom he may beget, as that the plays of childhood are a preparation for the prosaic work-life of the father? And as for seriousness, to the boy hastily swallowing his dinner or rushing through some uninteresting task to join his fellows in a game of ball or a trip to the river, it is the latter and not the former that are serious and real. It is a notable fact that most children take but a passing or trifling interest in what they eat, and scarcely remember their food of yesterday. It is a peculiarity of the adult masculine mind to be very intent on the bread-winning aspect of life and on the preservation of the species.

Perhaps nature exploits man for these particular aspects of life, which in themselves are but partial views. They might even be looked upon as necessary evils, subordinate in "purpose" to childhood, play, sport, art, and sympathy, which are more real and final.

In reference to the Groos theory of play, some critics have been misled by the fact that certain games, like baseball, seem to provide valuable training in such qualities as obedience, cooperation, quickness of decision, for attitude in defeat, and endurance. That the game cultivates these virtues to some extent is doubtless true. One can hardly suppose, however, that natural selection has operated to form an instinct for baseball because of its especial usefulness in providing such training. Other explanations for the fascination of this game are much simpler, as we shall see. Women, also, have need of these virtues, but they do not care to play baseball.

Professor Groos has more recently supplemented his work by a catharsis theory of play, already anticipated by American writers. According to this particular form of the catharsis theory, play is a kind of safety-valve for the expression of pent-up emotion, as for instance in the fighting plays of children, where the pent-up emotion is anger. According to this view, one would understand the emotions to be some kind of internal forces which would do damage if they could find no escape. It is not, however, probable that Professor Groos or any one holds this naive view of the emotions, and the whole relation may be more simply expressed if we suppose that the fighting plays are among the natural or spontaneous activities of children and as long as they are freely indulged in, the child is free from hurtful emotions. If these activities are repressed, then no doubt would occur certain internal disturbances of a less healthful character. Where spontaneous responses are inhibited, readjustments are necessary and emotions are present. When the spontaneous response is resumed, the emotion subsides. In this way children's plays might seem to have a catharsis effect. In spontaneous unrestricted play, however, there would seem to be no such element present or necessary.

In the sports of men, indeed, a decided Catharsis effect is present. They are essentially purifying. But, as we shall learn in these studies, the catharsis effect is primarily due to a restoring of disturbed balance in the psychophysical organism. It is thus more nearly described as rest than as purification. Play brings relief from that peculiar form of fatigue which follows from our modern strenuous life. It rests those parts of the nervous system which our daily work most stresses.

But adult play has probably a catharsis effect of another kind. It has been shown by the researches of Walter B. Cannon and his associates 1 that under the influence of strong emotion, say of fear or anger, a whole series of internal changes takes place in the organism, which are adaptive in their character and prepare the muscular system for the strenuous responses which the threatening situation demands. Of these the increased blood-sugar and the increased adrenin in the blood are typical. In the life history of our race these internal preparations for great muscular activity have been followed normally by the activity itself, say flight or combat. The circle is thus completed as nature meant it to be. But in our modern life of constant inhibition, where the emotions themselves are present often enough and the internal preparation for great muscular exertion takes place, the muscular responses themselves, owing to social restrictions and other causes, are necessarily greatly limited, if not altogether repressed. Hence arises a feeling of irritability, having its source perhaps in the poisoning of the blood by the presence of these unused activating substances. All kinds of active sports, therefore, involving muscular activity serve as substitutes for the original responses phylogenetically determined. Thus it would appear that sports have an actual catharsis effect in the case of adults, and that in children, while this effect is theoretically absent, it is, of course, actually present in increasing degree as the child becomes a man. This catharsis effect of play, laughter, and profanity should not, however, be interpreted in such a way that these forms of relaxation are considered to be mere drainage channels for shunting off accumulated energy. 1 All forms of play and sport, as well as laughter and profanity, have themselves been phylogenetically determined. They are indeed the older and more original responses, and their principal catharsis effect is not due to their draining off accumulated energy and using up the various energizing substances in the blood, but rather to the complete rest which they afford to parts of the brain over-stressed in our modern life of work.

The third theory of play has been called the Recapitulation theory. This takes full cognizance of the phylogenetic significance of play, and indeed is based upon it. As regards the latter, all future theories of play must take carefully into account the numerous and striking similarities between the plays of children and the pursuits and customs of primitive and prehistoric man as they have been pointed out by President G. Stanley Hall and his associates.

But the question arises as to the reason for this resemblance, and if the correct reason is not found, the whole significance of play may be lost. The theory in question does not explain this resemblance except by referring it to a so-called law, the law of recapitulation, according to which each individual passes through a series of stages in his development corresponding to the stages of racial development. Even in the sphere of embryology the validity of this law has been much questioned, and it is looked upon with increasing distrust when applied to the period of postnatal or psychological development.

It should be said, however, that this theory of play is the only one that has successfully attacked the specific problem of accounting for the form taken by children's play. Perhaps the most serious difficulty with this theory is its failure to explain the plays of adults and to correlate them properly with those of children.

Our main purpose in the present chapter is to examine more carefully the grounds of the resemblance between children's plays and the pursuits of primitive man and, more particularly, to explain if possible the similarity which exists between both of these and the sports of the mature man of the present time. To this end the following introductory definitions and propositions may be offered, which, if found useful and valid, will considerably simplify the psychology of play.

The term "play" may be applied to all those human activities which are free and spontaneous and which are pursued for their own sake alone. The interest in them is self-developing and they are not continued under any internal or external compulsion. Play will thus include practically all the activities of children and the larger share of those of adults, such, for instance, as baseball, football, tennis, golf, polo, billiards, and countless other games and sports; diversions such as travelling, hunting, fishing, yachting, motoring, flying, dancing; vacation outings, games, races, spectacles, fairs, tournaments, and expositions; the theatre, opera, moving pictures, lectures, and entertainments; the enjoyment of music, painting, poetry, and other arts; the daily paper, the magazine, the short story, and the novel.

The term "work," on the other hand, will include all those activities in which by means of sustained voluntary attention one holds one's self down to a given task for the sake of some end to be attained other than the activity itself. Such activities involve mental stress, strain, effort, tension, concentration, and inhibition.

The plays of children and the sports of adults are to be closely coordinated and explained by reference to the same general principles. There is a striking similarity between the plays of children and the sports of men on the one hand and the pursuits of primitive man on the other. This similarity is due to the fact that those mental powers upon which advancing civilization depends, especially voluntary and sustained attention, concentration, analysis, and abstraction, are undeveloped in the child and subject to rapid fatigue in the adult.

The question may be asked how, according to the above definitions of work and play, we shall classify that form of work which becomes so interesting as to be self-developing and requires no effort of attention to pursue it. A man may become so interested in his garden or in his inventions or in his professional pursuits that his work may take on some of the characteristics of play. Nevertheless, this kind of work demands the exercise of mental powers of a high degree of complexity, and is far more fatiguing than play or sport as above defined, though far less so than that kind of work which has been called toil, or drudgery, where interest fails and the strain of attention is at its maximum. Hence the chilcts activities and the play activities of the adult tend always to take the form of old racial pursuits.

If we look at the matter physiologically, it is very evident, in the case of the adult, that there are some brain centres, or some brain tracts, or some forms of cerebral functioning, that are put under severe strain in our modern strenuous life and that there must be some kind of activity which will relieve these centres, or these tracts, during a considerable portion of each waking day and involve other centres not so subject to exhaustion. Such activity we call play or sport. Perhaps the word "relaxation" would be a more exact description of it. For our present purpose it does not matter in the least what these centres are or what manner of cerebral functioning this is.

It is only necessary to note the evident fact that there is some kind of cerebral activity associated with those peculiar mental powers the development of which has made possible human progress. Nor, again, is it necessary for our present purpose to make any exact enumeration of these so-called higher mental processes which distinguish the modern civilized man. Generally speaking, however, they include a constantly increasing power of sustained attention of the voluntary kind, controlled association, concentration, and analysis, together with a constantly increasing power of inhibition. The individual becomes increasingly able to hold steadily in view the image of a desired end, to inhibit the old and habitual responses which are no longer appropriate to that end, to analyse a given situation in thought, so that the response may be to certain elements in the situation rather than to the situation as a whole, and thus to meet a given situation with a new response. Only the fully developed adult mind is capable of much thinking of this kind, and at best it is highly fatiguing and cannot be continued through many hours of the waking day, so that all, or almost all, the hours of the child's day and the larger number of hours of the adult's day must be filled with responses of the simpler, more elemental, and racially older kind. Consequently children's play and adult sport tend to take the forms of old racial activities, involving brain tracts that are old, well worn, and pervious.

It is well known that the present tendency in both historical and anthropological study is to place less emphasis on the differences in the mental constitution of different races of men. 1 All existing races and all historical ones, so far as we can see, are much alike in their mental powers. But from our present point of view these races are all modern. It is clearly evident that in comparing modern civilized man with the highest of the lower animals or with his prehistoric, if not even with his primitive, ancestors, there has been an unmeasured advance in the powers above mentioned. Even this assumption, however, is not necessary so far as our present theory is concerned. It is merely necessary to notice that in seeking relief from the fatigue involved in that sustained and voluntary attention, controlled association, analysis, and abstraction which are essential to our or to any advancing civilization, we fall back upon a set of activities which no longer involve these processes, but which through ages of use have become familiar and easy.

All the evidence that we have points to the validity of the law that those peculiar forms of mental activity which have developed late in the evolution of man are most affected by fatigue a law fully sustained by the study of psychasthenics and their incapacity for higher mental operations, as well as by the observation of people normally fatigued, while it is known that the disintegration of the nervous system in disease follows the reverse order of its development.

Hence we understand why children's play and adult sport take the form of hunting, fishing, camping, outing, swimming, climbing, and so on through the long list. The more elemental these activities have been in the history of racial development, the greater release they afford, when indulged in as relaxation, from the tension of our modern life.

Those forms of mental response which are developed late in the history of the race, and late in the life of the child, that tense and strenuous activity upon which modern progress depends, the power to hold ourselves by sustained attention and sustained effort down to hard and uninteresting tasks for the sake of some ultimate end, the consecration of the mental forces upon probed Science, philosophy and invention Kie inhibition of old and undesirable responses, all these bring quick and extreme fatigue, and demand rest for the corresponding parts of the brain. In sleep these higher mental processes enjoy almost complete suspension. But the exercise of these powers during the long hours of our waking day would result in speedy collapse. It is clear therefore that our daily activity must be made up quite largely of responses of the simpler type, which shall give exercise to our muscles and sense organs and invoke older and more elemental forms of mentality, and at the same time allow the higher ones to rest. Such is relaxation in all its forms, and of such consists almost wholly the life of the child. For the brain tracts associated with the above-mentioned forms of mental activity are undeveloped in the child, as they are in early man, so that we may say with considerable truth not that the child ought not to work, but that he cannot work.

In the following pages we shall review some of the instances of the striking resemblance between the habits of our human ancestors and the plays of children and men, beginning with the simpler illustrations drawn from the plays of children and proceeding to the more instructive ones connected with the sports of adults.

Haddon and Tylor have studied the history of the kite and the top and of marbles, and have shown their very ancient character and their connection with early religious and divinatory rites. The same may be said of casting lots, throwing dice, games of forfeits and games with common playing cards. The mental habits of our ancestors, as we know, survive in the counting-out rhymes, in the charms and talismans and superstitions of children. One recalls the magic formula used by Tom Sawyer for driving away warts: You got to go by yourself in the middle of the woods where you know there is a spunkwater stump, and just as it's midnight you back up against the stump and jam your hand in and say: and then walk away quick eleven steps with your eyes shut, and then turn around three times and walk home without speaking to any one, because if you speak, the charm's busted.

The mental habits of the child seem like echoes from the remote past, recalling the life of the cave, the forest, and the stream. The instinct exhibited in infancy, as well as in boyhood, to climb stairs, ladders, trees, lampposts, anything, reminds us of forest life; the hide-and-seek games which appeal so powerfully even to the youngest children recall the cave life of our ancestors, or at least some mode of existence in which concealment from enemies, whether human or animal, was the condition of survival; while the instinct of infants to gravitate toward the nearest pond or puddle, the wading, swimming, fishing, boating proclivities of every youngster, seem like a reminiscence of some time when our fathers lived near and by means of the water. During a long period in the evolution of life among the higher animals and in the early history of man, the one all-important factor was speedy for upon it depended safety in flight from enemies and capture in pursuit. This ancient trait has persisted and survives today in a deep instinctive joy in speed, whether exhibited in running or coasting or skating or in the speed mania which lends such delight to motoring, flying, fast sailing, and fast riding.

Again, the ancient life of pursuit and capture persists upon every playground in the familiar games of tag, blackman, pull-away, and a hundred others. Indeed, for the exhibition of this instinct, no organized game is necessary. Sudden playful pursuit and flight are seen wherever children are assembled. The ancient life of personal combat is mirrored in the plays of children in mimic fighting and wrestling. The passion of every boy for the bow and arrow, sling, sling-shot, gun, or anything that will shoot, reveals the persistence of deep-rooted race habits, formed during ages of subsistence by these means.

There was a time when man lived in close relation with and dependence upon wild and domestic animals. This period is reflected in many forms in the child's life, in his animal books, his animal toys, his Teddy bears, in his numerous animal plays. The former dependence of man upon the horse is shown in the instinct of the child of today to play horse, to ride a rocking-horse, or a stick, or anything. The child's first musical instruments, the rattle, the drum, and the horn, were the first musical instruments of primitive man.

These illustrations could be multiplied indefinitely. They show the limitations of the Groos theory of play, for none of the plays of this class have much to do in preparing the child for the life of today, or in giving him special practice for his future work. We ourselves are so much slaves of the past in our habits of thought that we do not easily realize how far from the actual life of the present day is this play-life of the child. The real world of today is that of the laboratory, the school, the library, the bank, the office, the shop, the street, the factory, the farm and the railroad. Notwithstanding the child's imitative bent, his world, as shown in his tales, his dreams, and the plays he loves best, is that of the forest, the stream, the camp, the cave, the hunting-ground, and the battlefield.

Those things which have such a vital and absorbing interest for the boy have had at one time in our racial history an actual life and death interest for mankind. Take, for instance, the jackknife. How many knives has your boy had and lost, and what rich joy there is in every new one! We see how the practice and preparation theory of play fails here. The knife has no significance in society now. It has degenerated to mere fingernail purposes. But at one time it meant life in defence and food in offence. Your boy's supreme interest in the knife is a latent memory of those ancient days. Those who could use the knife and use it well survived and transmitted this trait to their offspring. The same could be said of the sling, the bow and arrow, and of sports like boxing, fencing, and fishing.

Consider the fascination of fishing: This is not a practice and preparation for the real life of today, but a reverberation of phyletic experience. In a summer resort where the writer was a visitor the past summer, day after day the whole male population of the hotel resorted to the fishing grounds. They paid two dollars and a half a day for a guide, seven dollars a day for a motorboat, and a cent and a half each for worms. Surely a stranger uninitiated into our habits would have been amazed to see these returning fishermen at night indifferently handing over their catch to the guide. It was the fishing they desired, not the fish, and yet great was their woe when one large fish was lost in the act of landing. It is estimated by the New York "Times" that on Sundays and holidays when the weather is fine, twenty-five thousand people in New York City go fishing at a minimum cost of one dollar each, and of these no doubt more than ninety-five per cent go for fun and not for the fish. At some stage in the history of human development fishing was without doubt a general means of subsistence. Those who could catch fish survived and handed down this instinct. Likewise the fascination of gathering wild nuts and berries is out of all proportion to the value of them when gathered. But nuts and berries were once of vital concern to our fathers.

It is in baseball and football, however, that we best see the phylogenetic significance of play. The daily paper is a good index of popular interest. Here we shall often find perhaps seven, perhaps twenty columns devoted to baseball, while no other single subject whether in politics, art, literature, or science, aspires to two columns. How shall we explain the absorbing interest in baseball and football as well as in horse-racing and prizefighting? Here again, phylogenetic experience becomes the key to the problem of modern sports.

In baseball we have a game combining three of the most deep-seated racial instincts, the instinct to throw, to run, and to strike. During untold periods of the life history of our race, survival has come to him who could throw the straightest, run the swiftest, and strike the hardest. To throw something at something is almost as natural for a boy as to breathe. Throwing, batting, running are no longer of any service in this age of mind, but they were the conditions of survival in the distant past. Baseball reinstates those ancient attitudes and brings a thrill of cherished memories. Any one who has ever held a bat in hand and assumed the expectant attitude of the batter knows the peculiar thrill which is explained only by recalling that his distant ancestors in just that attitude beat down with a real club many an opposing foe, whether man or beast, and those who held clubs in this position and struck hard and quickly survived and transmitted this instinct. Dr. Gulick says:

Baseball is a complex of elements all of which date back certainly to our prehuman ancestors. The ability to throw a stone with accuracy and speed was at one time a basal factor in the struggle for survival. The early man who could seize a bough of a tree and strike with accuracy and great power was better fitted to survive in the brutal struggles of those early days than the man not so endowed. He could defend his family better, he was better fitted for killing game, he was better fitted for overcoming his enemies. The ability to run and dodge with speed and endurance was also a basal factor.

The instinct to throw, as the same author shows, belongs to boys only, scarcely appearing in the case of girls. The awkward throw of girls, like the left arm throw of boys, is well known. The plays of girls reveal their own set of instincts recalling the habits of primitive woman. "We are the descendants of those men who could throw and those women who loved children."

Football excites still greater enthusiasm than baseball because it reinstates still more primitive forms of behaviour. The fascination of football, like that of other sports which have a deep appeal to the human mind, is explained only by the facts of mental evolution. We have to go back in human history to those ancient scenes and those ancient pursuits which have left an indelible imprint on the human brain, and we have to remember that in our hours of relaxation we demand a complete release from those newer forms of mental activity which condition progress and civilization, and a temporary return to the older and easier ones. The one great elemental fact in human history is the fact of war. Mankind has come up through a history of warfare. It has been man against man, group against group, tribe against tribe, nation against nation, from the beginning. Man is at home on the battlefield.

There he has received his training and gained his strength. His soul is full of latent memories of strife and conflict. The football field is a mimic representation of this age-old field of battle. Here again is found the face-to-face opposition of two hostile forces, the rude physical shock of the heavy opposing teams, the scrimmage-like, melee character of the collisions, the tackling, dodging, and kicking, and the lively chases for goal as for cover.

Football is more fun than baseball and attracts larger crowds, because it is more dramatic, more like a fight. It awakens in us deep-seated slumbering instincts, permits us to revel for a time in those long-restrained impulses, relieves completely the strain of the will, and so serves all the conditions of relaxation.

By inner imitation the spectators themselves participate in the game and at the same time give unrestrained expression to their emotions. If at a great football game any one will watch the spectators instead of the players, he will see at once that the people before him are not his associates of the school, the library, the office, the shop, the street, or the factory. The inhibition of emotional expression is the characteristic of modern civilized man. The child and the savage give free expression in voice, face, arms, and body to every feeling. The spectators at an exciting football game no longer attempt to restrain emotional expression. They shout and yell, blow horns and dance, swing their arms about and stamp, throw their hats in air and snatch off their neighbours' hats, howl and gesticulate, little realizing how foreign this is to their wonted behaviour or how odd it would look at their places of business. So also the defeated players cry like babies, as did the heroes of ancient Troy.

The excitement of the spectators cannot be explained by the importance of the scenes before them, for, as in the case of the horse-race, they have little or no relation to the serious life of the present; but the scenes are those which were once matters of life and death. The prevalence of gambling in connection with football, as well as in horse-racing, prizefighting, and other popular sports, illustrates the reversion to primitive morals accompanying the return to early pursuits.

This prevalence of gambling and of other obvious evils 2 connected with intercollegiate athletics has suggested to some the desirability of abolishing these sports. A very different conclusion, however, seems to be forced upon us by the study of the laws of relaxation in its broader aspects. Not until we understand the psychology of alcohol and of war and of the foolish amusement crazes shall we recognize the full significance and the full value of athletic contests and intercollegiate rivalries. The evils mentioned are real enough and most deplorable, but it does not follow that they would not be present in other or worse forms in different connections if there were no intercollegiate athletics.

The intense interest aroused in intercollegiate sports is no doubt to some extent an echo of the old ancestral rivalries between social groups. They appeal, therefore, to deepseated human instincts and fulfil to a marked degree all the requirements of relaxation and recreation.

It should, of course, be remembered that the social value of these sports relates rather to the spectators than to the players. For the latter, indeed, they may become a form of work. But the participants as spectators are numbered by the thousands, and for all of these the games serve as valuable forms of relaxation. The substitution of intramural football and baseball for the intercollegiate games would result in the loss to a large extent of the valuable holiday and festival aspects of the latter sports.

Furthermore, the intense interest in intercollegiate football and baseball has resulted in a very wide actual participation in these games by the students in colleges, universities, and in public and private schools throughout the country.

The law that the more elemental the character of our responses, the greater their value as relaxation and release from the tension of the strenuous life, is well illustrated in the circus and amphitheater of the Romans. When we recall the sports of ancient Rome, we see again that in sport we have a psychological factor of the greatest importance and a profound psychological problem. Juvenal's phrase "bread and games" has become familiar. The popularity of any emperor was nearly proportional to his liberality in the matter of games and spectacles. Emile Thomas says: "After the sack of Rome by Alaric, the miserable remnant of the original inhabitants, and the peasants who flocked in from the environs to the number of ten thousand, loudly demanded games in the Circus, which had to be celebrated among the smoking ruins."

The Colosseum, whose magnificence receives a new meaning from our point of view, accommodated eighty-seven thousand people. The Circus Maximus was one of the most imposing of Roman structures. It is said that four hundred and eighty-five thousand spectators were in actual attendance at once upon its spectacles. 1 The shouting could be heard in the suburbs of Rome. The upper wooden seats collapsed at one time, killing eleven hundred people. Rome had theatres, too, but the largest of these, that of Pompey, had seats for only forty thousand spectators, and despite the political interest which attached to many of the theatrical exhibitions, we must believe that the interest in the theatre was insignificant when compared with that of the amphitheater and circus. Trajan gave a single entertainment lasting one hundred and twenty-three days.

Now, what was the character of these amusements which so fascinated the Roman populace? They were horse-races, gladiatorial combats, and the exhibition and contests of wild animals. Man's racial history has been one long battle with the lower animals, defensive for life and safety, offensive for food and sustenance. So far as the workaday world of the Romans is concerned, it was much the same as ours, taxing the same higher mental powers and demanding relaxation in the form of older and simpler pursuits.

In the gladiatorial combats we see the hand-to-hand encounters of early man, almost as far removed from the actual daily life of the Romans as it is from ours. In the display of wild animals and in their deadly combats with each other and with man, we see mirrored in Roman sports the old life of the forest and plain. The mood of the spectator at the Colosseum changes also to suit the character of the spectacle, and for the time he is no longer the civilized Roman of the second century, but boisterous, cruel, intoxicated with the sight of blood. So strong was the craving for the old feral scenes that professional hunters were kept in the remotest parts of Asia and Africa to capture alive every species of beast to be exhibited and killed for the amusement of Rome. Eleven thousand animals were produced by Trajan at a certain spectacle. Much has been said about the brutalizing effect of these games upon the Romans; but if we have correctly outlined the psychology of sport, we see in such games as these not a brutalizing agency, but an afterglow of brutality left behind. The modern circus, menagerie, and zoological gardens offer similar entertainment on a smaller scale, and appeal to the same instincts.

The human race has reached a stage of evolution in which such sports as gladiatorial shows, prize-fights, and 'bullfights hark too far back and are no longer endured, but before we condemn them too harshly it would be well to compare the number of men and animals killed in these ancient exhibitions with the number of men and horses killed in a modern war.

Success today does not depend upon swiftness of foot or swiftness of horse, yet our sports take the form of foot-races and horseraces. There was a time when swiftness of foot and swiftness of horse were vital. So in our sports these old scenes are reenacted. Stage managers, story-writers, and moving-picture shows seek always 'for a new thrill. It is sometimes thought that the new and unexpected is thrilling. The reverse is true. The thrilling is the old and elemental. When love and warfare fail, the story-writer can always fall back on the horse-race for thrills. The horse has little significance for the life of today and it is fast becoming less, but he has had an intimate relation with the life history of the race. It is difficult to read any well-told story of a horse-race or chariot-race, or any account of human rescue by means of equine or canine intelligence, without an emotional disturbance out of all proportion to the importance of the events. In fact they have no significance now. They belong to the past.

In this connection it is interesting to recall that some years ago an English magazine published the results of a census which it had made of the order of popularity of Browning's shorter poems. The list contained about fifty of these poems, including such matchless gems as "Evelyn Hope," "Abt Vogler," "My Last

Duchess," "Rabbi Ben Ezra," etc. But the first place of all the fifty was given to the poem entitled, "How they brought the Good News from Ghent to Aix," a poem without significance of thought or sentiment, but depending for its interest upon the incident of a desperate horseback ride from Ghent to Aix. The compelling force of this poem will be felt by the reader, if we quote some of the first and last lines:

* I sprang to the stirrup, and Joris, and he;
* I galloped, Dirck galloped, we galloped all three;
* "Good speed!" cried the watch as the gate-bolts undrew;
* "Speed!" echoed the wall to us galloping through; Behind shut the postern, the lights sank to rest, And into the midnight we galloped abreast;
* And there was my Roland to bear the whole weight Of the news which alone could save Aix from her fate;
* With his nostrils like pits full of blood to the brim, And with circles of red for his eye-sockets' rim.

Then I cast loose my buffcoat, each holster let fall, Shook off both my jack-boots, let go belt and all, Stood up in the stirrup, leaned, patted his ear, Called my Roland his pet-name, my horse without peer; Clapped my hands, laughed and sang, any noise, bad or good, Till at length into Aix Roland galloped and stood.

* And all I remember is friends flocking round;
* As I sat with his head 'twixt my knees on the ground;
* And no voice but was praising this Roland of mine, As I poured down his throat our last measure of wine.

Which (the burgesses voted by common consent) Was no more than his due who brought good news from Ghent.

From the phylogenetic standpoint which we have thus gained, both children's play and adult sport come into clearer light. Thus we understand why adult sport resembles the activities of early man. The older, the more basal, the more primitive, so to speak, the brain patterns used in our hours of relaxation, the more complete our rest and enjoyment. Just in proportion as the sport is primitive, so much greater is the sweet peace which it seems to bring to the troubled soul, simply because it involves more primitive brain tracts and affords greater release from the strenuous life.

So while we find one hundred and fifty spectators at an intercollegiate debate, we find a thousand at an automobile race, five thousand at a horse-race, thirty thousand at a great baseball game, seventy thousand at a great football game, and three hundred thousand at a gladiatorial show. The nervous tracts which function in such activities as hunting and fishing and swimming and boating and camping, in football and baseball and golf and polo, and in horse-racing and bullfighting, are deep worn, pervious, and easy. During countless generations the nerve currents have flowed through these channels. Witnessing these rude contests, pictures of former ages, or taking part in these deep-seated, instinctive actions brings sweet rest and refreshment. 'The racially old is seized by the individual with ease and joy." The soothing restfulness of the open grate fire is thus probably due to latent or subconscious memories of the campfire, which so long brought rest and comfort to the early man.

From this point of view, the dancing craze is less difficult to understand. In explaining such phenomena it will not do to rely too much on the behaviour of the crowd, as some writers have done. To call it a craze, a fashion, an epidemic, and to refer it to the laws of imitation which govern a crowd, is not to explain it. Imitation alone is a very feeble social force. It becomes a powerful force only when the imitated action satisfies some need. The desire to dance, whether it be conscious or unconscious, may be very strong, but, as long as it is under the ban of social disapproval, the desire may be largely repressed. When these social restrictions are removed, then the practice may become general, and if the desire is strong enough, it may spread like an epidemic. This is about as far as the law of imitation helps us in explaining a dancing craze.

Dancing is a pastime as old as the human race. The muscles involved are the larger muscles of the trunk and legs, fundamental, as they have been called. The brain patterns concerned are, therefore, the oldest and earliest in racial development. Progress has been, first, in the direction of the finer and more differentiated movements of the arms, hands, eyes, and vocal organs, and then, in our own times, more and more toward purely intellectual activity. Rest and relaxation, therefore, always tend to take the form of exercise of the fundamental muscles. As compared with other forms of relaxation which we have been studying, such as hunting, fishing, horse-racing, ball-playing, etc., dancing is ultra-primitive, both in respect to the fundamental character of the muscles involved, and also in respect to the simple rhythmical form of the movements. It affords, therefore, a complete rest of the higher brain and provides a very perfect means of relaxation.

If we consider the manner of life of civilized man of the twentieth century and compare it with that of one hundred years ago, we shall understand the peculiar fascination of the dance at the present day. From the beginning of his racial history, there has been one set of muscles which man has continuously used, however intermittent the use of the others has been, and these are the muscles of the legs. Until recent years he has been on his feet most of the time when not asleep standing, walking, running, climbing. Now he sits in a chair, working his brain or his eyes or his hands, or else he rides in a carriage, automobile, street-car, or train. It is doubtful whether this sudden and radical change can take place without disastrous consequences. At any rate, we can understand why dancing as a mode of recreation should in these circumstances appeal to us so powerfully as to take the form of an epidemic when once fashion has given its sanction.

When we speak of dancing as a very perfect means of relaxation, we refer, of course, to healthful forms of the dance as exhibited in the folk-dances and in the dances of children. The modern social dance as it exists in America, in which the sex element has become too prominent, associated also as it is with night hours, electric lights, dust, and bad air, has slight recreational value as compared with the earlier and healthier forms of folk-dancing. To understand the truth of this, it is only necessary to ask ourselves whether the dancers of today are likely to be the fathers and mothers of the future citizens of America. Sociologists are already well aware that we must look in quite another direction for these. The game of golf, again, has a peculiar restorative power surpassing all medical or other therapeutic arts. We may be physically and mentally weary from a morning's work. Despite the strenuous physical exertion of an afternoon at golf, our fatigue is lessened, not increased. Fresh air does not explain it. It is a return to the primitive outdoor life. We stride over hill and through ravine; we stumble into ditches; we carry a club and strike viciously at the ball; we follow the ball with the eye and search for it in the grass as our forefathers searched for their arrows and missiles; we use our legs and our arms; we let the nerve currents course through the more ancient channels; we revel unconsciously in latent memories and old race habits and come back to our work rested, renewed, and refreshed.

But you may say golf and bowling and baseball and prizefighting require skill and close attention and tax mind as well as muscle. But this is not the point. Our remote ancestors had skill. To see quickly and correlate nicely eye and hand, or eye and foot, was an early acquisition. It is not this that fatigues us in modern life. It is the everlasting, high-pressure grind. It is holding ourselves down to hard working and hard thinking and long-sustained tasks. It is analysis, concentration, effort, dead lift of mind, the kind of mental work that digs Panama canals, perfects automobiles and airships, discovers new laws of mind and matter in the laboratory, thinks out new fields for the investment of capital, scrutinizes countless court records for precedents in law which may clear our clients, holds the ship's captain on the bridge in times of peril, keeps the soldier at his post and the clerk at his desk through the long hours and the weary days. As the strenuous life increases in city and country, there is an increased demand for relaxation, whether in the form of baseball or football, horse-racing or gambling, or in the form of the automobile craze, or the auction-bridge craze, or the dancing craze, or the moving-picture craze. These are all methods of escape from the clutch of the modern strenuous life, exhibited in all countries, but most noticeably in America, for whatever it is that is driving the human race forward in the path of progress so rapidly and relentlessly seems to have gripped the Anglo-Saxon people particularly hard.

Even these many forms of relaxation are not sufficient to relieve the overwrought brain, and so in ever-increasing amounts we have recourse to artificial means of relaxation through narcotics, such as alcohol, tobacco, and other drugs. Alcohol, by its slight paralysis of the higher and later developed brain tracts, accomplishes artificially what is effected naturally by play and sport, that is, it liberates the older, freer life of the emotions and the more primitive impulses.

Thus, from our new point of view, the difficulties in regard to children's play disappear. The reason why children play and why their plays take reversionary forms is now evident. The higher brain tracts, those making work possible, are not developed. If a child does anything, he must play, i.e., his activity must take the form prescribed by the brain patterns already developed, and these are the old racial ones. He is equipped with a nervous mechanism adequate for old racial activities and for the most part with these only. The little girl hugging and nursing her doll is not the victim of an instinct whose purpose is to prepare her for later maternal duties. She is simply doing what her mother and her grandmothers have done since the beginning. If they had not done so, she would never have been born.

The child does not play because of surplus energy, for under normal conditions all his energy is expended in play; the child is a playing animal. Nor does he play because of an instinctive need of practice and preparation for life's serious duties, for the form of the latter is constantly changing while the plays of children remain much the same from year to year and century to century. Nor, finally, does he play because it is necessary for his complete growth that he should pass through the several stages of racial history. He plays because he is a child, and to the child's natural and active life we give the name "play" to distinguish it from the life of conscious self-direction, of strain and effort and inhibition which evolution has imposed upon the adult human being.

When we say that all of the activity of the young child takes the form of play, the statement should be regarded as a general one. As the term "play" is actually used, there are certain minor classes of responses which are not included. The child's instinctive shrinking from a large furry animal is as much a part of his original nature as his tendency to run and jump and climb and wade. His responses in the taking of food, likewise, and in protecting himself by crying are original inherited responses. But to crying and sucking and shrinking from objects of fear we do not give the name "play," because, being of the immediate life-serving kind, they bear a closer resemblance to those responses to which in later life we give the name "work," and we reserve the term "play" for that larger and characteristic class of activities which are distinguished from the conscious self-directive life of the man. The play reactions of children, therefore, belong to their original nature. Social heredity may account for the forms of organization of many of the plays of children as well as the sham character which they assume when compared with their originally serious form, but the elements of the great mass of the plays which are dearest to the hearts of children are truly instinctive. The educational; application of this theory of play presents difficulties than the older theories. It is not necessary that the child should live through and live out any series of savage stages. It is merely necessary that he should be kept active with the mental and physical equipment that he has, that work should not be too early imposed upon him, and that his plays should be so organized and supervised that, while retaining the elementary form of his instinctive responses, they may be physically, morally, and socially harmless.

For instance, a boy, if he is a boy, must throw. It is just a question of whether he shall throw stones at a cat, at a street-car, at little children, or whether he shall throw a curved ball to the catcher. The latter is harmless, the former dangerous. Again, a boy's instinct of 1 Compare James's Psychology, n, 429, n. rivalry is very strong. He must do something daring, get ahead of some one, as those of his ancestors who survived did before him. If a proper playground is provided, all these things may be done without injury to society. Again, in response to the dancing instinct, the children must be taught the graceful and healthful folk-dances.

In our modern cities supervised play has become necessary for social order for the reason that the old conditions of spontaneous, healthful play have been taken away.

Says Luther Burbank, quoted by George E. Johnson: Every child should have mud-pies, grasshoppers, water-bugs, tadpoles, frogs, mudturtles, elderberries, wild strawberries, acorns, chestnuts, trees to climb, brooks to wade in, water-lilies, woodchucks, bats, bees, butterflies, various animals to pet, hay fields, pine cones, rocks to roll, sand, snakes, huckleberries, and hornets; and any child who has been deprived of these has been deprived of the best part of his education.

As regards adults, the social applications of the theory are equally obvious. There must be large periods of relaxation from the high-tension life of today. If they are not provided in the form of healthful and harmless sports, there will be irritability, abnormal fatigue, and antisocial outbreaks. There will be auction-bridge crazes and dancing crazes and moving-picture crazes, and there will be ever-increasing resort to the temporary harmonizing effect of alcohol, tobacco, and coffee. Even in the life of the family the harmonizing influence of games is seen. The friction sometimes exhibited among its members, in some cases taking the extreme form of nagging, wrangling, and quarrelling, is no doubt due in large part to the fatigue of the higher brain. In such cases it will often be found that participation in some simple game, particularly an outdoor game, such as golf, tennis, or even quoits, will completely relieve the situation, bringing sympathy, harmony, and peace. In society, the larger family, the same effect must follow upon the larger participation in healthful sports. It is sometimes a matter of surprise to us in periods of national prosperity, when wages are good and work obtainable, that unrest increases, together with crime and insanity.

It may be because the high tension with its consequent fatigue is not relieved. What is needed is less work and worry and more healthful relaxation. Worry is a good example of the high-tension life that is a part of our civilization. Worry is only a perverted form of provision. It is well enough for preachers to tell us not to worry, but worry is one of the conditions upon which civilization depends, namely, solicitude and care for the future. As a nation we are just beginning to worry, for instance, about the depletion of our forests and soil, and it is well that we are doing so. But sometimes we become excessively solicitous about the future, whether it be about the rent or the winter's supply of coal or our future health or the health and morality of our children, and this is what is usually spoken of as worry. It is very wearing, for the reason that it brings constant strain upon delicate and recently developed brain tracts and makes relaxation imperative.

If we have correctly described the theory of play and the psychology of relaxation and their relations to the conditions of our modern life, it will be evident at once that the need will not be supplied merely by providing more playgrounds for children and more holidays and sports for grownups, vital as these are. The difficulty goes deeper and calls for emphasis of still other forms of relaxation than play and sport. There are many of these, such, for instance, as music, which is one of the best, and rhythmic dancing, when freed from objectional features. An ever-ready and convenient form of relaxation is the modern novel, in which the attention is sustained objectively as in the chase or the drama, but its value as relaxation is greatly less than that of the old and social storytelling. Society in all its forms is a healthful means of relaxation. All valuable games and sports are social and the mere mingling with our fellows lowers the mental stress and tension. Primitive man was wholly social and survived only in cooperative groups. The reversionary character of crowd behaviour has been made well known to us.

Religion may be mentioned finally as a mode of relaxation of the highest value. Religion is a letting go the stress and tension of the individual and resigning one's self to an outside power, whether that power be God or the Church. The function of religion in this aspect is that of a sustainer, and religion loses much of its usefulness if the individual, as is often the case, feels it his duty to sustain his religion. His religion must sustain him. Clubs, societies, fraternities of all kinds, exercise a similar function. The great charm of all fraternal societies is that they relieve the stress, the burden, the tension of the individual and shift the responsibility upon the society as a whole. The society is back of him, to some extent will do his thinking for him, decide moral questions for him, relieve him from fear.

Just as man has physically lifted himself from the earth, overcoming gravity, so mentally he has raised himself above the other animals by the fatiguing exertion of his higher mental powers. The first animals were marine animals. They floated in or upon the water without effort. Then came creeping land animals prone upon the ground but not so completely supported as in the water. Gradually the animal lifted himself upon four legs and at last, by infinite labour, erect upon two, and the tension is correspondingly great. The horse rests very comfortably upon his four legs if allowed to stand, and needs to lie down scarcely an hour in the twenty-four. Man sustains himself with constant effort in an erect position and must sit much of the time on a chair, and at night reverts to the original position of the worm, flat upon the bed. This illustrates the whole theory of relaxation. It is always some form of reversion to primitive attitudes, physical or mental, and it brings rest and peace and harmony.

The rhythm of moral and social progress probably follows the same law. Periods of rapid progress are followed by periods of rest and relaxation. From time to time we are shocked by waves of vice and epidemics of immorality. We hear suddenly of conditions of astonishing laxity of morals in the small towns of our Western States, which are supposed to be models of propriety, and we say that the world is going to the bad. But our judgment is too hasty. These things are really incidental to progress. What we witness is a kind of moral relaxation, a relapse to more primitive conditions, as a result probably of progress that is too rapid, of tension too great. Something like moral fatigue takes place and a reaction follows.

Just at present we are hearing it said that our country has gone "amusement-mad." Well, our manner of life has been very strenuous. The tension has been high. Something was bound to happen. Other forms of relaxation have failed us just when we needed them most particularly art and religion. We are told that the art of ancient Greece was the product of the Greek genius. Perhaps it was the cause of it. Both art and religion entered intimately into the daily life of the Greeks. They have departed from ours.

In fact the world has lately been getting too severely serious and laborious. Too much hard thinking is demanded to keep up the modern pace. Whether in journalism, in literature, in scientific research, in mechanical invention, in social and educational reform, in labour movements, or in the feverish struggle for wealth, the higher brain is taxed to a degree incommensurate with the possibility of physiological adjustment. Our physical constitution cannot so quickly adapt itself to this suddenly increased demand upon certain specific nervous functions comparatively new and unstable. Reactions of one kind or another are therefore inevitable. In America we have the amusement crazes, obsessions of dancing, motoring, baseball, football, moving pictures, etc., together with a healthy revival of athletic sports, playground and recreation movements, and interest in outdoor life. In Europe, where the temper of the people lends itself less readily to these forms of release, we have witnessed the reaction in its most repulsive form, in a debauch of bloodshed, and a return to the most brutal and the most elemental kind of behaviour, that of war, which rests the higher brain completely. It is really a physiological situation that the peace societies have to contend with. Mankind cannot so easily escape from its long past.

In conclusion, it should be said that it is doubtful whether the tendency shown in children's play and in adult sport to take the forms of old racial activities can be subsumed under such names as survival, reversion, or recapitulation. These biological terms are all too narrow, and they carry a certain reproach which does not pertain to the play and sport activities. It is a wholly unwarranted assumption that those peculiar forms of mental activity which in a special manner characterize the adult masculine mind are of any higher order than those which are exhibited in play in the broader sense in which we have used the term.

The latter represent more fundamental forms of human behaviour and perhaps more valuable. Just at the present time evolution seems to be tending toward the development of those high-tension masculine traits by which man adapts himself to his environment and which produce something which we call progress or civilization, a civilization, however, in no way remarkable except in the way of its frenzied reactions. It is the age of work, the age of stress and effort and tension, the expensive, centrifugal age, the age of outer conquest but not of inner harmony. At such a time, comforts, luxuries, and inventions abound, side by side with profound misery. Is it not possible to think of a higher civilization than ours a civilization faintly realized by the ancient Greeks where the play motive will be ascendant, where a greater degree of repose, of measure, and of harmony will be attained, and where humanism will be more prized than expansionism?

Sex Tourism

The term sex tourism is mostly associated to the prostitutes more particularly women in Asia. Although prostitution is illegal in most countries more particularly, for those minors, still, the said type of tourism is still in full bloom in many of the poor countries in the world. In fact according to the survey conducted in Germany and Switzerland, there are about 8% of the respondents who have answered that they had sex with someone whom they had only met during their holiday that could be a fellow traveller, a local and more particularly a prostitute (2003).

In fact according to statistics, in Costa Rica, the capital city of San Jose, there are about 2, 000 child prostitute alone, that are regularly sold to the foreigners as a part of their sex-tour packages (2007). One thing that have affect the fast growth of the said industry is when HIV/AIDS have arrived to Southeast Asia, the industries started to implement different health check up. Nowadays, the said type of tourism has also involved in the use of the Internet for their marketing strategy.

Educational Opportunity

Educational Tourism

During the past decades, the educational tourism have evolved and developed number of ways such as the student exchanges or the urge of the young people to travel to another country in order to study and learn as well as analyse the language and culture of other people; special holidays on the other hand, is the urge to travel to learn something new (1999). There is no doubt that educational industry has already become one of the most popular types of special interest tourism. According to and (1997), the world market for international education travel was estimated to increase from 4.8 million trips up to more or less 8 million trips in 1996, showing that it had increase 66% of its total trips.

Tourism industry has been one of the most important industries in the world during the past few decades that have helped many countries and nations to improve their economies by increasing sales, employment and the foreign currency earnings

(1991). Tourism has been part of the normal daily life of many people in the world (2006).

That is why most of the countries and places in the world are doing their best in focusing on their tourism industry because of the fact that the said industry has obtained the leading position of becoming the most important source of income and foreign investments (2006). (2006) believes that the growth of the tourism industry will continue to expand in the near future and will maintain its growth to become the most important industry in the world.

Special Interest Tourism

Special interest tourism is a controversial and a hot label that often used incorrectly or interchangeably to define a form of tourism that refers to the mass tourism (2000). According to the World Tourism Industry or WTO, special interest tourism can be defined as the specialized tourism that involved individual or group tours by those people who wishes to develop their given interests or visit sites and places that has a relation or connection with their specific interest or subject (2003). According to, people are travelling because of their particular interest for a particular subject that are available or can be seen in a given country or place (2003).

On the other hand those people who are into the special interest tourism are called special interest tourist. They are motivated by their desire and urge to pursue their particular interest, hobby or activity than can be a sport like, scuba diving, golf or mountain climbing or bird watching; another thing that can motivated them is their love for heritage interest like folk music, educational pursuit and periodical architecture. They are choosing their destination based on the can offer them a better and unique way of enjoying their hobbies and interest (2000 century).

Conclusion

There is no doubt that tourism had been the most important industry of any country that is why most of them are doing their best in order to maintain and preserve all of their resources that can attract the attention of their target tourist. With accordance to the three chosen tourism, I must say that all of them are in great performance in the international tourism industry. Perhaps of all the special tourism that I had chosen, the education tourism is the most fast growing and the most in demand in the world. On the other hand, the sex tourism is the most controversial and most judged.

Shopping

One-day Shopping Tourism as a Situation Specific Experience

Motives for a Shopping Trip : The motivational basis for purchasing and shopping has been studied by consumer behaviour researchers for decades. The seminal attempt to classify buyers according to their orientation was made by Stone (1954). He identified four different shopper types: the economic consumer, the personalizing consumer, the ethical consumer and the apathetic consumer. Later, several studies have been conducted in order to increase understanding on shopping orientation. According to Tauber (1972) shopping behaviour is motivated by a variety psychosocial need beyond those relating to the products being acquired. In this way, Tauber identified both personal and social motives to be influential in shopping behaviour. Personal satisfaction gained from shopping according to Tauber are: 1) the opportunity to enact a culturally prescribed role; 2) diversion from daily routines; 3) provision of self-gratification; 4) learning about new trends, fashions and innovations; 5) obtaining physical exercise; and 6) receiving sensory stimulation from the retail environment.

The satisfaction of a social nature arises from 1) social interaction outside the home; 2) communication with others having similar interests; 3) affiliating with reference group; 4) obtaining increases in social status; 5) achieving success in bargaining and negotiation. Later, Bellenger and Korgaonkar (1980) introduced their twofold shopper typology: economic shoppers, who dislike shopping or are neutral toward it and recreational shoppers, who enjoy shopping as a leisure-time activity.

Westbrook & Black (1985) introduced a motivation-based shopper typology based on Tauber's work. According to Westbrook

& Black, there are seven major dimensions of shopping motivation: 1) anticipated utility; 2) role enactment; 3) negotiation; 4) choice optimization; 5) affiliation; 6) power and authority; and 7) stimulation.

These dimensions may vary across individuals and shopping situations due to personality, learning, products being shopped and the types of retail institutions. Dawson, Bloch & Ridgway (1990) used Westbrooks & Blacks results as starting point in their research of how shopping motives and emotional states influence retail outcomes.

They divided motives to product-oriented motives and experiential motives. Product-oriented motives include 1) find variety of new products; 2) find unique crafts or foods; 3) see new things; 4) find good prices; and 5) keep up with new crafts or foods when experiential motives are 1) watch other people; 2) enjoy the crowds; 3) see and hear entertainment; 4) meet new people; 5) experience interesting sights, sounds and smells; 6) get out of the house. Babin, Darden & Griffin (1994) use same kind of duality in their research of shopping value.

Babin et al. argue, that shopping includes both 1) utilitarian outcome resulting from some type of conscious pursuit of an intended consequence and 2) an outcome related more to spontaneous hedonic responses.

As the entertainment aspect of retailing came more recognized, also the hedonic shopping motivations came more apparent. Arnold & Reynolds (2003) focused only on hedonic shopping motivations and developed a scale, which consists of 1) adventure; 2) gratification; 3) role; 4) value; 5) social; and 6) idea shopping motivations.

One remarkable feature in the studies on shopping motivation is that both utilitarian and hedonistic motivations are apparent and important in explaining different aspect of purchasing behaviour. According to Arnold & Reynolds (2003) the importance of the recreational and hedonistic aspects is emphasized in modern markets. Shopping goes beyond mere purchasing and product acquisition in that it emphasizes recreation and gratification. The growth of the size of shopping malls and the change of their style into more entertaining has led to increase in consumers' interest. It appears as, for example, long shopping trips and increase in time spent in shopping malls. Ikea is one of those shopping centres, which tempt customers from long distance to receive stimulation, buy products and spend leisure time. Travellers spend hours in a car, bus or train just to spend one day in Ikea. The aim of this paper is to understand the main motives of this kind of a shopping trip. The objective is to describe and analyse the motivation orientation of the people going on a one-day trip to Ikea by bus. This study represents a new approach of shopping orientation study in that it concerns the whole trip, not only the store.

Motivational Orientation for One-day Shopping Trip to Ikea

This one day shopping tourism trip to Ikea cannot be specified solely as tourism or shopping. For some consumers, the trip might be just travelling and for others it is mainly shopping. Shopping is experiential and satisfying in nature and not only instrumental in getting the products and services needed. In this way it can be seen to be something in between everyday and holiday. It contains tourism-like features when both movement and changing places are included. On the other hand, shopping is an important activity in tourism, shopping and dining have said to be the most popular activities among tourists. In its broadest sense, shopping is seen as a significant element of tourism. Sometimes shopping may be the foremost motivation for travelling. When the prime reason for the trip is to shop, tourist shopping has been defined as 'shopping tourism', while 'tourism shopping' is used when shopping is just one of many other activities undertaken during the trip.

The similarities between shopping and tourism are evident especially in outshopping, i.e. when the shopping trip is extended beyond the boundaries of one's local retailing area. What is evident is that consumers do not go to a shopping trip just for purchasing or goods. It can be presumed that on a shopping trip motives to travel and motives to purchase are both present. In this research the interest lies in the tension between the recreational motives and the purchasing oriented motives on a one-day bus trip to Ikea. On these shopping trips, travellers spend hours in a bus, shop hours in Ikea and spend hours on the way back home. The first challenge here is to analyse the ability of the motivational orientations to categorize differently motivated travellers.

In order to analyse the motivational orientation of Ikea travellers a Likert-scale consisting of 25 items based on previous research on shopping and travelling motives was developed. Altogether 104 persons were interviewed on bus on their way to Ikea. The motivational data was factor analysed in order to reveal the orientation dimensions. Thinking about the aim of this study, two factor model appeared to be the most clear to interpret. Only the most heavily (>.50) loaded statements.

The two factors explain 38 per cent of the total variance.

Items describing recreational reasons for participating a shopping trip, push from everyday life and pull of the experiential aspects of a shopping trip were loaded on the first factor. In order to capture both the pull and push motivations the factor is termed as "variety from everyday". Items loaded on the second factor conventionally included elements of purchasing behaviour, namely information gathering and product buying. This factor is named as "purchasing". The two factors resemble well the motivational orientations of recreational and task-orientation found by Kaltcheva & Weitz (2006).

In order to reveal different shopping traveller groups a cluster analysis was conducted by using the factors as variables. The five cluster solution presented, offers a grouping that can be justified with good reasons argued for.

The two factors of purchasing and variety from everyday life turned out to be able to discriminate between the clusters of consumers. However, because of the relative small sample size we are not able to make any far reaching interpretations of the clusters. The results suggest, however, that the recreational factor of variety from everyday life seems to be somewhat better discriminator than the task-related purchasing factor. Most of the travellers attended on the Ikea trip in order to buy something. Especially consumers in group A went to Ikea in order to purchase something. On the other hand group B consumers were not inspired by purchasing. They were presumably there just to escort or to elapse time. The C and D shoppers emphasized the recreational and experiential aspects of the shopping trip with the difference that for the C consumers purchasing was more important. On the other hand, the E consumers regarded the shopping trip more as an everyday activity that has to be attended to in order to get something needed.

Clusters are relatively close to origin. It can be assumed, that travellers' motives on this kind on shopping trip to Ikea are not strongly related to variety from everyday life or to purchasing, but various things combine in the motivation structures of the travellers. Falk and Campbell (1997) argue that while shopping, hedonistic and utilitarian motivations become so closely intertwined it is not reasonable to separate them. Consumers often justify their shopping with some rational reason, which might also increase the amount of utilitarian motives. Shopping trip is a sum of several elements, which is why it should be considered as different, partially overlapping processes.

Shopping Trip as an Experience

Since the hedonistic motives to shopping became apparent, the consumer has been seen as an individual emotionally involved in a shopping process, in which the multisensory, imaginary and emotive aspects are sought and appreciated. Shopping is not only buying, but also a socioeconomic means to socialize, enjoy oneself and the company of another person. In this way, shopping can be seen as an experience with an important emotional meaning, founded on the interaction with the products and services consumed. According to Schmitt (1999), an experience is a sum of different elements: sense, feel, think, act and relate.

In order to gain deeper understanding of a shopping trip as an experiential phenomenon, 104 Ikea travellers were interviewed on the way back home from Ikea. The travellers were asked to describe their trip and the best and worst things of it. These descriptions were analysed with content analysis using the elements of experience by Schmitt (1999) as a loose conceptual grid. All of these elements were present in Ikea traveller's descriptions. In addition, to own and to be privileged came up in the descriptions.

Owning has an important role on a shopping trip: buying things and the joy of possessing get travellers into a good mood.

Thinking on a shopping trip is both creative and thoughtful. A shopping trip is imagination, gaining new insights and pondering of things. A shopping trip to Ikea is full of stimulation for senses: people try different tastes, see attention awaking new things, smell the scents of new goods, touch coverings of soft pillows and smooth leather couches and listen to the sounds of the department store. Sitting in a bus is a large part of physical action on a shopping trip to Ikea. However, the trip also includes a lot of other kind of action: eating, talking and laughing. To relate is an important element in a shopping trip. Good company might make the trip worth going and friends are needed for backup while making purchasing decisions.

Feelings on a shopping trip can be everything from wonderful and lovely to awful and horrible.

Travellers' descriptions of their trip express a large spectrum of experiences. Every consumption experience is unique and includes thinking, action, relating, feeling and sensing in varying degree. We can assume that this consumption experience itself is somehow valuable, although the desired products are not always found, the prices are too high or the time runs out too fast. Also Westwood (2006) argues that for shopping tourists, already sense of being somewhere different was a defining feature of their experience. Ikea travellers have an experience that makes them somehow privileged compared to those, who have not visited Ikea.

Wonderful Shopping or Endless Torture?

It is amazing, how many different elements are attached to one shopping trip to Ikea. Pleasantness or unpleasantness of the trip is a consequence of many different elements. Sometimes one element affects a lot and sometimes small things create large entities. The pleasantness of the trip might derive from good company, meeting an old friend or spending time with family. Good plans, new ideas, reasonable purchases and money saving make the trip nice. People can relax and enjoy buying and travelling on the Ikea trip. Seeing new products and the large store is exciting and shopping in good company cheers up. The store's selection is nice to watch; scents from cafeteria arouse hunger and food tastes amazingly good after wandering. For some of the travellers, motivational orientations defines the pleasantness or unpleasantness. One of the travellers, who was strongly oriented for variety from everyday life found, that the best thing about the trip was *"The trip itself (possibility to get away from home once in a while)"*, when the worst thing was, that Ikea was only *"An ordinary store"*. One of the purchasing-oriented travellers described the best thing about the trip *"I got all the things I needed"*.

But for many of the travellers on Ikea-trip, situational factors seem to define the pleas ant and unpleasant elements of the experience. One traveller, who was not purchasing oriented at all, thinks that the best thing about the trip was *"many good purchases"*, when the worst thing was that *"all of the plans did not come true, I could not find suitable things"*.

Sometimes one good or bad occurrence is the one that is remembered about the trip. For some travellers, the fact that restaurant closed earlier than they assumed, was definitely the worst thing about the trip, despite of their motivational orientation. In one trip, there were some problems with the seats on the bus on the way back and everybody could not sit next to their friend. This was worst thing about the trip to many travellers, although they were purchasing-oriented.

This might be due to the experiential and intensive nature of the one-day shopping trip. This trip is not solely purchasing or leisure, it combines rationality and emotionality. This trip includes many different aspects, and the comprehensive experience is a combination of all of these.

According to Buttle (1992) shopping trips are basically made in terms of logical force, but motives for shopping are also linked to particular shopping context. Our findings support Buttles conclusions: most of the Ikea travellers are purchasing oriented, and attend the trip to buy desired products. Tourism, on the other hand, is considered to be hedonic activity, which determines the shopping context. On the shopping trip to Ikea, travel context brings in the hedonic motives for the trip.

Travellers' motivational orientation differs in the way they wish to gain also immaterial consequences on the trip. Most of the travellers are oriented to buy something, but they are not all interested in the recreational aspects of the trip. According to Westwood (2006) leisure-like aspects are more important than purchasing while shopping. This might be true with shopping-oriented travellers, but our results indicate that there are also purely purchasing oriented travellers on a trip to Ikea. The fact, that some consumers try to justify their shopping with rational reasons, might affect to this.

Because of the small differences in Ikea-travellers' motivational orientation, we suggest that a shopping trip should be seen as different processes, which might also be overlapping. We examined these processes as experiential aspects of a shopping trip. Ikea travellers' experience includes the elements suggested by Schmitt (1999) and in addition the elements named to own and to be privileged arouse from travellers descriptions.

These elements can be assumed to occur from the special characteristics of the shopping trip. Pleasantness and unpleasantness on this kind of intensive one-day shopping trip seems to arise from situational factors. For some travellers, motivational orientation defines the best and worst things about the trip. But it is not unusual, that same elements affect the pleasantness or unpleasantness, despite the motivational orientation of the travellers.

This might be due to the experiential nature of the trip. One-day shopping trip to Ikea is not purely a shopping trip; it is an intensive experience, which includes many different elements.

Offering experiences is a great opportunity for retailers to succeed. Experiential retailing aims to offer customers satisfactory total consumption experiences by chancing the store atmospherics.

Types of Tourist

Tourism is a travel for predominantly recreational or leisure purposes. Tourism also refers to the provision of services in support of this act. Tourism is defined as the study of man (the tourist) away from his usual habitat, of the touristic apparatus and networks responding to his various needs, and of the ordinary (where the tourist is coming from) and nonordinary (where the tourist goes to) worlds and their dialectic relationships. Such conceptualisations extend the frame beyond the earlier trade-oriented notions or definitions mostly devised to collect data and calculate tourist arrivals, departures, or expenditures. Significantly, it is this holistic view which accommodates a systemic study of tourism: all its parts, its interconnected structures and functions, as well as ways it is influenced by and is influencing other forms and forces relating to it.

Tourism Behaviour

The concept of behaviour in tourism considers customers and their behaviour specifically as it relates to tourist activities. Some distinctive behaviour topics include cross-cultural interaction, authenticity, tourist-guide interaction and post travel attitudes. This subsumes both the observable behaviour of tourists and their mental and psychological processes involving decision-making, motivations and cognition. The study of tourist satisfaction provides a link to business and management research. Knowledge of the behaviour of tourists in space and time is valuable to assist planners and managers of attractions and environments. Tourist behaviour and experience is assessed by survey studies as well as observational and field research.

Decision Process

Many models have been proposed to simulate the decision-making process for tourism-related products. However, this is a very complicated procedure, and it increases in complexity as more people become involved. The concepts of image, utility maximisation, knowledge acquisition and others are all involved. In addition, various socioeconomic characteristics affect decision making in different ways. Tourism has become one of the world's most powerful components of economic development. Many countries have established tourism development as a high priority concern.

However, increases in discretionary time and money, as well as the variety of vacation choices, have given the potential traveller more flexibility of choice. As a result, the factors influencing travel decisions are becoming more complex. If a travel or tourism organisation wants to influence a travel decision, it needs to understand who is making the decision and how that decision is made.

The 'decision process' has been described as a simple association between a stimulus and a response. It has also been described as a very complex interaction among many behaviour determinants (, 1966). An effective travel decision-making model must incorporate important factors affecting the decision (such as sociodemographic, sociological and psychographic characteristics) and provide an understanding of the relationships between these variables. Travel decisions may also be affected by factors such as travel characteristics, destination attributes and past travel patterns. One of the key steps in tourism planning and marketing is to develop travel behaviour choice models by analyzing these travel factors.

Consumer Behaviour

Consumer behaviour can be viewed as the study of how, why and how often individuals make decisions to spend their available resources (such as money, time or energy) on consumption-related items (and, 1990). Many factors affect the consumer decision process. Factors can come from marketing (including such things as perceived product quality, price and distinctiveness), social sources (which includes family and reference groups), individual differences (such as sociodemographics, lifestyle and personality types), or psychological processes (like motivation, or destination perceptions). Sociodemographics, travel characteristics and psychographic variables have all been recognized as important factors influencing travel decisions. One of the strategic approaches in tourism planning and decision-making is to develop travel choice models by analyzing these travel factors. Models can be defined as 'systems of hypotheses relating one or more dependent variables to several independent variables' (1989).

In studying travel and tourism, dependent variables could be the choice of a tourist destination, hotel or accommodation, the likelihood of taking a future trip, the length of stay or the total number of visits. On the other hand, independent variables could include factors such as sociodemographics, psychographics, travel characteristics, destination attributes or economic variables.

Tourism Motivations: Factors affecting the Decision Making Process: According to the sociologist Max Weber, motivation lies at the core of human behaviour. Consequently, the study of motivation is central to any social scientific undertaking since it provides understanding, explanation and prediction. It goes beyond the how questions of description to the why questions of interpretation and causality. As one domain of interpersonal activity, tourism is no exception to this general observation. Indeed, 'why do people travel?' is probably the most fundamental issue in tourism research today (2000). (1994), points out that there are several concrete social influences conditioning the decision to travel. He identifies the family, reference groups, social class, the surrounding culture and the work place as the most important of these. The latter is particularly significant since it is conductive to compensatory and spill over effects in various types of travel.

1. Social interaction is commonly identified as a tourism motivation. Early research on the latter incorporated the underlying hypothesis that an individual has a need for love and affection and the desire to communicate with others. Further explorations revealed enhancement of kinship and friendship relationships and the facilitation of varied and increased social interaction as motives which directed vacation choice and behaviour.
2. Cultural motivators are strong push factors for the development of tourism. Cultural motivators lead the tourist into learning about and experiencing the culture of societies other than their own.

Senior Tourism

An exponential increase in the number of senior citizens throughout the world has made this group an attractive niche market for tourism with its own particular needs. Tourism marketers in countries like Australia, Canada and the United States are beginning to sharpen their focus on older people. Seniors roughly constitutes up to a third of the adult population in each of these countries. Many of these seniors have the desire and means to travel for pleasure, discovery and learning. The main purpose of travel is Holiday. Seniors stay more in lower cost accommodation. They tend to stay more with friends, relatives or their own property.

Trip Characteristics

1. Senior Tourists travel longer.
2. Senior Tourists travel to more destinations.
3. Senior Tourists have less ties to employment.

Senior Tourists are people of later age (after 55) who travel for leisure and whose earning and family obligations decrees and finally disappear. A-first-distinction can be made in young-old (aged 55-64), old (aged 65-74) and very old (aged 75 and over).

Economic Aspects

The WTO forecasts that earnings from international tourism will grow an average of 6-7% annually – double the growth rate for the world economy as a whole. In the coming decades tourism activity will become one of the main economic sectors of the world. Senior Tourists are attractive as consumers because:

1. They have the financial means.
2. They have time.
3. They have a better education than in the past.
4. They belong to a generation, which has travelled.
5. They are relatively healthy and know that activities like tourism and recreation contribute to a healthy lifestyle.

Senior Tourists differ in age (chronological-biological), health, economic status, tourism experience and cultural background.

People do not change their travel behaviour because they turn 60 or retire. Travel experience and patterns will have an important influence on travel behaviour.

Youth Tourism

Youth Tourism has taken many forms over time, most of which seem to have been a simple expression of youthful energy and curiosity about the world beyond their bounded society. Their travels were usually a form of alternatives to prevailing tourism. Historically, these involved travels to medieval universities and such institutions as the "Grand Tour", with its year abroad for young scholars and their tutors.

Youth travel itself is not a new phenomenon. For centuries, young people have been travelling around the world with their families, in groups, or on their own. The World Tourism Organization (WTO) defines the 'young' tourism market as travellers 16-25 years old, who take a trip of at least one night's stay. The Canadian youth market is defined as young people 30 years of age and under, who are travelling outside the family unit, not for business, and not primarily to visit friends or relatives, and whose travel includes at least one overnight stay.

Youth Travel Market

Different groups within the youth travel market have unique characteristics and motivations for travel, and require different products to suit their needs. The youth travel market is divided into two broad categories: independent you travel and youth travel group.

Youth Group Travel

This group is consisting of six or more unrelated young people travelling together. Youth travel group is divided into two groups: student travel or school-based youth group travel and non-school based youth group travel. Youth travel is specifically sanctioned by the sponsoring school, board or school district. School based youth group travel may be driven by curriculum-related activities an/or semi-curricular or extracurricular activities like music performances and sports competition.

Travel and activities are generally undertaken as a group, accompanied by teachers, school personnel and/or adult chaperones. Non-school-based youth group travel is often referred as youth travel grope. This travel is organized by a group such as a sports team, church group, cultural/musical performance troupe or Scouts/Guides. Travel is often undertaken as a group, but may also occur in smaller groups, led by parents or other adult chaperones. Youth group travellers are price sensitive, in the sense that they are more strongly influenced by price related issues that the average business or convention traveller.

Independent Youth Travel

Sometimes referred to as 'free independent youth travellers', or foreign independent youth travellers', independent youth travellers travel alone, or in small informal groups. Today's independent youth travellers tend to be well educated, well informed, and Internet savvy. Students between the ages of 18 and 26 mostly comprise this group, although some are young professionals who are either unemployed or taking time off between school and settling down.

Most independent youth travellers head for destinations farther from home stay longer and spend less daily but more in total than the average adult tourist spends. They appear to be price sensitive for travel, housing and food, but less for entertainment, shopping and attractions. Domestic independent youth travellers tend to plan shorter trips, to one or two specific destinations. Foreign independent travellers tend to have longer stays, and are experience-driven.

Independent Youth Traveller Characteristics

1. Between 15 and 30 years old.
2. Well-educated – most often students or previous students.
3. Travel independently, or with 1-2 friends.
4. Risk-friendly, experience oriented.
5. Responsive to destination/experience based marketing initiatives.
6. Detailed pre-trip planning.
7. Lower incomes, but willing to save/combine travel with work in order to finance travel.
8. Lower daily spending, but longer stays resulting in higher overall spending per trip.

Organised Mass Tourists

The organized mass tourist was the least adventurous and was confined to his environmental bubble, while the drifter was most adventurous and felt at ease with strangeness. The organized mass tourist preferred guided tours, air-conditioned bus with fixed itinerary because of the need of maximum familiarity and minimum novelty.

The degree to which strangeness and familiarity prevailed in the tourist role determined the nature of the tourists' experience as well as the effect on the host society. Cohen (1979) further distinguished five modes of tourist experience by analyzing the different meanings which interest in and appreciation of the culture, social life. The typology further confirmed the different behaviour of travellers in relation to their motivation

Individual Mass Tourist

The individual mass tourist was similar to the organized mass one but he allowed more flexibility in his time and itinerary and so his tour was not well preplanned. He would make the major arrangements through a travel agent, as familiarity was dominant in his total trip experience, but he still accepted somehow the experience of novelty.

The explorer tried to leave the environmental bubble by associating himself with the local people visited and the language they spoke. However, the explorer was still cautious to avoid too rough a visiting experience, and therefore he normally needed comfortable accommodation and reliable transportation.

The Explorer

The explorer tourists are thole one, who travel to or into (unfamiliar or unknown regions), esp for organized scientific purposes. Archeologists, Environmental schientist etc. are the examples of this group.

Exploration is the act of searching or travelling a terrain for the purpose of discovery, e.g. of unknown people, including space (space exploration), for oil, gas, coal, ores, caves, water, (Mineral exploration, botanical exploration, or prospecting), or information.

Although exploration has existed as long as human beings, its peak is seen as being during the Age of Discovery for Europe's contact with the rest of the world, and Major explorations after the Age of Discovery for scientific exploration in the modern era.

The Drifter

A Drifter is an itinerant person. Such people may be called drifters, tramps, rogues, or hobos. A vagabond is characterised by almost continuous travelling, lacking a fixed home, temporary abode, or permanent residence. Vagabonds are not bums, as bums are not known for travelling, preferring to stay in one location.

Historically, "vagabond" was a British legal term similar to vagrant, deriving from the Latin for 'purposeless wandering'. Following the Peasants' Revolt, British constables were authorised under a 1383 statute to collar vagabonds and force them to show their means of support; if they could not, they were jailed. Under a 1495 statute, vagabonds could be sentenced to the stocks for three days and nights; in 1530, whipping was added. The assumption was that vagabonds were unlicensed beggars.

By the 19th century the vagabond was associated more closely with Bohemianism. The critic Arthur Compton-Rickett compiled a review of the type, in which he defined it as men "with a vagrant strain in the blood, a natural inquisitiveness about the world beyond their doors." Examples included Henry David Thoreau, Michael John Arthur Bujold, Walt Whitman, Leo Tolstoy, William Hazlitt, and Thomas de Quincey. A notable 20th century vagabond was the Hungarian mathematician Paul Erdos.

Allocentric vs. Psychocentric

Allocentric tourist – enjoys varied activities and gets a thrill from the unexpected

Psychocentric tourist – nonadventurous and self-inhibited

Allocentric tourists are constantly searching for the new destination, as package tours start spreading into past midcentric and even allocentric destinations. Examples of this include the Caribbean becoming increasingly more midcentric (people between the extremes) as travel becomes less expensive.

- o In 1974, Stanley Plog developed a theory which allowed the US population to be classified into a series of interrelated psychographic types. These types range from two extremes:

- o The 'psychocentric' type is derived from & apos; psyche & apos; or ' self-centred & apos; where an individual centres thoughts or concerns on the small problem areas of life. These individuals tend to be conservative in their travel patterns, preferring 'safe' destinations and often taking many return trips. For this latter reason, market research in the tour-operating sector labels this group as ' repeaters & apos;.
- o The 'allocentric' type derives from the root 'allo' meaning 'varied in form'. These individuals are adventurous and motivated to travel/discover new destinations. They rarely return to the same place twice, hence their market research label ' wanderers & apos.

The Expectation-Evaluation Paradigm

Tourists and vacationers go through a complex decision-making process in determining their level of post-purchase satisfaction. Most tourist satisfaction models follow a positivists approach, in which tourists are viewed as rational beings who evaluate their level of satisfaction or dissatisfaction through a disconfirmation paradigm. That is, tourists purchase a trip with certain expectations (i.e., destination, amenities, and activities), and subsequently evaluate satisfaction based on whether than absolute truth, and that such research produces findings "with a focus on meaning and understanding the situation or phenomenon under examination".

He recommends building multiple methods approaches that involve the researcher with those being researched and focus on in-depth study of a small sample.

Stewart and Floyd (2004) capture the rationale for including post-positivistic philosophies within recreation and leisure studies with their observations: "The anxiety amongst leisure researchers is a reflection of a broader crisis within the social sciences about any account that claims to have directly or completely captured someone's lived experiences and social reality". They cite an increasing interest in post-positivistic philosophy as a means for addressing this inability to fully represent people's lived experiences.

Employing a post-positivistic philosophy, this study focuses on understanding and interpreting the process and factors of satisfaction evaluation, rather than on prediction and control. Utilizing mixed qualitative methods, this study examines the complexity involved in tourists' satisfaction with their travel experiences, moving beyond the rational decision-making principles found in positivistic approaches such as Moutinho's, towards an interpretivistic approach.

"Travellers want more than merely observing things and listening to lecture, they want to get actively involved". Tourists may have expectations about the level of active involvement they will experience during a trip that would lead to a disconfirmation paradigm, however active involvement seems to be a more complex variable in the evaluation of satisfaction than what can be captured and measured using Moutinho's model.

For this reason, it has been chosen as a variable to be further explored. Geva & Goldman (1999) define group dynamics as "...the relations and interactions among group members, the cohesion and morale of the tour group, manner in which free time was spent...". Bettenhausen (1991) suggests that belonging to a group had a great impact on an individual's sense of self, in shaping behaviour and attitudes, in creating a shared culture, and in creating the "rites, rituals, and social roles that provide continuity and order". Arsenault and Gale (2004) report findings from their study of Travel Suppliers and Tour Operators, which indicate a relationship between small group interaction, bonding, friendship formation, and satisfaction via the dimension of positive memory creation

The Tourist Experience

Tourism is a quest for experiences that are in contrast to, and sometimes an extension or intensification of, daily experience. In this sense, tourism is a pioneering example of the emerging "experience economy". The quality of experiences constitutes the key to the success of tourism development. However, despite the importance of the "tourist experience," this is still an ambiguous term. Although various constituents of the tourist experience, such as motivations (curiosity, novelty, change, authenticity meaning, identity, self), satisfactions, feelings, and emotions, have been well researched in psychology, anthropology, sociology, and other disciplines, the literature on the tourist experience as a *gestalt* phenomenon has still been understudied. This is not to deny that there exists a small literature on the tourist experience per se. But many questions still remain unanswered. For example, how is the formulation of the tourist experience related to itineraries?

Itinerary is a frequently used term in the tourism industry, especially in tonnst brochures, but it is rarely seen as an academic term. The reason for this situation could be simple. The itinerary is seen as too self-obvious, too simple, and too trivial to deserve serious academic treatment. At best, it is treated as a component of tourism linking to tour operation. Such a common-sense view of the itinerary should be challenged! however. Rather than being trivial, itineraries act as important media through which the tourism industry interacts with the tourist in the production and consumption of the tourist experience. Itineraries shape the formulation and organization of the tourist experience and become an arena in which the tourist experience is socially produced. As *temporal-spatial carriers* of tourist experience, itineraries are significant in the ways that tourism is consumed and in the ways that tourists' experiences are shaped.

Surely, the tourist experience cannot completely be equated with, or reduced to, itineraries, but it is equally true that the tourist experience is shaped by itineraries. There are at least two reasons that the itinerary deserves study in its own right. First, a number of paradoxes involved in tourism have their roots in itineraries. These paradoxes involve dualisms including authenticity and inauthenticity, autonomy and passivity, freedom and determinations, agency and structure. For example, while tourism is regarded as a quest for authenticity, what is experienced often ends up as "staged authenticity" of the front zone, partly because of the temporary and transient nature of itineraries that constrain tourists from penetrating the back zone of toured reality. While tourism is hailed as freedom, it often ends up as the loss of freedom, partly because of the rigidity of itineraries. While tourism is thought to restore the autonomy and agency that have decreased in daily routines, it creates its own constraints over autonomy and agency because of the constraining, pre-determining, and disciplining nature of itineraries. As Minea and Oakes put it in this volume's introduction, tourism is a performance through which various binaries, such as subject and object, are constantly re-enacted. Relatedly, itineraries are performances in which the paradoxes of modernity are enacted and embodied. The itinerary is thus one of the best dimensions of tourism from which the paradoxes and ambivalence of modernity can be revealed.

Second, as spatial-temporal carriers of tourism commodities, itineraries constitute the media that bridge experiences and goods, services and products, hospitality and attractions, movement and rest, time and space, the quantitative side and the qualitative side of tourism, the ordinary supportive consumption and extraordinary peak consumption, tourist consumers and tourism suppliers. Thus, the itinerary is one of the best domains of tourism from which the mechanisms of social, economical, and cultural production of tourism can be better understood.

This chapter deals with the issue of how the production and consumption of itineraries bring about and reinforce a series of paradoxes in tourism, and how the formation of itineraries are related to wider social, economical, and cultural processes. Just as tourism reveals the ambivalence of modernity and globalization, the same is true of the itinerary. The itinerary provides an alternative perspective from which the paradoxes of tourism can, perhaps more clearly, be revealed.

The following pages consist of three parts. The first concentrates on the issue of how itineraries constitute the *commodity form* of the tourist experience and how the commoditization of itineraries leads to a number of paradoxes. The second examines how itineraries become a way of circulation of tourism products and the associated paradoxes. The third focuses on the role that itineraries play in shaping the consumption of tourism, and the consequential "consuming paradoxes". Finally, in the conclusion, the paradoxes of tourism are discussed in relation to the rationalization of the tourist experience within the context of postmodernity.

Itineraries as the Commodity form of Tourism

In contemporary societies, the tourist experience is sold as a commodity, which is a result of the commoditization of travel and associated pleasant experiences under the condition of modernity. However, what is the commodity *form* of tourism? This is still an unanswered question. For a commodity to come into being, it must have a form.

For example, for a commodity to become the object of desire, it must be designed in order to take a particular appearance of colours, shape, size, and so on. This type of appearance can be called the *material form* of a commodity. However, in addition to the material form of commodities, there also arise *dematerialized forms* of commodities. In postindustrial economies, the commoditization of information and services leads to the *dematerialization* of commodity forms. The increasingly dominant part that the economy of services plays in postindustria] economies makes the nonmaterial form of commodities increasingly significant. As an integral element of the service industry, tourism also assumes a nonmaterial form, which is exemplified by itineraries.

The itinerary is a system of links between the temporal and spatial arrangements of tourist activities on the tourist journey. From the perspective of the tourism industry, an itinerary is a salable product that links, bridges, and puts together the various components that are necessary to the consumption of tourism. These components include accommodation, transportation, restaurants, attractions, entertainment, and tourist sites. Obviously, for tour operators and travel agencies, itineraries are the commodity form of mass tourism products.

But they are the nonmaterial form, despite the fact that tourism contains such material elements as food, means of transport, and hotels. The itinerary is nonmaterial because it is "virtual", existing in both tourists' and suppliers' imaginations; illustrated in tourist brochures, guidebooks, or TV programs; and only instantiated or materialized in the stage of consumption. Although itineraries are the non-material form, this does not mean that itineraries have nothing in common with the material form. The material commodity form consists of the arrangements of material elements. By contrast, the nonmaterial commodity form is constituted by the temporal and spatial arrangement of procedure, process, and activities. Thus, itineraries, as the nonmaterial commodity form of tourism, are temporal-spatial connections.

They constitute the temporal-spatially organizing processes in which discrete tourist "raw materials" are integrated and sold as a packaged commodity. At the same time, they themselves become the boundaries organized and constrained by the larger economic, social, political, and cultural contexts. Why does tourism take the commodity form of itineraries? The answer should be found from the process of the commoditization of travel experiences.

First, the commoditization of travel experiences is confronted with the problem of *intangible* experiences. In order to turn intangible experiences into "tangible" products in managerial terms, a certain organizing form must be imposed upon the journey.

Thus, itineraries are a way in which travel experiences are objectified, operationalized, and temporally and spatially "materialized." In a literal sense, we cannot sell experiences or pleasures per se, but we can sell the itineraries that are the "containers," carriers, or confines of experiences and pleasures. In short, itineraries are the "tangible" temporal-spatial carrier of intangible travel experiences, which can be produced, circulated (in the form of tourist brochures), and sold in the tourist market. Second, the essence of the commoditization of travel experiences is to make profit through creating an exchange value of tourism commodity. In so doing, travel experiences, as a qualitative subjective state, must be turned into precisely quantifiable and priceable products. Itineraries thus become the quantifiable, profitable, and saleable products of travel experiences.

Third, the commoditization of travel experiences reduces risk and uncertainty arising out of journeys. In order to transform the "raw materials" of risky and uncertain travel into tourism commodities, itineraries become a necessary form through which risks, chances, and uncertainties linking to journeys are eliminated or diminished. For examples, flight seats, hotel rooms, and restaurant tables are secured; safety and hygiene are ensured; access to attractions is guaranteed with tickets booked in advance. With itineraries, the risk-related and uncertain journeys are turned into clearly arranged, certain, standardized, and predictable commodities of tourist experiences.

Itineraries thus embody the rationalism in capitalist commoditization, and hence act as a rational way in which the tourism industry controls and manages mobile experiences. Itineraries are particularly attractive to *mass tourists* who want to create order out of chaos, risks, and uncertainties on their journeys to unfamiliar environments, even though they might also want to defy that order at the same time.

Itineraries are thus an indispensable commodity form of modern tourism and act as an integral dimension of the commoditization of the tourist experience. However, while tourism is successfully commoditized with the help of itineraries, it also faces a paradox derived from itineraries. Part of the essence of the tourist experience is to get out of daily routines, order, schedules, and constraints. As mentioned above, in order to turn the tourist experience into a commodity, it is necessary to make tourism assume a commodity form, namely, itineraries. The latter, however, imposes an emergent routine, order, schedule, and constraint upon the tourist experience.

Thus, tourism, the very act of escape from daily constraints, ends up as an alternative constraint. In relation to the *elimination of chance, risk, and uncertainty* and the increase of security and certainty, tourism is wheeled to the position of diminishing the real charms and appeals of travel, namely, a suitable extent of risk-taking, challenge, improvisation, independence, flexibility, freedom, creativity, and authenticity. Thus, while tourism is put on with the commodity form of itineraries, it paves a way to the demise of the authenticity of travel. As a response to such a strong commoditization of tourism, an increasing number of tourists tend to abandon overscheduled and itinerized mass tourism and adopt more individualist, independent, and flexible forms of travel.

These individual tourists take responsibility for then-own itineraries and leave enough room for adapting and changing primary schedules. The increasingly popular "backpacking" form of travel is such an example. This process can be called the *decommoditization* of itineraries. What Edensor (1998,105-14) describes about tourist behaviours at the Taj is a typical example of differentiation of decommoditized itinerary from commoditized itinerary.

For package tourists, visits to the Taj are highly regulated, predetermined, restrained, and disciplined in time and space. As a result of commoditization of itineraries, package tourists are usually allowed to stay for a quite limited time and to walk around within a limited range when they visit the Taj. By contrast, backpackers have much wider room for improvisation and for changing their itineraries as much as they wish.

For ex ample, they usually spend much more time and cover a wider spatial range at the Taj. Decommoditization of itineraries is thus a tourist action that seeks to transcend the rigidity, constraints, and disciplines of the itinerary of package tourism and that seeks more individual freedom, autonomy, and creativity. However, after getting rid of the itineraries of package tourism, independent travellers find themselves involved in an alternative form of commoditization.

For example, independent travellers often have to buy guidebooks in order to plan an itinerary. Here, guidebooks, such as Lonely Planet and Rough Guides, are themselves a specific way of commoditization of itineraries, or more precisely, the commoditization of the *knowledge* of potential itineraries. In guidebooks, itineraries become the content, rather than the commodity form, of guidebooks. The consumption of this content accompanies independent travellers' journeys. The itineraries described in guidebooks are thus the *hidden* itineraries of the tourism system that shape and organize independent travellers' concrete itineraries.

These *hidden itineraries,* such as the network of schedules, traffic lines and prices, and booking systems of transportation and hospitality, constitute alternative constraints on travel. While the itineraries of package tours are the first level of touristic constraints, the itineraries of the tourism system as a whole are the second level of touristic constraints. Thus, while independent travellers can get rid of the first level of itineraries (overt itineraries) that are sold by travel agencies as packaged tours, they cannot get rid of the second level of itineraries (covert itineraries), itineraries that are hidden in the tourism system and are described by guidebooks and other travel materials.

Itineraries as the Way of Circulation of Tourism Products

Itineraries are not only scheduled journeys, but also mark a spatialization of those journeys. To put it another way, itineraries are about "what" will happen "when" and "where." While the issue of the scheduled journeys has been touched on above, we now turn to the issue of the spatialization of tourism, namely, the issue of "where" tourist activities will take place.

Itineraries are not only the commodity form of tourism, but also the form of access to tourist attractions. Itineraries are the way to circulate tourism products in tourist markets. In the market of goods, it is commodities that are circulated and delivered to consumers for consumption. In the market of temporal spatial experiences of tourism, however, it is tourist consumers that are "circulated" and "delivered." They are taken to tourism products, that are not deliverable in a literal sense. Thus, when tourists travel to destinations, are in a sense "delivered" to tourists. Itineraries can thus be regarded as a way of the circulation of tourism products, despite the fact that itineraries are themselves an integral part of those products.

As a result, once tourist sites are visited by tourists, the "experiences" of these sites are in reality "delivered" and "circulated" to the tourist simultaneously. Therefore, the directions of tourist flows or itineraries are of significance to tourist destinations.

Itineraries are thus not only the way in which people move, but also the way in which landscapes, cultures, and heritage are "circulated". The integration of places into the networks of tourist itineraries turns the places into "experiential commodities" circulated among tourists. Thus, it is no small wonder that tourist destinations compete for access to the network of tourists' itineraries. The simultaneity and synchronization of *circulation* and *consumption* of the tourism products makes the directions and coverage of tourists' itineraries vital to the success of tourism development.

Paradoxes may occur when tourist destinations vie for inclusion into the network of tourists' itineraries. In reality, to compete for this inclusion is to develop a favourable image that is in congruence with targeted potential tourists' tastes and demands.

In this sense, to promote the circulation of a product of "tourist destination" is an issue of developing and establishing a desired image about the destination. In general, a favourable tourist image of a destination tends to allow tourists to include this destination into his or her itineraries, whereas a negative image, on the other hand, tends to deter potential tourists from visiting the destination. However, a favourable image of a destination may involve a paradox.

For example, in sightseeing tourism, the inclusion of a destination into his or her itineraries this time simultaneously implies the exclusion of this place next time, for sightseers always want to seek variety and novelty. Therefore, while a favourable image increases a destination's attractiveness, it may at the same time pave a way to the demise of that attractiveness. That is why a destination has its own life cycle. In postmodernity, with the help of mass media and the Internet, images increasingly become cultural fashions, whereas cultural fashions are always transient and temporary. Moreover, with the bombardment of images, images seem to become an autonomous world, a world that is "virtual reality." Thus, while image-making on the part of a destination is originally aimed at directing potential tourists' journeys and competing for the inclusion of the destination into their itineraries, it may often end up as distracting those tourists because they may get lost in the bombardment of tourist images. In this situation, word of mouth regains its significance in a world with too much information and too many images.

Itineraries as Menus for Tourism Consumption

Tourism is essentially an activity of consumption. What is consumed in tourism consists of two types of "materials." The first is the "material" serving of such daily consumption needs as eating, drinking, and sleeping. This does not mean that the material of this kind needs to be same with that of everyday life. Rather, a certain variety is necessary. Moreover, the consumption of this material takes place in a nondaily context, that is, the context of a journey, mobility, and an itinerary. New meanings of the consumption of the daily material can be derived from such a nondaily context. The second is the "material" of attractions at destinations and the journey itself. This type of material is beyond the reach of daily consumption. The consumption of the first type can be called "consumption *on* the journey," and the consumption of the second type can be called "consumption o/the journey." The consumption *on* the journey is the primary tourism consumption, and the consumption o/the journey is the secondary tourism consumption. The former is the extension of daily consumption to the journey; it is the base and support of the secondary consumption. By contrast, the latter is a transcendence of daily consumption; it is an extraordinary consumption. Both kinds of consumptions constitute *mobile* consumerism, or mass consumption *on the move.*

In both the primary and the secondary consumption, itineraries function as the temporal-spatial carriers of the two. In the primary tourism consumption, itineraries act as the nondaily *context* where daily functions of consumption are performed. In the secondary tourism consumption, itineraries become not only an *object* for consumption (journeys, services, and experiences), but also a *means* of "consumption *elsewhere*" consumption that takes place in other places and that transcends daily consumption. The secondary tourism consumption can thus be called *"peak consumption"*.

The rise and the spread of mobile or touristic consumerism relates to the rise of tourist citizenship in contemporary societies. Tourist citizenship means a specific type of consumer citizenship, a democratized right to consume extraordinary experiences that transcend one's daily reach and that are accessible only through travel. In relation to this, itineraries act as the *carrier* of extraordinary experiences. However, problems arise with the question of "what is the extraordinary experience?" The extraordinary is always relative. What is extraordinary for children could not be so for adults. What is extraordinary for the first-time travellers could not be so for experienced travellers. For island residents, the sea is not the source of extraordinary experience. However, the sea is so for inhabitants from desert areas. Therefore, the extraordinary is relative to different potential tourists with different experiential backgrounds and characteristics. Relatedly, in tourism marketing, tourism is segmented into different typologies and packaged as various types of products in order to serve the varying needs of potential tourists with different tastes.

As a result, the functions of itineraries as illustrated in tourist brochures are similar to the functions of menus in restaurants. Just as menus help customers in selecting courses of foods that best fit their tastes and preferences, so itineraries presented in tourist brochures serve clients in choosing types of tourist experiences that best satisfy them. In short, itineraries function as menus for tourism consumption.

According to Levi-Strauss (1983), for foods to be edible, they must be cooked. In this sense, cooking is a cultural practice. The same is true of potential tourist resources. For these resources to be consume-able by potential tourist consumers, they must also be culturally "cooked." Itineraries are thus one of the cultural ways of "cooking" these resources. Just as menus represent certain cuisines by means of which foods are cooked, itineraries embody touristic "cuisines" by means of which potential tourist resources are "cooked" and "packaged." As itineraries are often displayed and illustrated in tourist brochures, it is more precise to regard itineraries *as presented in tourist brochures* that are the "menus" of tourist experiences.

Just like a certain type of cuisine produces some consistency in foods, itineraries also embody a certain theme or consistency in tourist experiences. A "touristic cuisine" that produces this consistency is "thematized." As a result of thematization, each itinerary is often centred around certain common themes, such as the itineraries of "Beautiful China," "Classic China," "China Adventure," and "the Silk Road." All these itineraries select some of the components from the "raw materials" of China and combine them as a thematic itinerary. Itineraries are thus the cultural combination of tourist experiences, in which the criteria for inclusion and exclusion of the components of tourist resources are culturally, as well as economically, determined. In short, it is culture that determines what type of packaged tourist experiences suit what kind of potential tourists. Via such criteria of selection, discrete tourist spots are integrated as a whole and objectified as an itinerary. Itineraries thus reflect people's views, evaluations, and imagery of the world.

They are the categorization of peoples, cultures, places, and heritage in the world. In this sense, itineraries form *institutional circuits* in which contemporary people are "circulated" to examine and renegotiate the meanings of their relationships with the world. Itineraries are not only culturally structured as thematic experiences, but also dramatized as progressive stories. Itineraries are *scripts* in which the tourist journeys—like courses for a meal—can be organized as the beginning, the middle, the climax, and the end. Accordingly, tourists are performers who make their own stories with the itinerary unfolding across time and space. Just as dramatization creates meaning, the intensified dramatization of human experiences in itineraries indeed helps foster and reproduce meanings in human Use. Therefore, the consumption of itineraries is in reality a way of *consumption of meanings,* that are created beyond the confines of daily life and that make human life more colourful and meaningful.

However, with the mass production and consumption of itineraries or tourism, there arises a paradox of objectification of meanings, a paradox inherent in what Simmel (1990) calls "the objectification of culture" in western modernity. Itineraries are the temporal-spatial carriers of tourist experiences and their associated meanings. Under the condition of the commoditization of tourism, itineraries are often supplied in massive, homogenized, and standardized ways. The new marketing strategy of the segmentation of tourism does not forsake these standardizations but merely divides them into several domains. As a result, the meanings related to itineraries are objectified, standardized, and thematized.

In pre-modern ages, every single journey was linked to unique, subjective, and personal meanings. Under the condition of modernity, by contrast, such subjective and personal meanings of travel are increasingly diminished. Instead, tourism is packaged as various types of itineraries with thematic, categorized, homogenized, and objectified meanings In tourism advertisements, there are a number of "musts."

Once these "musts" are seen, this means "you have been there." If you go to Paris, you "must" find the scene of a romantic couple kissing each other. If you go to London, you "must" enjoy beers in a typical English pub. If you go to Beijing, you "must" see the torrent of bicycles on streets, Tiananmen Square, the Forbidden City, and the Great Wall at Badaling. All these "musts" signify the typical, objectified, standardized, and commonly acceptable meanings derived from the journeys to these places. Itineraries are thus organized in terms of socially, culturally, and objectively sanctioned and defined "worthiness" of visits. This site is included in our itineraries, just because everybody says it must be seen. That activity is also an item of our itinerary, just because everybody thinks such a kind of activity is a "must" in such a place. To miss such a "must" is not only a pity, but also a loss of value we pay for the journey Thus, in a hidden way, itineraries lead to a cultural and social conformism to objectified and stereotyped meanings that are already circulated within society, mass media, and the tourism industry.

However, for individual tourists, the problem could be, "why 'must' we see this site or participate in that activity at such a place?" "Could we look at the place from our own perspectives and find something meaningful with our own eyes?" Yes, you could. However, even independent travellers are in pursuit of the experiences that are informed by guidebooks, brochures, maps, and holiday programs on TV that are seen at home.

Thus, it becomes obvious that tourism is a kind of cultural practice in which each tourist participates to reproduce the code of meanings regarding the status quo, what is "sacred," and what is "heritage." The meanings derived from itineraries are thus unavoidably objectified and stereotyped. Accordingly, the consumption of these meanings serves to reproduce consumerist values of a society. Thus, tourists begin with a search for personal meanings but end up with the disappearance of *personal* meanings. Tourists want to keep a distance from reality but end up with a stronger conformity to the objectified semiotic order that a society needs. Such a paradox is one of exemplifications of what Miles (1998,5) calls the "consuming paradox." In this, the consumers' pursuit of freedom through economic means ends up maintaining "a dominant order that potentially constrains personal liberty". He describes the consuming paradox as the idea that, on the one hand, consumerism appears to offer us individuals all sorts of opportunities and experiences, on the other hand, as consumers we appear to be directed down certain predetermined routes of consumption which ensure that consumerism is ultimately as constraining as it is enabling. (Miles 1998,147) Itineraries embody the same consuming paradox.

As the form of circulation and consumption of tourism products, itineraries are the bearer of touristic consumerism. On the one hand, itineraries offer tourists "menus" for free choices and ease and order on the journey. On the other hand, itineraries direct tourists to the "predetermined routes of consumption" (Miles 1998,147), which may trigger complaints about the very ease and order linking the itineraries because of their constraints on freedom and spontaneity. Itineraries initially offer tourists menus for free choice, but they finally deprive tourists of freedom of choice on the journey. Itineraries are thus constraining as well as enabling. While tourism becomes a reaction to the ambivalence of modernity (Wang 2000), it itself brings about its own ambivalence.

The quest for the tourist experience is essentially a reaction to the Logos-modernity which is about the realm of institutions characterized by reason and rationality (Wang 1996, 2000). However, in so doing, the tourist experience is itself rationally organized. The tourist experience appears to be an escape from the overwhelmingly rationalizing institutions, but finally ends up as the rationalization of that experience, with the tourism industry being its rational agent. Itineraries, then, become a way in which the tourist experience is rationally organized. In this sense, the paradoxes of tourism derived from itineraries represent the paradoxes of the Logos-modernity that is characterized by overarching rationalization in contemporary societies.

In effect, the rationalization of experiences often turns the tourist experience into its opposite, namely, the non-flexible and rigid schedules and itineraries.

The Tourist as Outsider or Guest

Everyone who has ever travelled to another country knows that feeling. The feeling of being the outsider, the one who doesn't blend it, that everyone knows is totally outta place. And most of us know that when some tourist shows up in your home town, you feel the exact same way about them. Some try their best to blend in, others don't care that you laugh at them.

The Tourist Resort Zone

The Descriptive Approach

Tourist destinations are in a state of continuous change. This development is more intense in the case of island destinations due to their geographic limitations

Transport is a fundamental component of tourism, providing the vital link between the tourist generating areas and destinations. Hence there are very close links between the transport and tourism industries where a two-way relationship exists. On the one hand good accessibility, which is determined by the transport services provided, is essential for the development of any tourist destination. Conversely for the transport industry, there can be substantial benefits from tourism because of the additional demand which this type of travel can produce.

Aviation is an increasingly important mode of transport for tourism markets. Whilst geography has meant that, in modern times, air travel has always been the dominant mode for long distance travel and much international tourism, moves towards deregulation, and in particular the emergence of the low cost carrier sector, have also increased aviation's significance for short and medium haul tourism trips. Thus, developments in aviation are having very major implications for many leisure and business tourism markets. However, the characteristics and needs of leisure travellers are generally so very different from business travellers that this necessitates a separate consideration of these markets if a detailed understanding of the relationship with aviation is to be gained.

In spite of the obvious closeness between the aviation and the leisure tourism industries, there are very few specialist texts on this subject. Most tourism focused books consider aviation as just one component of the tourism industry which needs to be discussed, whereas aviation specialist texts rarely concentrate on just leisure travel. In addition there is very little literature that gives a detailed appreciation of the complexities and potential conflicts associated with the development of coherent and effective aviation and tourism policies. Therefore it is the aim of this book to fill this important gap which exists with a comprehensive, in-depth study of the relationship between aviation and leisure travel.

4

Emerging Dimensions of Promotion in Hospitality

Introduction

We have discussed in the previous units in detail, that tourism industry is one of the major segments of the Indian economy. It is a major contributor to foreign exchange earnings provides employment to millions directly and indirectly and acts as a vehicle for infrastructure development. Recognising the importance of the tourism industry, the Government of India has taken many policy measures such as Tourism Policy 1982, Tourism Plan of Action 1992 and Tourism Policy 1997. Through these policies, the government called for effective coordination of public and private participation to achieve synergy in the development of tourism. These plans identified new forms of tourism products for taking advantage of the emerging markets. Business tourism, health tourism, rural tourism, pilgrim tourism, adventure tourism, and sustainable tourism are some of the new products devised for changing demand. Let us study these emerging dimensions in the tourism sector.

Objectives

After studying this unit you will be able to achieve following objectives:

- Understand emerging trends in tourism.
- Learn about new products and old traditional tourism products.

- Know the importance of sustainable tourism development.
- Understand the concept of nature tourism.
- Develop environmental consciousness.
- Develop skills to locate important tourist destinations on the map.
- Know that tourism can be an instrumental for developing secularism and national integration and universal brotherhood.

Emerging Dimensions

Tourism will expand greatly in future mainly due to the revolution that is taking place on both the demand and supply side. The changing population structure, improvement in living standard, more disposable income, fewer working hours and long leisure time, better educated people, ageing population and more curious youth in developing the countries, all will fuel the tourism industry growth.

The arrival of a large number of customers, better educated and more sophisticated, will compel the tourist industry to launch new products and brands and re-invents traditional markets. The established traditional destinations founded on sun-sea-sand products will have to re-engineer their products. They must diversify and improve the criteria for destinations and qualities of their traditional offers. Alongside beach tourism, the tourism sector will register a steady development of new products based on natural rural business, leisure and art and culture. Thus the study of new markets and emerging markets and necessity of diversified products are the basis of our strategy, which can enhance and sustain, existing and capture new markets. Let us discuss some of the new tourism products.

Spiritual Tourism

Globally people are increasingly mentally disturbed and looking for solace in spiritual reading, meditation and moments of divine ecstasy. Our country has been known as the seat of spiritualism and India's cosmopolitan nature is best reflected in its pilgrim centres. Religion is the life-blood for followers of major religion and sects. Hinduism, Islam, Buddhism, Jainism, Zoroastrianism and Christianity have lived here for centuries. The visible outpouring of religious fervor is witnessed in the architecturally lavish temples, mosques, monasteries and Churches spreads across the length and breadth of the country. India is not only known as a place rich in its culture with varied attractions but also for many places of worship, present itself as embodiments of compassion where one get peace of mind.

Thus India has been respected as a destination for spiritual tourism for domestic and international tourists. Spiritual tourism is also termed as religious heritage tourism. It includes all the religions mentioned above; religious places associated with, emotional attachment to these centres and infrastructure facilities for the tourists. This can also be referred to as pilgrimage tourism, as clients are not looking for luxury but arduous journeys to meet the divine goal or simple life.

The essence of spiritual tourism is inner feeling through love. Love should not be rationed on the basis of caste, creed and economic status or intellectual attainment of the recipient. Religions come into existence for the purpose of regulating human life; what are common to all of them are the principles of love. Thus through religious tourism there is a sincere effort to bring better understanding among various communities, nations and thus foster global unity.

Hinduism is one of the oldest religions of India. Over 5000 years of religious history created wonderful temples and survived through ages all over India. The most popular spiritual tours are those that are centered on holy Ganges River. Badrinath, Kedarnath, Haridwar, Gangotri, Yamunotri, Allahabad, Varanasi. Jaganath temple at Puri, Bhubaneshwar, Konark in Orissa, Mata Vaishnodevi of Jammu and Kashmir, are some of the important pilgrim centres in north India. There are many spiritual sites in South India as well which dates back beyond the 10th centaury.

Rameshwaram, Mahabalipuram, Madurai Meenakshi temple in Tamilnadu and Tirupati in Andhra Pradesh are some pilgrim centres. Every year millions of tourists, both domestic and international, visit these places. India is special to Buddhists all over the world and India is the destination for pilgrimage because Buddhism emerged in India. The country is dotted with places that are associated with the life and times of Gutham Buddha; Lumbini-the birthplace of Buddha, Saranath where Buddha delivered his first sermon, Buddha Gaya where lord Buddha attained enlightenment and Vaishali where he delivered his last sermon and announced his nirvana.

Sikhism also emerged in India. The Golden Temple in Amritsar, the Hemkund Sahib, and Gurunanak Devji Gurudwara at Manikaran, which is also known for its hot water springs with healing properties, the holy city of Patna Sahib and Anandpur Sahib are important for Sikhs. The Jain temples of Dilwara and Mount Abu in Rajasthan, the Gomateswara temple at Karnataka, draw thousands of Jain followers. Even small communities like the Bahais have their own Lotus Temple at Delhi.

The Sultanate and Moghul empires built many historical monuments and mosques during their reign, all over the country. Red Fort, Fatehapur Sikri, Jama Masjid, TajMahal, Charminar etc., bear testimony to the blend of the Indian and Islam traditions of architecture. The followers of Islam have many mosques and shrines of Sufi Saints, like Moin-Uddin Chisti and Nizamuddin Aulia. For Christians, spiritual tours to Goa among other place like Mumbai and Kolkata are must. Among the most popular sites in Goa is the church of Our Lady of Rosary, the Rachel Seminary, and Church of Bom Jesus.

In addition to pilgrim centres there are personalities like the Satya Sai Baba, Osho, Shirdhi and others. This shows that spirituality and religion in India is a serious pursuit. The State Governments concerned, charitable trusts, temple trusts have made elaborate arrangements for accommodation, transport and ritual ceremonies. These organizations are also running hospitals, educational institutes, ashrams, meditation centres which benefit local community. More than 500 religious places have been identified and efforts are being made to develop these centres by Central and State Governments with private participation.

Adventure Tourism

Youth tourism has been identified as one of the largest segments of global and domestic tourism. The young travellers are primarily experience seekers, collecting, enquiring unique experiences. Adventure and risk have a special role to play in the behaviour and attitudes of young travellers. The growing number of young travellers is being fuelled by a number of factors such as increased participation in higher education, falling level of youth unemployment, increased travel budget through parental contribution, search for an even more exciting and unique experience and cheaper long distance travel.

Youth and adventure tourism appears to have considerable growth potential. The rising income in some major potential source markets such as the Central and Eastern Europe, Asia and Latin America, combined with the lower travel cost, growing student populations around the world particularly in developing countries, has fuelled the demand. India: a heaven for adventure tourism India has been an attraction for travellers from all over the world. Though in the field of international tourism, the segment of adventure tourism in India is getting only a fraction of such traffic. The trend has been showing an increased movement year after year with the development of facilities and greater awareness about adventure tourism options. Indian tourism offers both international and domestic adventurers a wide choice of adventures. Water sports, elephant safari, skiing, yachting, hail-skiing, gliding, sailing, tribal tours, orchid tours, scaling the high peaks of Himalayas, trekking to the valley of flowers, riding the waves in rapids, and camel safari in the deserts are breath taking opportunities for nature enthusias. Ladakh, the Garwal hills, the Himachal hills, Darjeeling, Goa, Lakshadweep, Andaman and Nicobar, Jaisalmer and wildlife sanctuaries and reserves are some of the places that offer adventure tourism.

Himalayas are the centre of India's main adventure activities as well as out- door recreational tourism. Our rivers, backwaters, Indian Ocean, Arabian Sea and deserts are unique attractions for the various branches of adventure. Trekking holds out the greatest potential in terms of numbers. It requires little infrastructure and carries its benefits to remote hills and mountain regions. Many of them are economically poor and backward. For our own youth it also helps in inculcating a spirit of adventure, respect for nature.

Indian Mountaineering Federation, Ministry of Tourism and State Governments are trying to improve trekking facilities and ensure safety and protection of travellers. The Institute of Mountaineering also organises courses for guides to train them in basic rock climbing safety procedures, environmental knowledge, and flora and fauna conservation. The major trek heads in the Himalayan region include Kashmir valley, Kirshwasser Zanskar, Ladhak, Lahul and Spiti, Champa and Manali, etc, Trekking in the Himalayas is a quite enjoyable. Let us now discuss some important adventure activities:

Mountaineering Expedition

This is the first and foremost activity in the Himalayas. In India, the expeditions are controlled and regulated by Indian Mountaineering Federation, which is the nodal body. Foreign expedition groups have to request the Indian Mountaineering Foundation (IMF) to book the required peak and IMF confirms the peak, by charging the royalty depending upon the number of persons and height of peak. Ministry of Defence, Home Ministry, of External Affairs are also involved in this process.

River Rafting

The Himalayan river's offer River rafting that run through the beautiful terrains, sandy white beaches, boulder studded rapids, river confluences, deep gorges, and some revered temples and towns. White-water sports are popular in Rishikesh, Manali, Zanskar Teesta, Beas, Central Ministry of Tourism has great extremely extended support to import inflatable rafts, canoes, kayaks, and accessories to boost water sports. Lakshadweep and Andaman have been promoted for scuba diving and wind surfing.

Water Sports

To boost water sports, water skiing and sailing both in seas and lakes, and river facilities has been provided. Chilka Lake in Orissa, Kollam in Kerala, Bhopal Lake in Madhya Pradesh, Dal Lake in Kashmir are some of the places where facilities have been provided for water sports. In Himachal hills Heli-skiing is also being promoted in season. The Garwal Mandal Vikas Nigam provides regular skiing courses during the season. It can be said that India is a new destination for adventure tourism. The Ministry of tourism, The Himalayan Task Force and Himalayan Tourism and Adventure Tourism Board (HMTAB) meet every year to discuss conservation, promotion for Himalayan tourism, and conservation of ecology.

Nature Tourism

In search of new tourism products, travellers and suppliers are today seeking to reshape the meaning of nature as a tourism attraction. Modern nature based tourism focuses on experiencing flora and fauna in natural settings. The nature based tourism related to nature, its attractiveness so that the visitors experience it in its natural settings. Eco-tourism takes into account unspoiled natural and socio-cultural attraction. Today the term nature tourism is often used synonymously with eco-tourism. Today nature tourism is the fastest growing segment of the tourism sector. It comprises around 40-60% of all international tourism.

Diversity of India is to be seen not only in its people, culture, religions, language and life style, the diversity starts in the land itself. The snowbourd peaks of the Himalayas, tropical rain forests, and hot deserts and breath-taking beautiful coasts. Each diverse geographical region generates a different picture and exploring them provides a unique experience. Now all these are packaged for tourists to provide eco-friendly holidays in India.

Wild life

The diversity of wild life in India is as rich as that of its flora and fauna. The great wealth of Indian wild-life can be imagined with the sight of majestic elephants, the dance of peacocks, the camel strides, the roar of tigers, at unparalleled acts of beauty. Watching birds and animals in their natural habitat is an experience in itself. The vastness of wild life and wilderness is India unparallel in the world. All these account for the immense opportunities for wild life tourism in India.

The immense heritage of wild life in India comprises 80 national parks and another whopping 441 wild life sanctuaries including bird sanctuaries. These reserves and forest areas are spread across the breadth and length right form the foot hills of Himalayan, the

Jim Corbet National park to six national parks in Andaman, from Ranthambhor national park in Rajasthan to Hazaribag wild life sanctuary in Bihar. India also boasts of the unique ecosystem at Sunderbans which is a UNESCO world heritage site and home to the largest number of tigers in the world. The Himalayan region is renowned for being the national habitat for a variety of wild life, elephants, snow leopards, deer, panther, wild buffalos, wild ass, one horned rhinoceros, porcupine, snow leopards, etc. The Kaziranga Game Sanctuary is ideal habitat for the rhino that the nature lovers and environmentalists are fascinated by.

The great Indian bustard and the black buck of Kerera sanctuary attract a lot of tourists. The Madhav National Park (Shivpuri Park) is another rich habitat for the wild life. The royal animal, tiger happens to be symbol of strength and speed. Amongst the best-known tiger reserves in India is Bandhawgarh in Madhya Pradesh. It is also known as the crown in the wild life heritage of India.

The variety of birds in India is enormous. Several hundred species of bird can be spotted across India. Indian wild life has its share of native birds along with migratory birds. The region of Andaman is home to rare species of birds like Narcondum hornbills, Nicobar pigeons and megaspores. The Himalayan region is well known as the natural habitat for the pheasant griffon, vulture and ravens. Dudhuwa wild life reserve, Keoladeao, Ghana national park, the Bharatpur bird sanctuary in Rajasthan is home to indigenous and migratory water birds. These bird sanctuaries are attracting tourists from far and wide.

Fishing and angling

Among the amazing array of nature tours offered in India are those that offer angling and fishing. The waters of Indian sub-continent are mind-blowing grounds for the nature sports. The adventures settings range form the majestic Himalayan valleys, snow fed streams and high altitude lakes and wide coastal stretches of the Arabia Seas and Bay of Bengal. Amidst the beautiful hills of the Himalayas is tented accommodation along the river beds, excellent option for adventure holidays in India. The Cauvery fishing lodge near Mysore, the hill stations of Munnar, and streams and lakes of Kerala and Kashmir are a paradise for anglers.

Hill Stations

At heights that range from 600 m to 3500m above sea level, most of the hill resorts of India are tourist destination in India. The hill stations add to the nature tour of India with majestic mountains and ravishing rivers. Mountain ranges of Shimla, Kullu Manali, Dalhousie, Palampur in Himachal Pradesh, Nainital-Almora-Kausani in Kumaon hills of Uttar Pradesh, Pachmarhi in Madhya Pradesh, Darjeeling are important for their snow-dusted peaks, lakes, parks and hot springs. The waterfalls, sulphur bath and all provide such an experience, which will linger in one's mind. Green heavens are on not only in the forest but the Islands are also a source of the best eco-tourism destinations. The tourism activities in Lakshadweep bring you close to nature. Andamans that are covered with rainforest, ringed by coral reefs, marine life, swimming and sunbathing are good experiences.

We are promoting tourism but while promoting tourism in eco-sensitive areas the emphasis is to control the volume of tourists so that the fragile balance of the area is not disturbed. The whole objective of nature tourism is to have purposeful travel to natural areas. Taking special note of this very objective of the eco-tourism while utilising the economic opportunities we should ensure conservation of natural resources. People travel to those areas, which enlightens, educates and entertains them. The new changed concept of nature tourism revives the tired source of the eco-tourism. It also provides basic economic upliftment to local people and other stakeholders who are directly dependent on this natural heritage. This strong relationship is targeted throughout eco-tourism.

Government Initiatives

Ministry of Tourism formulated eco-tourism guidelines for regulated and sustainable tourism. Tour operators operating in the fragile zones have adopted the (American Society of travel Agents) eco-practices for eco-tourism practices. These are: -

- Leave only foot prints, take photographs, but do not take away from natural areas and heritage monuments.
- Encourage local culture

- Respect local traditions
- Help in the conservation efforts
- Do not buy products made of endangered plants and animals.
- Try to respect natural habitats and support those products which promote the cause of environment and protection Ecotourism
- Madhav National Park
- Andaman & Nicobar Island
- Bharatpur
- World heritage site
- Narcondum hornbills
- Munnar
- Kanha
- Shivpuri
- Sunderbans
- Bird sanctuary
- Angling
- Wild life sanctuary

Rural Tourism

Rural tourism has been identified as one of the priority areas for development of Indian tourism. Rural tourism experience should be attractive to the tourists and sustainable for the host community. The Ninth Plan identified basic objectives of rural tourism as: -

- Improve the quality of life of rural people
- Provide good experience to the tourist
- Maintain the quality of environment.

Indian villages have the potential for tourism development. With attractive and unique traditional way of life, rich culture, nature, crafts, folk-lore and livelihood of Indian villages are a promising destination for the tourist. It also provides tourism facilities in terms of accessibility, accommodation, sanitation and security. Rural tourism can be used as a means to:-

- Improve the well being of the rural poor
- Empower the rural people
- Empower the women
- Enhance the rural infrastructure
- Participate in decision-making and implementing tourism policies
- Interaction with the outside world
- Improve the social condition of lower sections of the society.
- Protection of culture, heritage, and nature.

To tap the immense opportunities, coordinated actives of all agencies involved in the development are required. A carefully planned and properly implemented development will definitely benefit the community economically and improve the quality of life in the villages.

The success of such development depends upon the people's participation at grass root level for the development of tourist facilities and for creating a tourist friendly atmosphere. Development of rural tourism is fast and trade in hotels and restaurants is growing rapidly. Increase in the share of earnings through rural tourism will no doubt; provide an attractive means of livelihood to the poor rural community. It increases the purchasing power at all levels of community and strengthens the rural economy. Development of infrastructure facilities such as rail, electricity, water, health and sanitation will definitely improve the quality of life.

Government Initiatives

Central Government and State Governments have been encouraging rural handicrafts and fairs and festivals that have direct impact on preservation of heritage and culture of rural India. It also draws tourists from all over the world. Regional fairs, festivals help the growth of tourism, provide a ready market for the handicrafts, alternative income to the community, and facilitate regional interaction within the country.

The state governments have been monitoring closely the ecological relationship, socio cultural impact and conducting feasibility studies before selecting tourist sites. The state governments also ensure that: Tourism -

- Does not cause the tension for the host community
- No adverse impact on the resources
- Psychological satisfaction for the tourist.
- The large inflow of tourists would not put a stress on the local system
- Local community should not be deprived of basic facilities for the benefits of tourist
- The rural tourism does not disrupt the rhythm of community life

Thus the Central Government and State Governments have taken various steps for the promotion of tourism and attainment of the goal of sustainable tourism development.

Sustainablle Tourism

The concept of sustainability means that mankind must live within the capacity of the environment that supports. Sustainable development has been defined briefly as "that which meets the needs of the present without compromising the ability of future generations to meet their own needs".

The definition brings out certain important aspects of sustainable tourism: -

- Conservation and enhancement of resources for the future generation
- Protection of biological diversity
- Equity within and between generations
- Integration of environmental, social and economic considerations.

The concept of sustainable development is all about conservation and stewardship of resources for the future. The support for ecologically sustainable development emerging strongly in the tourism sector, as it is the logical way of balancing environmental concerns with growth and development of the industry.

Environmental problems facing the world today are of such magnitude that urgent actions have to be taken at the highest levels to counter this fatal degradation. But it is not just enough for government organisations to work towards sustainable development. Every individual, every neighbourhood, and every community has to contribute in every away possible to get close to the goal. Since the earth summit, the concept of sustainable development has been placed firmly on the global agenda. This issue is assuming great significance in the development of tourism in India also.

Tourism activities depend upon nature and natural heritage, it is essential to ensure that tourism development is ecologically sustainable –ecological process must not be neglected. Similarly tourism offers real experience of unique culture of the country. Hence the development should ensure that social and cultural sustainable tourism development compatible with the culture and values of the local people. The World Tourism Organization (WTO) defined sustainable tourism development as "that which meets the needs of present tourist and host regions while protecting and enhancing opportunities for the future. It is envisaged as leading to the management of all resources in such a way that economic, social and aesthetic needs can be fulfilled while maintaining cultural integrity, essential for ecological process, biological diversity and life supporting system".

Thus tourism has to be human and adapted to the needs of the tourist, respond to the needs of the local communities, be socio-economic and culturally well planned and environmentally sound. The tourism must offer products that are operated in harmony with the local environment, community attitudes and culture so that they become permanent beneficiaries and not the victims of tourism. The basic cultural identity of these local people should not be adversely affected. Sustainability also ensures economically sustainable-development process in the efficient management of resources and such management to ensure that the resource supports the future as well as the present generation.

Thus sustainable tourism aims to: -

- Improve the quality of life of people.
- Provide good experience to the tourists
- Maintain the quality of environment that is essential for both tourists and the local community.

Tourism can be one of the effective tools for building a prosperous community economically, socially and culturally. It must be environmentally sustainable and based on the sustainance of the natural and cultural base. Each destination should examine whether it has adequate attractions and facilities for tourism and there is a potential for tourism generating markets to be open to exploitation. The carrying capacity is the central principle in environmental protection and sustainable tourism development. It determines the maximum use of any place without causing negative effects on resources on community, economy and culture. Thus tourism has to be environmentally sustainable in both natural and cultural environment

Basic Guidelines for achieving sustainable tourism The following are certain guidelines that have to be followed to achieve sustainable tourism:

- A general tourism policy incorporating sustainable tourism objectives at national regional and local level should be followed.
- Targets established for the planning, development and operation of tourism involving various government departments, public and private sector companies, community groups and experts could provide widest possible safeguards for success.
- Primary consideration should be given to the protection of natural and cultural assets.
- All tourism participants will follow ethical and sound behavioural and conservative rules regarding nature, culture, economy, and community value system.
- The distribution of tourism development project should be rationed on the basis of equity.

- Public awareness of benefits tourism and how to mitigate its negative impacts should be pursued.
- Local people would be encouraged to assume leadership roles in planning and development.

In the Tourism Policy, 1982 the guidelines in Eco-tourism have attempted to achieve sustainability in tourism. It indicates that the key players in the ecotourism are Central Government and state governments, local authorities, developers, operators, visitors and local community. Each of them has to be sensitive to the environment and local traditions and follow the guidelines for successfully development of sustainable tourism.

Summary

Tourism industry is one of the major segments of our economy, it contributes major part of foreign exchange and generates employment and helps infrastructure development. Government of India has formulated policies to boost the tourism industry. Tourism will expand greatly in future mainly due to the great revolutions that are taking place in demand and supply.

Thus the study is a critical issue in tourism industry. And new product development and innovation is essential for survival. Health tourism in India is promoted as high-tech healing destinations, which provide world-class treatment at low cost, incorporating the Indian system of medicine-ayurveda, naturopathy, unani, sidha and allopathy. India is the seat of spiritualism. It is the confluence of different religions: Hinduism Sikhism, Islam, Christianity, and Jainism, etc. The followers of religion built many lavish temples, mosques, monasteries and churches across the country.

These are attracting both domestic and international tourists. In India, adventure tourism and nature tourism have been identified as the largest segment of global and domestic tourism. The geographical diversity makes India as a heaven for adventurers. MICE tourism is a fast emerging sector; especially after the liberalization of the Indian economy and Indian tourism industry is equipped with all facilities to welcome business tourists. Sustainable tourism is a new concept, which says that the tourism development should meet the needs of the present without compromising the ability of future generation to meet their needs.

Key Words

The various key words which are mentioned in this lesson are:

- Yam
- Dhyana
- Samadhi
- Niyam
- Asana
- Pranayama
- Prathyahara
- Arduous
- Exotic
- Ecstasy
- Fervor
- Rejuvenation
- Expertise
- Therapy
- Multi specialty
- Preventive health care.

5

Promoting Rural Tourism

Introduction

This revision of *Promoting Tourism in Rural America* covers the major issues in rural tourism including agritourism, cultural/heritage tourism, ecotourism, planning, marketing, economic impact and more. It provides web links to more than *fifty* full-text "how to" information guides, manuals, and handbooks for assisting local officials, communities, and citizens involved in tourism development and includes a section of resources organizations.

The reader may also access additional tourism resources including success stories/case studies, funding and assistance programs, and statistical information located on the Rural Information Centre's Tourism Resource page at

This source guide was revised and updated by Patricia LaCaille John November 2004.

Rural Information Centre Publication Series Number 60, Revised Edition. Last Modified: May 22, 2008

Tourism Development Overview

Advantages and Disadvantages of Tourism Development

The pros and cons of tourism development in rural America are varied. Tourism provides income and diversification to rural communities. Most of the dollars generated from outside visitors stay within the local economy.

In addition to gains from direct sales to visitors, many indirect benefits are realized from tourism. Visitors contribute to the tax revenues collected and can influence the quality of life by financing community facilities such as swimming pools, golf courses, restaurants, and shopping facilities. Community events intended for tourists, also attract local residents. Many potential industries prefer locations that provide high quality services and recreational resources. If the community is a pleasant place, the visitors may become a permanent resident.

Tourism offers other indirect benefits. For example, the need to provide services to tourists creates new jobs in the community. Although they may not be high paying employment opportunities, these jobs satisfy the need of students and dual-earning families for part-time or seasonal employment.

On the other hand, developing and maintaining the tourist industry in a community requires added costs and puts pressure on public services. The cost of surveys, impact analysis, promotions, insurance, fund raising, and operations are some points to consider.

Managing Resources Requires Planning

Advanced planning maximizes the advantages and minimizes the disadvantages of developing rural tourism.

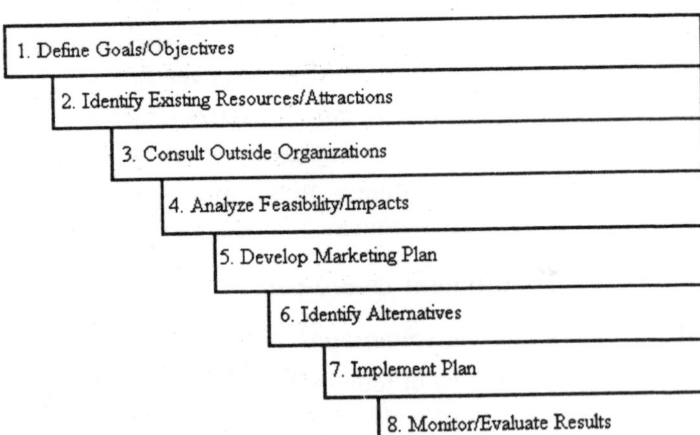

Steps in Planning and Developing Tourism

Tips and Technologies

Many communities can develop tourism into a major industry using these techniques:

- Understand the potential for tourism development
- Inform and educate the community to create support
- Secure investments for public and private sources
- Manage natural, human, and financial resources
- Build an image for the community

Where to Start

Leaders must first assess the potential for tourism in the community. What businesses serve travellers and how much additional revenue will it generate? Are these enough services to satisfy the potential demands? What are the goals and objectives of the community? Talk about tourism with other members of the community. Tourism requires support, and one way to gain support is by informing and educating the citizenry. Introduce the idea to the Chamber of Commerce, at civic clubs, at city council, or at other community organization meetings. The community and its leaders can broaden support for tourism by securing financial commitments from public and private sources.

Existing Resources

Managing natural, human and financial resources is an important component of tourism development. Most communities have existing resources and attractions that can draw visitors, such as:

- natural settings
- scenery
- parks and recreations
- historical identity
- cultural identity
- ethnic identity
- volunteers
- students

- retirees
- events
- festivals
- fairs
- shops
- hotels
- local industries
- art galleries

What Does Your Community Have to Offer?

Conduct an inventory of the things that your community has to offer to tourists. Describe each type of attraction in terms of quality and quantity. Separate them by "core elements" (primary reasons tourist are attracted) and "secondary elements" (supporting resources; those that contribute positively to the tourists' travel experience). Look ahead at the resources that might be enhanced or used more fully.

Surveys and Models

Surveys and models are used in the process of tourism planning to determine:

- Community attitudes toward tourism
- Recreational use value and demand
- Tourism patterns
- Travel costs
- Economic impacts

Types of survey methods include telephone interviews, questionnaires, and mall interviews.

Telephone interview are low in cost, and provide a quick turn-around. In order to simplify the responses, the interviewer offers a minimum number of choices to each question in the survey. The interviewer also sends a letter before the call is made to state the date and time of the survey and ask the customer's cooperation. Questionnaires can be used to identify the different types of tourists, or market segments. The surveyor lists responses that can be checked off by the visitor. This type of response is easy to tabulate. The survey may include questions that ask:

- Where does the visitor live?
- What attracts the visitor to the community?
- How does the visitor find out about tourist attractions?
- What type of businesses/facilities does the visitor use?
- What kinds of accommodations/services are needed?

The survey tests the questionnaire to determine the typical responses and to modify the questions. Face-to-face interviews are useful if visual aids are necessary, for instance, in evaluating what promotional materials are pleasing to the consumer. These interviews are conducted at a central location, such as in a shopping mall.

Developing a Marketing Plan

An important step in tourism planning is determining target market segments. Experts begin by defining the market areas that will draw the most visitors.

They then divide the market into trip length categories. Finally, they define the clientele that will be attracted to the community. Use the chart below as a guide:

Geographic Market Areas

Day Trips

- short — within 50 miles
- long — up to 200 miles

Pass Through Visits

- day visits
- overnight stays

Overnight Trips

- weekends
- vacations

Outdoor Recreation Activities

- Water Recreations
- Camping, Hiking, Bicycling
- Hunting
- Winter Sports
- Horseback Riding
- Picnicking
- Hang Gliding, Ballooning
- Nature Study
- Photography, Painting

Entertainments

- Cultural Heritage
- Historic sites
- Events
- Fairs, Festivals
- Shopping
- Picnicking

Other Travel Purposes

- Visit Friends & Relatives
- Business

When the expert has determined the market segments, leaders of the community are ready to make a written marketing plan. This plan helps them to see the best combination of marketing strategies, prices, places and promotions to use.

Which characteristics are unique to the community? Using the plan, the leaders are able to develop a theme that ties the community's businesses and services together.

It is important to involve all facets of the community in the decision making process. Remember that everyone and everything the visitor has contact with projects and promotes something about the community.

Keep your promotional messages short and targeted to the community theme. Use your theme to promote your community:

- on brochures, billboards, posters
- ont-shirts, hats, stickers, coupons
- at demonstrations, contests, the library
- for public announcements on television, radio or community calendars.

6

Advertising and Promotions of Wellness Tourism

Introduction

Tourism is the fastest growing industry internationally with destinations not only in industrialised countries, but also in less developed countries in East Africa, Central America and South East Asia.

Developing countries which were previously seen as less likely destinations or were closed to tourism altogether are now considering the marketing of their natural and/or cultural attractions to receive a share of this global industry. Adventure tourism, and cultural tourism take advantage of this development. Each year more exotic places are offered on the tourism market for those who have seen everything else, or prefer destinations 'off the beaten track'. The close contact with locals in isolated areas and their customs seems to be one of the main attractions of developing countries, and this is used extensively in marketing strategies.

At the same time, the scientific study of tourism has developed such that tertiary education institutions worldwide offer degree courses in tourism studies. The perspectives and approaches one can adopt to study the topic are as diverse as tourism itself. Jafari (1990) presented an overview of disciplines and approaches in the study of tourism. The disciplines offered are of considerable diversity but 'health' does not rate a mention in this model of approaches.

Tourism and Health

Literature dealing with the combination of tourism and health abundantly covers health aspects of travellers to particular locations, health education, medical aspects of travel preparation, health problems in travellers or in returning tourists, and economic or administrative consequences of tourists' ill health. In short, 'Tourism and Health' usually focuses on the travellers' wellbeing. However, despite this necessary and applaudable development in protecting travellers from health problems, one needs to consider that there are people on the other end of the journey who may be subjected to a change in their health status as well, due to visiting fellow humans. 'Tourism and Health' rarely includes the hosts in its consideration. Tourism's potential impact on the health of the local host communities can be direct or indirect. One example of direct impact is the possible transmission of diseases from travellers to locals. Nowadays, the emergence of new infectious diseases or the reemergence of diseases thought to be eradicated are causing great concern, and travel is a major contributor to their spread. Lea (1988) rightly pointed out that tourism has the dual effect of promoting the provision of improved health care in Third World destinations but, in addition, acts as a vehicle to spread some forms of disease. Other possible direct health impacts are chronic diseases or disabilities, and accidents causing injuries or deaths of local tourist guides in the course of their employment in tourism. Indirect impacts can be attributed to the social, cultural, environmental and economic impacts which are the usual focus of accounts on tourism impact.

Methodology

Aim of the Study

The aim of this study was to ascertain the current knowledge on health impacts of tourism in developing countries, to provide information on gaps in this knowledge as a baseline for future research, to identify research topics which could be investigated by researchers from health, tourism and other disciplines, and to propose elements of a framework for the assessment of health impacts of tourism.

Design of the Study

First, a literature review was conducted. Publications related to the topic were identified in the fields of health and tourism. A few sources were located through networking with people working in disciplines pertinent to the subject. The key areas for the search were: travellers' health; tourism and health; tourism in developing countries; economic, environmental, sociocultural impacts of tourism; public health; and tropical medicine. The literature was reviewed to identify any references made in relation to the topic under study to recognise unresearched issues and, if possible, to obtain ideas for an innovative approach of investigation. Only publications in English, German and Spanish were sought and utilised.

Second, a field trip was undertaken to test the findings from the literature analysis against fieldwork in Easter Island/Chile and Peru. First, a range of tourism destinations (including some very popular and others only visited by few individual travellers) were examined with the aim of detecting evidence of positive or negative impacts of tourism on the health of the local population. The emphasis here was on potential environmental impacts; potential health hazards due to running a tourism destination, e.g., construction, equipment, transport; and possible transmission of diseases. Second, semi-structured interviews were conducted with health practitioners, tour operators and conservationists to elicit their assessment of tourism's health impacts. Discussions centred around medical aspects, such as changes in disease pat terns, introduction of previously nonendemic infectious diseases, and work place health and safety aspects; tour operators' recollection of possible anecdotal evidence of health impacts; and conservationists' views on tourism in environmentally fragile destinations.

Tourism's Health Impact- a Review of the Literature

The Impact of Travel on the Health of the Hosts: An Historical Overview

Travel is inseparably linked with human existence. Historical accounts of travel and migrations as the main source of epidemics are numerous. The Roman Empire was struck by the bubonic plague, spread along the trade routes of the time, leading eventually to the dramatic and largest epidemic of the 'Black Death' in the 14th century. It had started in the Gobi desert in 1320 and reached Europe 30 years later, where it is estimated to have killed one-third to half of the population in some European countries.

Venetian authorities who observed outbreaks after the arrival of ships from the East assumed that travel may have to do with the spread of the plague. The first regulations governing the arrival of ships were introduced in Venice and Rhodos in 1377, detaining ship, passengers, crew and cargo at a distance for 40 days ('quaranta giorni' became quarantine) before being allowed into the harbour.

The conquest of the 'New World' is probably the best known event in history which has been linked to the spread of fatal diseases to non- immune peoples. It was clear from the first written accounts of the Spanish invasion of the Americas in the 15th century that the native peoples were not only killed in battle and through hard labour or physical punishment but also succumbed to a great extent to introduced infectious diseases to which they lacked immunity. In some parts of the New World, infections such as smallpox and influenza reduced the native population dramatically. When this lead to an acute shortage in the work force, the ensuing slave trade from West Africa lead to an even greater range of diseases. The arriving ships, for example, not only brought the yellow fever virus but also its vector *Aedes aegypti*.

Similar transmissions occurred in the Pacific region some hundred years later. It is not clear from historic travel logs if early explorers were aware of their potential role in the transmission of diseases. Beaglehole (1934) in his account of the exploration of the Pacific clearly focused on the exploratory aspect of journeys into the area with only one mention of "the visits of European ships destroyed utterly and horribly its primitive freedom from pestilence".

Captain James Cook seems to have been the first to actively at tempt the prevent ion of a transmission of infectious diseases from crew to native populations by confining any person found to be diseased to the ship while the rest of the crew was permitted to go ashore. Apart from syphil is, other often deadly diseases such as measles and dysentery were transmitted from Europeans to native people.

Uncertainty about the transmission of diseases did not seem to exist 100 years later when it was purposefully employed as the following excerpt illustrates. In 1860, three captains arrived at Port Resolution on Tanna (Vanuatu) to occupy the island. Alexander (1895) cited Rev. John Paton reporting: Our watchword is, "Sweep these creatures away and let white men occupy the soil". They then invited a chief by the name of Kapuku on board one of their vessels, promising him a present, and confined him for twenty-four hours without food in the hold among natives ill with measles, and finally sent him ashore without a present to spread the disease. The measles thus introduced spread fearfully, and decimated the *population of the island*. Epidemics occurring in isolated 'virgin' populations, i.e., populations without immunity to a certain disease, are not confined to the Middle Ages. Forty years ago on Easter Island, Heyerdahl (1958) observed the influenza epidemic which accompanied the arrival of the yearly supply ship from the Chilean mainland:

The conongo *was the natives'* great terror- the annual influenza epidemic which always accompanied contact with the mainland. It came and went with the regularity of clockwork. After the ship's visit it always raged through the village for a month or two. It got into chests, heads, and stomachs: everyone was ill, and there was always a toll of *human lives before the* conongo passed and left the people in peace for the rest of the year.

A mumps epidemic in 1957 on St. Lawrence Island (Alaska) was started by a boy returning from the mainland after undergoing surgery. Similar outbreaks on other 'virgin' island populations in Alaska occurred in 1965 and 1967-68. Although it is generally argued that it is unlikely that there are any 'virgin' populations left due to the contacts of people around the world, partial or selective immunity still allows the transmission of diseases by people on the move. Today, business and leisure travel is claimed to be the driving force in the spread of disease and the (re)emergence of infectious diseases.

Potential Indirect Impacts of Tourism on the Health of the Host Community

The impacts of tourism are a popular topic in the literature, usually covering the economic, environmental and social aspects. However, few discourses are based on research evidence. Cater (1987) attributed this to the difficulty of studying impacts due to their complexity. An additional problem is that social and cultural dimensions are difficult to quantify and, therefore, out of reach of most researchers employing conventional methods. Using the tourism literature as a baseline, one can develop the arguments further and identify ways in which these impacts can affect health in positive or negative ways.

Economic impacts affecting health Economic benefits are certainly the primary cause for the promotion of tourism in developing countries. The benefits are mainly seen in the gain of (often desperately needed) term problem is water pollution. The following examples are taken from a compilation by Maurer (1992). Frequently, tourism developments in developing countries do not have an appropriate system for sewage and waste management and they use rivers and the sea for disposal. This can pose two problems. First, fish and molluscs eaten by the local population as a source of protein may be unsuitable for consumption due to pollutants deposited in these animals. Second, swimming in polluted water can lead to ear, eye, skin and gastrointestinal infections in even epidemic proportions. Herbicides used on golf courses have been shown to pollute the freshwater supply and impact on health directly or through food obtained from the water. The pollution of waterholes in deserts through the tourists' use of soap and shampoo poses another problem.

Redirection and overuse of freshwater for hotels, swimming pools and landscaping purposes in tourism facilities can lead to the local population having less or no clean drinking water which in turn puts them at risk of contracting diseases. Lack of water also impacts on the local agriculture leading to poor crops and a scarcity of food.

There is a need to substantiate examples such as those mentioned above. Very little research evidence supports numerous anecdotal accounts of environmental problems caused, at least partially, by tourism. More specific investigations into pollution and redirect ion of drinking water need to be carried out. Also, resulting health problems need to be documented carefully to support strategies for improvement.

Garbage generated by tourists poses another public health hazard for host communities as, apart from its unaesthetic appearance, it creates breeding tourist areas in Argentina, 96.3% of respondents to a survey claimed that tourism was to blame for increasing costs, but the results have to be treated cautiously as the study had only a return rate of 23%. There seems to be a paucity of research supporting anecdotal accounts of economic impacts of tourism. Research needs to be conducted into changes of living costs and their effect on locals. For example, D'Sousa (1985) reported from Goa that, in addition to a lack of improved health, local tax payers paid for tourists' free medical care.

A different type of negative economic impact on health was reported by Loval and Feuerstein (1992): "There is said to be a drain of trained nurses away from the health sector in some Pacific areas as they seek jobs in tourism". No other reference could be found supporting this claim. Considering the expenses of training health personnel, it is important to know if this is a common trend in developing countries where salaries of health professionals are known to be very low. The problem of locals leaving their traditional activities of fishing or farming for seemingly more lucrative work in the tourism industry has been presented in the literature.

Environmental Impacts Affecting Health

Unfortunately, tourism seems to be the culprit for a number of environmental problems that pose health hazards to local communities. A serious longforeign exchange and the creation of employment. Archer (1986) claimed that "tourism generates a considerable secondary economic activity in a destination country" with income percolating to the public sector, business and private households. Consequently, locals' possession of foreign or local currency earned in the tourism industry enables them to purchase more or better food leading to a better health status (although more money may also mean more junk food). It also allows them access to better health facilities if earnings from tourism have been used to improve the services. Hundt (1996) presented Jamaica as an example where tourism development has lead to prosperity and improved health of the population.

However, the same author admitted that "more important is the realisation that the profits of tourism generally are not used to improve the health status of the poor, marginalised natives in host countries". The following example from Peru may illustrate this statement. In 1995, the country received almost half a million tourists.

The area around Cusco is certainly one of the main attractions of the country and the majority of foreign tourists include a visit in their itinerary. Tourism generated income, however, does not seem to percolate to everybody in the general population in the area if the nutritional status of children in the Cusco Health District (as investigated by Wolff, Pérez, Gibson, Lopez, Peniston and Wolff, 1985) is taken as one outcome criterion. Tourism development may eventually lead to increasing living costs. In two sites for disease-carrying arthropods and rodents. Harrington (1993) reports the pollution of the Amazon through tourists. In 1980, the South American Explorers Club collected approximately 400 kg of unburnable garbage on the Inka trail in Peru. An aspect not yet located in the literature is the possible danger of injuries (cuts, lacerations) caused by garbage. This may be of particular concern if people contract infections but are unable to access or pay for the treatment required.

Clearing for tourism developments or sports facilities causes serious ecological changes and can lead to flooding or landslides destroying crops, homes and lives. Apart from that, mosquitos which are potential vectors for diseases tend to move into cleared areas. When people (locals and tourists) move in to utilise the cleared land, they are at risk of contracting serious diseases such as malaria or yellow fever if the mosquitos are infected. The cutting of firewood along the world's trekking routes adds to the deterioration of forest already damaged due to cutting of wood for domestic purposes as can easily be seen in Nepal or Peru. At present, no statistics could be found indicating the exact extent of destruction of forest or bushland for tourism purposes.

On the other hand, tourism can have positive environmental effects, when generated income is used for environmental planning and education, or for the construct ion of appropriate sewage systems. Investing in the conservation of natural areas and safe tourist facilities in these areas ultimately benefits the physical and mental well-being of locals and visitors alike. Hellen (1995) argued that research into tourism in the developing world "opens up the prospect that global tourism may itself become a vehicle for investment in environmental health programs and securing improved health for all". So far, there is a striking paucity of examples supporting this vision.

Socio-cultural Impacts Affecting Health

This third major category of impacts is similarly widely discussed in the literature. Generally, it is stated that tourist-host encounters may lead to better understanding between cultures, remove prejudices and promote cultural pride eventually leading to the preservation or a renaissance of the local art/craft. Despite these positive arguments, it seems that tourism's impact on society and culture in developing countries is mainly perceived as negative. It is acknowledged that social and cultural change is a phenomenon attributed to modernisation in general but it seems that the frequent and fast exchange of encounters of people from different backgrounds accelerates this change at a rate not always favourable for the host communities. Obvious health problems accompanying these changes originate in the appearance or increase of prostitution, alcoholism, drug use and violence.

Also, lifestyle and food preferences of visitors seem to be imitated often leading to higher body weight, greater percentage of body fat, and high blood pressure, conditions previously unknown in these communities. Farrell (1982) named Hawaii and other areas in the Pacific as an example of areas where these changes occurred. Little additional research evidence on unhealthy lifestyles due to the influence of tourism could be located.

Mental health problems are less frequently discussed. Changes in the traditional lifestyle or loss of identity through changes in social and cultural values can put a considerable mental strain on people. Negative implications through changes in social and cultural values include potential mental health problems. Currently, it is unclear how many confirmed diagnoses of mental alterations could be attributed to long-term impacts of tourism.

Physical and mental health problems caused by the forceful removal of peoples to make way for tourism are equally neglected in the literature. Examples of this practice can be found around the globe. A more recent case was reported from Botswana where Kalahari Bushmen appealed to the UN to save them from being evicted from their ancestral lands which were to be used for tourism purposes. Forced relocations of indigenous people in the Peruvian Amazon area are a common method to make space for tourist lodges. Research into changes of locals' health status is very scarce. Numerous questions arise when evaluating anecdotal evidence on sociocultural impacts. An important issue that needs investigation is if changes to lifestyle, the adoption of unhealthy food preferences, increase in prostitution, alcohol and drug use, and violence can clearly be attributed to tourism, or if they are symptoms of 'development' and modernisation. It is also of interest to ascertain if tourists engage in activities contradicting local rules and taboos, and of what type and frequency these actions are. Additionally, there has to be a closer investigation into the occurrence of people's forceful removal from their home and land for tourism purposes.

Potential Direct Impacts of Tourism on the Health of the Host Community

Health conditions which can affect local people directly and not as secondary implications of other impacts of tourism, are diseases, accidents, and conditions related to employment in tourism. The potential direct health impacts of tourism are mainly those occurring through the spread of infections by travelling individuals. These infections can be imported from the tourists' country of origin, or they could be contracted while travelling. The main infection risks for travellers in developing countries as compiled by Warren and Mahmoud. All of those can be transmitted to local individuals. There are diseases that are easily spread and are common, others require a range of factors and circumstances to be transmitted and are less common. Some diseases may have a minor impact on the individual and/or can be treated easily, others are difficult to treat and/or have serious impacts on the individual. The ease of spread of a range of diseases which can be transmitted from travellers to hosts and their level of impact on the host individual.

The mode of transmission of some conditions is common knowledge and well researched, the spread of others has not been discussed in the light of tourist-host transmission, possibly because some diseases are less common. Nevertheless, sometimes only one case of infection may be enough to introduce a virulent agent to people without the necessary immunity and lead to a major epidemic. This potential risk warrants the consideration of all possibilities of disease transmission. An additional factor needs to be addressed when discussing the potential spread to people in developing countries, and here particularly indigenous communi ties. Poor hygiene, unfavourable economic conditions, inadequate housing and nutrition predispose people already to a range of diseases such as tuberculosis, parasitic infections or hepatitis, with individuals often having several acute and chronic conditions at the same time. It is obvious that an additional load of pathogenic agents, especially when the immune system is compromised, can only aggravate health problems.

Field Studies on Tourism's Health Impact

One objective of this study was to test if the findings of the analysis of published material applied to real situations in developing countries.

Health Problems Linked to Tourism in Easter Island and Peru

On Easter Island it was found that the (only) campground on the island at Anakena Beach had no fresh water supply, and the sanitary facilities provided, according to the locals, had been locked for a long time. On weekends, hundreds of locals and tourists gather at the beach usually staying the whole day. This was discussed with staff at the hospital who reported a relatively high prevalence of diarrhoea on the island but had attributed this to vegetables imported from the Chilean mainland. After discussing the lack of sanitary facilities which becomes even more obvious with the added tourists, they agreed that it was worthwhile to investigate this potential health hazard. Staff, however, saw the main problem regarding tourism and health as the transmission of Sexually Transmitted Infections (STIs) from tourists to locals.

This anecdotal evidence has not yet been systematically investigated. The issue of the availability of health facilities came up during conversations with locals in the market. It could be concluded that tourism on Easter Island has not improved the locals' health facilities. This may have to do with the fact that tourists generally stay only a short time, either because of the limited facilities on the island or because they are only having a brief stopover on the connection Tahiti- Santiago de Chile. If seriously ill, the people joked, they had "only two options, Santiago [some 3700 km away] or the cemetery".

Health professionals in Peru also maintained that cases of STIs were increasing and tourism was seen as a major contributing factor to this development, but they were unable to substantiate these claims. Toonen *et al.* (1996) conducted a health baseline study in the Camisea area in the Amazonian jungle where the Shell Company is prospecting. The potential risk of the native population to contract STIs was seen as very high because of people coming from outside (here mainly oil workers). The study does not clarify if locals also spoke of tourists, the term 'visitadores' in the study refers to prostitutes. Other diseases repeatedly named as being spread by people moving around were malaria and leishmaniasis. The important aspect of tourist-host encounters die each year in the Andes including mountain guides. The health of tourism workers, however, can also be in danger in the developed world. More than 50 climbers and guides died within a few weeks in the European Alps in the summer of 1997. Another form of 'occupational health hazard' has been observed on the Argentinian side of the Iguazu Falls where, at a certain point, locals drive tourists in an open boat equipped with a small engine close to the edge of the falls. The engine barely is able to get the boat out of the current and back to shore. A thin rope along the edge clearly is not sufficient to withstand a boat should the engine fail.

Increasingly, developing countries with access to spectacular reefs market their underwater attractions to encourage diving holidays. When the income of a diving guide depends on the number of dives, the minimum surface interval that is required for health reasons may not always be observed, putting them under considerable health risks. A lack of decompression chambers in developing countries, partly due to the failure of enforcing their installation, as Rudkin and Hall (1996) reported from Pacific islands, is of concern not only to the visiting diver but also to the local guide.

In many areas in the developing world, customs prevent people's exposure to physical danger by placing a taboo over a certain area. If such an area happens to become of interest to tourism, the reluctance of locals to go to such places may be overcome by the need to earn money. Two guides together with one tourist died in January 1995 at Mt. Yasur on Tanna/Vanuatu, killed by falling rocks ejected from the volcano. This author has witnessed local guides refusing to accompany visitors to the summit of this volcano.

In tribal areas in the jungle could not be examined during this field trip but needs urgent attention. This is so because some villages now seem to contact tour operators suggesting cooperation, and operators sensitive to potential problems need to be provided with information to facilitate their decision making. Environmental impacts of tourism in trekking areas with problems due to unregulated garbage disposal and the lack of sanitary facilities were suggested in the literature and could be observed in reality. The problem applies to areas with opportunities for short hikes as well as to trails representing major tourist attractions such as routes in the Cordillera Blanca/Huaraz or the Inka Trail near Cusco. The need for urgent action has been recognised in both areas and plans are already under way to implement solutions to the problems. A program is currently being designed to install sanitary facilities along well-used trails. This is of particular importance when the areas represent the main water supply for a large region.

Implications for Local Tourism Employees' Health

The neglect of local tourism workers' health in the literature is obvious. The importance of the consideration of this topic became apparent during the field trip. It seems that many tourism workers in Peru (and other developing countries) earn their living as tourist guides, often in destinations with little tourism infrastructure such as nature based adventure tours. Tourists are given advice about the dangers they may encounter on these trips. But tourists are only exposed to those hazards for a very short time compared to the guides. Their health risks increase through the frequency of exposure due to their job as well as the terrain they are working in.

Adventure tours to the Amazonian jungle are very popular. Like tourists, guides are exposed to health hazards such as snake and other animals' bites, diseases such as malaria or leishmaniasis, and car or boat accidents. Several cases of snake bites and accidents with boats and trucks were named by a tour operator in Cusco.

Probably the highest health risk exists for mountain guides who risk altitude sickness, injury or death in their attempt to lead tourists to spectacular summits. Peak season means a higher income but also a higher health risk. Shlim (1996) reported that in just one storm in the Nepal Himalayas on 10-11 November 1995, 22 foreigners and more than 45 Nepalese guides and porters died in different regions due to heavy snowfall, avalanches and mudslides. It was claimed that up to 30 people and porters should be assessed and monitored. The identification of potential occupational health problems and a documentation of the spread of diseases contracted during employment in tourism to family and community, would assist in strategies to minimise health hazards.

Towards a Framework for Understanding Tourism's Health Impacts

Anecdotal Versus Research Evidence

This study suggests that, at the moment, there is very little research based evidence on the impact of tourism on locals' health in developing countries. Sources that can be found related to the topic are mainly anecdotal, underline the need for further research. Diseases which had been reported as transmittable through people's movement, were found again in the field. Also, the health problems of local tourism workers proved to be a reality, and research into this area appears to be overdue. Although their numbers may be small compared to the entire population who may be at risk of infectious diseases, the concern over their work safety warrants further investigations. A retrospective and ongoing documentation of illness/death of local tour guides classified into areas of expertise, such as mountain, scuba diving, jungle and so on, should be established and a data bank created with links to neighbouring countries which have similar problems. Also, the health status of guides Health hazards for white water rafting guides have been described in the literature.

Sisson, Nichols and Hopkins (1983) reported schistosomiasis (blood flukes) infections among US rafting guides on the Omo River/Ethiopia. A year later, Istre, Fontaine, Tarr, and Hopkins (1984) described an outbreak of acute schistosomiasis among rafters on the same river, pointing out that commercial organisations were about to start business. This means that local guides, although partially immune, are exposed to repeated infections. A different potential health problem was identified in porters. For example, on the Inka Trail (with the highest altitude above 4000m.) one can find children carrying backpacks considered too heavy for well nourished healthy adult tourists. This may cause problems in later life such as bone deformation and chronic backpain which can prevent the individual from pursuing regular work.

The examples mentioned give a little insight into this complex area. Unfortunately, no research on this topic could be found. This may be because accidents or other health problems affect individual people, not groups or whole communities, cases are dealt with individually but not linked with other similar events. Because of the absence of data on frequency/occurrence, it is also difficult to make a risk assessment based on assumptions alone. Considering the fact that in developing countries there is rarely any organised support for such workers, health insurance or compensation for themselves or their families, this matter needs urgent attention if tourism is not to be seen as yet another type of exploitation. On the other hand, however, it is to be expected that some local guides can indeed make a living without putting themselves at risk and, subsequently, even lead a much healthier life than before. The findings of the field work e.g., Pryor's (1980) account of residents' attitudes in Rarotonga, Cook Islands, or the many accusations about the role of (Western) tourists as transmitters of STIs and

AIDS. Although there is no doubt that tourism contributes to the spread of diseases, facts are hard to obtain. Using Doxey's (1975) index of tourist irritation as a framework, one has to assume that anecdotal negative evidence on health impacts may have a lot to do with locals' antagonism toward tourists for whatever reason.

Comments, therefore, should be (or should have been) examined from this perspective to allow for a more realistic interpretation. Antagonism may even lead to the perception of transmission of diseases with entirely different aetiology. In this connection, one also needs to consider the well known conflict between national park management and the needs of the locals living within a park or in close proximity. For example, the conservation of flagship species such as the tiger or rhinoceros has to be weighed against the loss of lives of locals caused by those animals. Likewise, loss of livestock and crop destruction have impacts on the population's health status. In the context of this report, it is necessary to identify what events occur within the framework of conservation and which ones can clearly be attributed to tourism.

Numerous gaps have been identified in the current body of knowledge on the impact of tourism on the health of the local population in developing countries and topics for research have been suggested. It has been established that research into potential indirect health impacts has to go beyond the economic, environmental and sociocultural impacts already widely discussed in the literature, and focus specifically on their health implications. Research into potential direct health impacts should concentrate on epidemiological studies into the transmission of diseases through travellers and on investigations into the work place health and safety aspects in relation to local tourism employees.

In addition, a wide range of general issues is the focus for basic and applied research providing additional information to achieve a more complete picture of health impacts. Examples are offered here to illustrate the variety of study topics available to researchers from different disciplines. Historians could explore how visitors in the past (invaders, explorers, missionaries) changed the local health status. At present, it seems information on this topic can only be found by chance when studying old documents or travel diaries. Addressing present day concerns, social scientists should establish if there is indeed an association between locals' negative attitudes towards tourism and anecdotal evidence of negative impacts (and then test those claims through epidemiological research).

Another focus of interest is an examination of national and regional tourism strategies in developing countries with respect to the consideration of the local public health and specific strategic activities to prevent a deterioration of the health status. Public health interests could lie in: the comparison of the impact of different levels of low, moderate, and high degrees of tourism in small/isolated communities; the investigation of advice given to tourists in their home country or at the destination regarding their impact on local health; an assessment of tourists' knowledge of their potential role as transmitters of diseases; the identification of services offered for tourists' health care and the examination of their utilisation and availability for locals; the documentation of tourists using local health care facilities; or a comparison of the distribution of health care professionals and health services in touristic and non-touristic areas within one country. Finally, tourism education should be included in research on the topic and curricula in tourism degree courses examined regarding their inclusion of health aspects. These study topics can be researched not only in individual projects focusing on a particular geographic area but allow for comparison between areas with the aim of collaborative efforts in dealing with identified health problems linked to tourism. The addition and consideration of country specific research needs which may be proposed by local health authorities will be of particular importance when deciding on a specific topic for research.

The Need for Research as a Basis for Tourism Planning

The goal of tourism planning is usually said to be economic, sociological, biological and cultural sustainability. Ethical concerns have been raised in connection with tourism development in the 'Third World'. The four goals in tourism development:

(1) enhanced visitor satisfaction,

(2) improved economy and business success,

(3) protected resource assets, and

(4) community and area integration clearly include participation of and approval by the local population. Any development that does not protect local people and environment could be classified as unethical.

It becomes clear when examining available tourism strategies and plans that tourism planning is an immensely complex activity. Publications on two areas visited during the field trip have been reviewed with respect to their coverage of issues which may directly or indirectly affect the health of local populations.

Aguilar, Hinojosa and Milla (1992) suggested a wide range of strategies and actions to develop tourism in the 'Inka Region', an area extending over the Departments of Cusco, Madre de Dios and Apurímac, but no reference relating to health could be found. The 'Plan for Touristic and Recreation Use of the Huascaran National Park' applies to the national park in the Cordillera Blanca/Huaraz which predicted 104,000 conventional tourists and 4,000 adventure tourists (mountain climbers) for the year 1996, and 320,000 conventional tourists and 12,000 adventure tourists for the year 2005. As this plan relates to a national park, it comes as no surprise that considerable emphasis is placed on the environmental impact of tourism (garbage, lack of toilets, water and sewage system). It also recommends that conditions are to be established "for the rural population to participate in tourism in a manner which permits sustainable development". Both aspects influence the local health status but health as such is not mentioned explicitly. The plan also suggests that local guides be registered in order to monitor uncontrolled activities in the park. Such a register, i f implemented, could be an excellent opportunity to monitor their health status.

Research is the basis to appropriate tourism planning. It is obvious that the lack of research into health issues has prevented their inclusion in tourism strategic plans.

Methodological Considerations

The benefit of studying a little investigated area is that there are few conceptual restrictions for the researcher but a great opportunity for creativity and innovative approaches when defining research topics. Research in some of the areas suggested, clearly poses enormous methodological challenges for the investigator, not least because of the transient character of tourism. Here again creativity is needed in employing a range of different research approaches, going beyond the conventional. Two will be mentioned here. For example, for some of these topics an action research approach based on Critical Social Theory could be adopted. The philosophy behind Critical Social Theory is that empowering people helps them to change their situation, to help themselves. A classic text is Paolo Freire's (1972) *Pedagogy of the Oppressed* on the empowerment through education. In a similar way, communities affected by negative health impacts from tourism could work at overcoming these by adopting the problem solving approach based on empowerment. The core of action research is the employment of a problem solving approach whereby the researcher guides the representatives of a group/community (who also become part of the research team) through the process of change until a satisfactory outcome is achieved.

The usefulness of a Geographical Information System (GIS) for epidemiological purposes is now widely accepted. The inherent geographical element of tourism and the aspect of movement represent factors very suitable for the employment of GIS for research purposes on this topic. Furthermore, its use would allow the combination of epidemiological and tourism variables. At this stage, it could not be established if GIS has ever been used in this form. However, the combination of medicine and geography is not new. Hellen (1995) discussed the use of applied medical geography in, for example, disease hazard mapping, and emphasised the need for a "multidisciplinary approach to safeguarding the health of individuals and ensuring the sustainability of tourism to potentially hazardous areas", albeit from the perspective of travellers' health. It is quite clear that the range of research questions suggested in this paper indicates that a lot of these need to be approached in a multidisciplinary fashion. This would also provide a unique opportunity to cooperate with local professionals and to train locals as research assistants to enable them to continue research and monitoring on a long-term basis.

Towards a Framework for Understanding Tourism's Health Impacts

The purpose of research is to generate and test theories. Applied research emphasises its practical applicability to the field of study. Consequently, research undertaken on this hitherto under-investigated topic will contribute to a body of knowledge which may eventually be expressed in a more abstract form as theories and represented as models for easier understanding. The theories, in turn, will have to be tested and refined.

Bushell and Lea (1996) quite rightly pointed out that there is more to 'tourism and health' than traveller illness and suggest a reorientation towards 'traveller and host wellness'. They then continue to present a tourism health model linked to the concept o f eco logical public health as a framework for research. It defines 'tourism and health' as the interface between (1) tourists, (2) hosts and (3) the natural environment. The model takes into account arguments by Brown (1985) supporting an epidemiology of health in contrast to the traditional epidemiology of diseases. Based on these arguments, the authors also propose a forced field approach considering the perspectives of promoting/preventing wellness/ illness as a guideline for investigations, and request that a new public health framework be integrated in the existing field of 'tourism and health'. Without doubt, this is one possible avenue. However, it can be argued that this model is rather one-sided as it focuses on health with little evidence of including tourism aspects (apart from the tourists). The model may represent the broad field of tourism and health but it does not depict enough detail to accommodate attributing factors which are mentioned by Bushell and Lea, such as typology of tourists or destination categories. It does not seem refined enough to offer directions for further research incorporating both fields (tourism and health) sufficiently. A framework can be seen as a system where all components are interdependent and interlinked in a way that variations in one component affect the rest of the system. Based on the results of this study, a framework for understanding tourism's health impacts in developing countries will most likely consist at least of the following major components: tourists, type of tourism, operators/developers, local population, local authorities, the environment, the level of tourism, and the country's current economic status.

Tourists (As Individuals/as Groups)

Tourists are probably the most active part in this framework as they are the ones actually moving around and coming into contact with places and people. A range of factors need to be considered as attributes of this constant visit or host encounter: tourist typology; tourists' health status and educational status; knowledge required for a particular trip; advice given; activities sought and their implications; speed of travel; size and numbers of groups; mode of transport chosen; accommodation (e.g., enclave vs homestay); travel patterns; travel corridors; travel seasons; and the degree of contact with the local population. Some of these factors are deliberately chosen by the individual, others occur unintentionally or have been decided for the tourist.

Type of Tourism

A further component is the type of tourism occurring in a particular location, from individual adventure travel to mass tourism. This has an effect on the degree of contact tourists have with locals as well as the potential of introducing diseases or causing other negative impacts, for example, on the environment. Although mass travel implies that large numbers of people travel, the accumulation of large numbers usually only occurs at very popular destinations, and these visitors may not come in contact with locals at all or rarely. The impact of mass tourism on health is likely to be indirect, i.e. through economic, environmental or sociocultural affects. Adventure tourism is pursued by travelling individuals, alone or in very small groups, but their destinations are usually in more remote and isolated areas where they are also much more likely to come in c loser contact with local communities. These interactions most likely prepare the ground for potential direct impacts such as the transmission of diseases. Tourist activities are another dimension impacting on local destinations. Pearce and Moscardo (1989) developed a tool to investigate the Structure of Tourism Activities for Regions (STAR). A list of attributes allows the classification of activities. Some of those at tributes are based on interactions between tourists and the environment (and hence important in relation to possible impacts), but no attribute is allocated to a possible interaction with the local population. As this interaction obviously does occur, on a continuum from very little to very close, not only should this dimension be added to the STAR (Structure of Tourism Activities for Regions) instrument, but it is an important factor in the assessment of health impacts of tourism. It may be useful to design a modified STAR tool that allows the creation of profiles of activities and their impact on host communities' health. The dimensions of such a tool would be factors such as impact on the environment, degree of contact with locals, or potential risks to local employees.

Operators/developers A further important component are those individuals or companies/organisations who develop tourism destinations and provide services and facilities from travel agencies to transport companies and the accommodation industry. Clearly, the primary purpose of those businesses is to make a profit out of the tourism they promote. Ideally, operators should be mediators between tourists and hosts, if only to ensure sustainability of the operations. In reality, however, it seems that the links with the tourists are much closer, tourists and operator s are involved in a business transaction with one supplying what the other demands. Operators have a great responsibility when it comes to planning, developing and running tourism products as these rarely occur without impacts on the local populations. Very often, operators decide on activities offered, destinations visited, accommodation constructed and mode of transport provided. They, therefore, do represent a very important element in the health impact framework due to their intermediate position between visitors and hosts.

Local Population

Here, we are looking at the more passive, receiving end of the activity 'travel'. The following aspects are of importance: the geographical location; immunity and health status; level of education; previous contact with visitors; dependence on tourism; degree of contact with tourists; attitudes towards tourism; the difference between the cultural and social values of visitor and host; locals' involvement in tourism planning. Brown (1985) strongly emphasised that a suitable approach to an epidemiology of health "must take account of complexity, open-endedness, multiple interactions, value choices, social rules and types of personality...". Nothing less should be applied to the local host population.

Local authorities (health tourism) So far, little attention has been paid to the role of local health and tourism authorities in the protection of the health of the local population. It is important to recognise the role of these authorities. Although the aims of both authorities may not seem to have much common ground, with one developing and promoting tourism and the principles of business in mind, and the other in charge of the public health status, if they are to achieve sustainable tourism which benefits all parties involved, a close cooperation between both is necessary. This applies particularly to activities such as monitoring the local health status in tourism destinations and implementing strategies of improvement if necessary; investigating health impacts (in cooperation with other agencies, such as conservation groups); approving of tourism destinations only after a positive outcome of a health impact assessment; or terminating an operation when its impact is detrimental. In this respect, local authorities play a central role in the monitoring of tourists, locals, and operators as well as environmental issues.

Environment

The environment represents an essential resource for tourism. Budowski (1976) proposed three possible relationships between tourism and nature, *conflict, coexistence* and *symbiosis,* claiming that the majority of relationships are those of coexistence moving toward conflict. It seems not much has changed 20 years later. Changes in the environment affect humans' health as a short- or long-term consequence. It is, therefore, important that every effort is made to closely observe the environment for changes attributable to tourism to allow for timely act ion in order to reduce the health risks to locals and tourists.

Economic Status

In order to achieve the required monitoring discussed above, not only is a substantial budget necessary but also professional expertise in fields such as health, tourism, and conservation. The same requirements apply i f research is to be conducted into topics suggested throughout this paper. A lesser developed country may well recognise negative impacts of tourism on the health of its people but may be in no position to do anything about it, not least because it is desperately dependent on tourism and foreign currency. Therefore, ways will have to be designed that allow countries with little expertise and economic abilities to still have strategies at hand to minimise a decrease in the local health status attributable to tourism.

These components and their relationships with each other can be seen as starting points for investigations A growth of research based knowledge on tourism's health impacts (as well as putting this area on priority lists of funding bodies) will allow the generation of theoretical frameworks in a reasonably near future. Such frameworks are necessary for applying this knowledge to practice, particularly for assessing health impacts. The ultimate goal will be to conduct such an assessment for prospective or current tourism developments in the same way as is already done for economic, environmental or, to a lesser extent, sociocultural impacts as, literally, prevention is better than cure.

Lacking such an assessment framework at the moment, other solutions have to be employed. Short-term solutions may centre around creating an awareness in tourists, locals and operators. In the longer term, other interventions may be necessary. Simmons' (1996) advice was meant for the protection of the environment but is equally applicable to health when he suggests the provision of 'honeypots' to draw people away from vulnerable spots. In practice, this could mean, rather than searching for isolated tribes in a rainforest, providing tourists with high quality interpretation centres.

The increase in tourism worldwide is likely to continue and the positive aspects of tourism in developing countries are acknowledged. However, it seems that health is being ignored in the process of tourism development, both "in terms of the local people and in the potential impact of travellers on the already scarce health resources" as Rudkin and Hall reported from the South Pacific. If visitor-host encounters lead to a decreasing health status of the hosts, action needs to be taken in order to promote people's well-being and, consequently, the sustainability of tourism destinations for the benefit of the visitor *and* the host. Otherwise, the World Tourism Organization's objective" to accelerate and enlarge the contribution of tourism (international and domestic) to peace, understanding, *health,* and prosperity throughout the world" cannot be met

Medical Tourism and its Negative Impact on the Rural Primary Health Care to the Poor Families in Rural India

Medical tourism refers to the practice of people travelling abroad to obtain medical care and services. In the past medical tourism has mainly consisted of wealthy people travelling to countries such as the United States and paying for the use of advanced medical facilities. Nowadays, there is an increasing trend whereby patients are travelling to middle and low-income countries to obtain low-cost health services with short waiting times. Medical and surgical procedures can cost between five to ten times less in India than the United States.

Some destination countries such as India have actively promoted medical tourism. This is because it can bring about benefits including increases in revenue, foreign exchange reserves and tourism. It is estimated that medical tourism generates over US$60 billion in business. In addition, it has led to the creation of high-tech private medical facilities in India.

Questions remain about whether local populations actually benefit from these facilities and national health systems from the revenues that they generate. Experience from India suggests that private hospitals attract health professionals away from the public health sector and rural areas in India. This internal brain drain creates shortages of trained health workers, thus reducing access to healthcare for local populations in rural India and exacerbating inequalities.

In India some private hospitals agreed to provide services to poor people for no costs and in turn received government subsidies in the form of land, tax breaks and medical equipment. However, the facilities oriented towards medical tourism (technology intensive tertiary services) do not meet the health needs of the average poor rural Indian and evidence suggests that few poor people have benefited from such care. It is important that the government does not overlook the negative impacts that health tourism can have on local populations, in particular on access to services and availability of public health professionals. They should also find ways of ensuring that the revenues accrued from health tourists are channelled into the public sector through national laws and regulations The article describes a trend, where large numbers of patients from wealthy countries, such as America, are travelling abroad to diverse countries including India, in search of less expensive health care. The article uses examples of India and Thailand to examine the implications of medical tourism in these countries. It shows that in both countries medical tourism has caused private hospitals to emphasise treatment over prevention, and promote technology-intensive tertiary services at the expense of primary health care. This has created distortions in the allocation of resources and spending that doesn't match the needs of local people.

UK conference discusses 'disastrous' impact of the myth of 'HIV health tourism' HIV health tourism is one of the Government's main justifications for "a harmful, costly and inhumane charging policy." The UK Government's policy of charging so-called 'health tourists' for HIV treatment and care is a "public health disaster" based on myth not fact, Yusef Azad, Director of Policy and Campaigns for the National AIDS Trust (NAT) told last week's British HIV Association (BHIVA) Autumn Conference during a session on treating migrant populations and their eligibility for care.

HIV health tourism is one of the Government's main justifications for "a harmful, costly and inhumane charging policy," according to a new NAT report, *The myth of HIV health tourism.* The results of that policy were highlighted at the conference by a panel consisting of an HIV clinician, a human rights lawyer, a GP who has cared for many asylum seekers with HIV, an HIV-positive migrant advocate, and Mr. Azad.

Since April 2004, overseas visitors, refused asylum seekers, undocumented migrants and visa overstayers have no longer been entitled to HIV treatment and care from the National Health Service (NHS) in England, although treatment for all other infectious diseases and sexually transmitted infections continues to be free to everyone on public health grounds irrespective of residency status. (The NHS in Scotland and Wales have different policies.)

Earlier this year, a High Court ruling resulted in HIV-positive refused asylum seekers being entitled to free HIV treatment and care for as long as they remained in the UK. But the judge refused a claim that there was a human right to NHS treatment, saying that any discrimination in the rules was justifiable so as to discourage 'health tourism'.

Yet a new NAT report that "separates facts and evidence around migration from fears and misinformation", argues that there is no evidence to demonstrate that HIV health tourism to the UK exists. Allegations of 'HIV health tourism', says the report, "make a serious charge against the integrity and truthfulness of many HIV-positive migrants to the UK, effectively alleging that stated reasons for migration to the UK are at best a pretext and at worst totally untrue. Given the discrimination and marginalisation experienced by many migrants we must question very carefully any claim which might add to social hostility".

The report also notes, "the claim of health tourism has been central to the Government's policy of charging refused asylum seekers and other migrants without lawful residency status for healthcare. The Government argues that free NHS care for those without what they deem to be a legitimate reason to migrate to the UK acts as a 'pull factor', encouraging illegal immigration and discouraging refused asylum seekers from leaving. Charges for NHS care for certain categories of migrant were introduced to end the 'pull' of free NHS care and address the so-called problem of 'health tourism'.

"Is there really evidence of HIV health tourism which would justify on grounds of immigration policy the singling out of HIV for NHS charges alone amongst all serious or sexually transmitted infections?" asks NAT. Over the course of twelve pages, the paper robustly argues that there is no evidence to demonstrate that 'HIV health tourism' is "a significant or real motivation for migration to the UK" and considerable evidence to demonstrate otherwise, "in particular the lower rates of HIV prevalence compared with country of origin, the long average delays [an average of five years] between arrival in the UK and accessing HIV testing and care, and the evidence available on the actual motivations of migrants coming to the UK".

Dr. Le Feuvre, a Kent GP, told the conference that NAT's conclusions match his own experience. "We had tens of thousands of [refugees and asylum seekers] coming through East Kent in the last ten years. I only personally remember one person amongst those tens of thousands who seemed to be coming here for medical treatment and the majority of people diagnosed with HIV, and who left the, left with it being diagnosed after their arrival and not before." One of the paper's recommendations is that "since the provision of free HIV treatment has no bearing on migration trends, the basis for the Government's policy of charging for HIV treatment is wholly undermined. It has been demonstrated elsewhere that the policy actually increases costs to the NHS and endangers public health. The Government must review its policy on NHS charging so as to exempt HIV treatment from charges."

The impact of this policy was brought into sharp focus at the BHIVA conference by Professor Jane Anderson of Homerton University Hospital, east London, who provided a case study to illustrate the desperation faced by HIV-positive undocumented migrants in England. She told the conference about a 35 year-old East African woman who was refused a prescription by a medical team outside of London when she had only three days supply of antiretrovirals left and no means to return to her country of origin. "We gave her an immediate prescription for antiretroviral drugs...and gave her a travelcard from our charitable fund so she could get food and support from other charitable sources," she said.

She argued that HIV care in the UK should be for everyone. She noted that the new UK HIV testing guidelines, which include a list of 'indicator diseases' prompting the offer of opt-out testing "is only ethically acceptable if positive individuals are immediately linked into appropriate HIV treatment and care. Yet," she asked, "we are meant to send them to a place where they're going to get a big bill. Is this appropriate practice?"

Adam Hundt, a human rights lawyer provided an overview of the complex rules and regulations governing access to secondary NHS treatment and care, which he described as "a bit of a minefield". He noted that there are situations, people, and diseases exempted from the charging regulations including treatment given at an emergency department, 34 infectious diseases (including TB and viral hepatitis) and all sexually transmitted infections apart from HIV which he said, "is a policy decision".

There is also an exemption for continuing a course of treatment, including treatment for HIV, as long as someone has lawfully entered the UK. "Unhelpfully," he noted, "there's no definition of what 'a course of treatment' is." The Government recently clarified that 'treatment' does not necessarily mean antiretroviral therapy, but in fact, can mean continued monitoring of immune and clinical status due to an HIV diagnosis.

He noted that there is also much confusion amongst clinicians over what constitutes 'immediately necessary treatment' which should be provided to anyone regardless of their ability to pay. "It basically specifies that if someone requires treatment because their condition is life threatening, or because if treatment is not given immediately it will become life threatening, or because permanent and serious damage would be caused by any delay then they must be given treatment regardless of whether they can pay or not and then be charged for it later," he said.

Dr. Ian Williams, BHIVA's Chair, recently wrote to the Department of Health to argue that HIV care should be considered immediately necessary in the same way as maternity care. "I think the most important thing to remember," noted Mr. Hundt, "is that it's a matter of clinical judgment which should not be second-guessed by administrative staff."

In the discussion that followed, Prof. Anderson pointed out the paradox of one Government department, the Department for International Development, supporting universal access to HIV treatment and care overseas, but another two Government departments, the Department of Health and the Home Office "denying that care free here and also sending people back through various legislation and legal decisions to places where there's no care. Why can't we have domestic policies that are the same as foreign policy?" she asked.

Environmental Impacts of Medical Tourism

Although medical tourism is a boon for people who cannot afford expensive treatments in their own country, there are certain disadvantages to it. One of the biggest disadvantages is the environmental impacts of medical tourism, which is always negative.

Most people going for medical treatment abroad tend to combine travel and tourism along with the medical procedure. This means that the country where you go for the treatment has to build more hotels to accommodate the ever growing number of patients cum tourists. The government resorts to deforestation to build more hotels and provide better civil amenities because medical tourism is a way of earning revenue and foreign exchange. In addition, medical tourism is also responsible for contributing to increased air emissions, noise, solid waste and littering, releases of sewage, oil and chemicals, even architectural/visual pollution; all which has negative impact on the environment.

Medical tourism creates great pressure on local resources like energy, food and other raw material, which could be already in short supply in that country. Even natural resources like water, especially fresh water, is affected as medical tourism like any other tourism generally tends to overuse water resources for hotels, swimming pools, and personal use of water by the tourists. This results in shortage of water and degradation of water supplies as well as generating large volumes of waste water. From fiscal aspect, medical tourism is good for a country but the environmental impacts of medical tourism are always negative.

Social Impacts of Medical Tourism

While people from America use medical tourism to get low cost medical care, people from Canada and Britain, where public healthcare systems are present, take advantage of medical tourism to avoid long waiting lists in their own countries.

Health insurance companies are now trying to understand how they can offer medical tourism to people and one of the plans they have in mind is to introduce lower premiums for certain services if the people go abroad for them. This will have a great impact on healthcare insurance premiums as well as hospital profitability.

However, the social impacts of medical tourism are in countries where people go for medical treatments. These countries are poor and developing countries where citizens cannot afford medical treatment, food, shelter or clothing. If medical tourism can bring about a change in their lives, it would be the perfect scenario. Hospitals specializing in medial tourism should use their earnings to provide free and adequate health services for the poor.

The other social impact of medical tourism is positive. Medical tourism is instrumental in creating jobs for people. This means as the developing country grows to accommodate increasing number of medical tourists, it creates more jobs for the locals. In addition, the medical tourism healthcare providers keep upgrading their capabilities and facilities which can be used to treat the domestic patients too at a reasonable price.

Impacts

Health Impacts

During the haze period, quite a number of people experienced respiratory related problems; asthma attacks, bronchitis. Many too suffered from coughing/wheezing, runny noses and sore throats. People complained of eye irritation and reddening of eyes.? Those with respiratory problems, heart conditions, skin conditions (Eczema) and the young and old would be severely affected by the haze. Professor Euston Quah, head of economics department of Nanyang Technological University, mentioned that there was even a possibility of stunted growth for children's lungs if the children were repeatedly exposed to haze for a long time.

From our interview with Doctor Chris Huang, he felt that this statement is not true. Haze is not likely to stunt the growth for children's lungs, except for babies because their lungs are not fully developed yet. Hence, when they are exposed to particulate matter from the haze and their lungs are irritated, the result might be the scarring of their lungs. Furthermore, it might lead to other serious health conditions such as pneumonia, which could cause permanent damage to lungs. Nonetheless, this does not stunt the lung growth of the babies.

The haze pollutants contain particles such as ozone and sulphur dioxide (also greenhouse gases) may cause damage to the heart and lungs. Particulate matter 10 (PM10), the more commonly-found particle in the smoke haze, happens to be the most dangerous threat to lungs. When breathed in, PM10 might cause lungs to function at a decreased rate, causing shortness of breath!

During a serious haze situation, civilians would be advised by the government to stay indoors and limit outdoor activities so that the people are less exposed to unhealthy, polluted air. Nonetheless, PM10 is still able to enter buildings through fresh air vents.

In the First week of October 2006, when the haze was at its worst in Singapore, approximately 15 000 citizens complained of illnesses associated with the heart and lungs.

Haze has been linked to premature death recently according to HazeOnline website. If a person is exposed to too much pollutants from the haze, that could lead to premature death. The two main causes of this premature death are the two gases sulphur dioxide and nitrogen oxide which are part of the haze.

Environmental Impacts

The haze situation in Southeast Asia mainly resulted from the burning of the trees in Indonesian forests. The gases that evolved from the combustion are sulphur dioxide, ozone, nitrogen dioxide and carbon monoxide. These are greenhouse gases and hence contributed to global warming and affected the atmosphere tremendously. This in turn speeds up global warming, causing shifting climate changes and unpredictability of the weather.

There is loss of biodiversity due to the forest fires. Flora and fauna are burnt and lost in the fires. We might have endangered even more species of animals and also destroyed rare species of organisms. This will cause a disruption in the ecosystem.

The haze pollutants cause a negative change in air quality in the neighbouring countries. This would also affect the human's respiratory system. Humans need fresh air, but if the air quality is not good, the human's health will be affected detrimentally. Therefore, there would be a rise in patients with respiratory and eye problems caused by the inhalation of haze pollutants.

PM 2.5 mostly causes reduction in visibility. Reduction in visibility might also cause trade transport to travel with lots of difficulty. Trading ships may crash accidentally into objects if sailors are not alert and careful about their course, especially when it is so difficult to see ahead during the haze. As for airplanes, the haze would hinder the sight of the pilot, making it difficult to manoeuvres the aircraft, hence compromising the safety of the passengers.

Impact on Tourism

When haze hit Thailand on 12th of March 2007, flights were disrupted (13 cancelled) and had to be delayed. Tourists normally tend to shun countries with images of smoke and civilians wearing surgical masks, hence resulting in the decline of the tourism rate in the countries affected by the haze. Due to the fact that flights were cancelled, many tourists were left stranded at the airport since they had already checked out of their hotels while locals could still return back to their homes.

Though immediate cancellations were less observed, this showed that people planning for trips may reconsider their holiday destinations. Fewer tourists have visited Thailand, posing a problem towards Thailand's tourism, and the root of the problem is haze. Should the haze problem be solved, then Thailand's tourism would not be affected negatively.

An interviewed tourist was very annoyed with the haze situation because there was no sight of the sun after 9 days when he had come to Singapore to enjoy the sun.

In 1997, 13 flights from Singapore were cancelled due to the poor visibility from the haze. In that same year, airports in Malaysia such as West Kalimantan were closed. Also, 9 out of 11 Indonesian airports closed due to the haze. Visibility had worsened to 300 meters. There was even an Indonesian plane crashed which involved the lives of 234 people. The cancelling of flights and closing of airports prevented tourists from coming in to Singapore, causing a fall in tourism.

Economical Impacts

There would be a surge in medical costs since there would be many people going to the doctors for treatment of cough, and other haze-related illnesses. As a result, less people would turn up for work, reducing the efficiency of the different industries during that period.

People would flock to pharmacies to purchase eye drops to sooth their irritated eyes; face masks to filter the air they inhale, facial masks to prevent their faces from getting too dry and air purifiers to purify the air inside air-conditioned buildings. Retailers and businesses may be affected due to the fact that most people try to stay indoors (definition: at home). However, there are some people who would rather stay indoors (definition: shopping centres) and spend their day there doing shopping, having meals, watching movies, et cetera. However, retailers in neighbourhood or places which are not air-conditioned will be affected adversely.

During the haze period, theme parks, sports facilities and coaches, alfresco dining restaurants and sightseeing tours had losses between 10 to 50 percent.

Singapore lost an estimated S$425 million during the 1997 haze period which lasted 3 months. US$210 million tourism; US$95 thousand recreation; US$5 million health; US$41 million visibility-airplanes and ships cannot navigate properly. The highest PSI was 226.

Should the haze last for a month, economic losses for Singapore would be maximum of $70 million, according to Professor Quah. Imagine, if a worse haze were to last for more than a month, what would be the consequences be like to the country?

Bibliography

Brown, L.A. : *Innovation Diffusion: A New Perspective,* London and New York, 1981.

Brunt, Paul: *Market Research in Travel and Tourism,* Oxford, Butterworth Heinemann, 1997.

Carl H. : *Internet Distribution of European Travel and Tourism Services,* Research Centre of Bornholm, Denmark, 1999.

Chakravarti B.K. : *Hotel and Hospitality Management,* A.P.H., Delhi, 2011.

Cukier, J. : *Tourism Employment in Bali: Trends and Implications,* London: Thompson, 1996.

David L: *International Tourism Policy, New York,* Van Nostrand and Reinhold, 1990.

Donald E. : *Public Personnel Management: Contexts and Strategies,* Upper Saddle River, NJ: Prentice Hall, 1998.

Donald M.: *Customer Service in the Hospitality and Tourism Industry,* Englewood Cliffs, Prentice Hall, 1994.

Douglas C: *Practical Tourism Forecasting,* Oxford, Butterworth Heinemann, 1996.

Eberts, Marjorie: *Careers in Travel, Tourism, and Hospitality,* Lincolnwood, VGM Career Horizons, 1997.

Fesenmaier D., Klein, S. : *Information & Communication Technologies in Tourism,* Springer-Verlag, Wien-New York, 2000.

Ghimire, Krishna: *The Native Tourist*: Mass Tourism within Developing Regions, London, Earthscan, 2001.

Graham M S: *Language of Tourism,* The, Wallingford, CAB International, 1996.

Harrison, Lyndon: *Tourism Means Jobs,* Chester, Lyndon Harrison, 1996.

Ireland, Lewis: *Quality Management for Projects and Programs*, Upper Darby, PMI, 1991.

Judi Radice: *Restaurant & Food Graphics*, Glen Cove, PBC International, 1994.

Judy A: *Tourism: Management of Facilities*, London, Pitman: M & E, 1993.

Karski, A: *Urban Tourism* - A Key to Urban Regeneration?, 1990.

Klein, S. : *Information & Communication Technologies in Tourism*, Springer-Verlag, Wien-New York, 2000.

Kotler, Philip: *Marketing for Hospitality and Tourism*: New Jersey, Prentice-Hall, 1998.

Kotler, Philipl: *Marketing Places: Attracting Investment, Industry & Tourism etc*, New York, free press, 1993.

Larkham, P J: *Building a New Heritage: Tourism, Culture & Identity in the New Europe*, London, Routledge,1994.

Leivadi, S: *Sociology of Tourism, The: Theoretical And Empirical Investigations*, London, Retailed, 1996.

Lewis, Robert C.: *Cases in Hospitality Marketing and Management*, New York, John Wiley, 1997.

Lucas, Rosemary E.: *Managing Employee Relations in the Hotel and Catering Industry*, London, Cassell, 1995.

Madhukar Manoj : *Hospitality Industries in Next Millennium*, Rajat, Delhi, 2001.

Marcussen, Carl H. : *Internet Distribution of European Travel and Tourism Services*, Research Centre of Bornholm, Denmark, 1999.

Margaret Wade: *Medieval Travellers: The Rich and Restless*, London, Hamish Hamilton, 1982.

Marjorie, E.: *Careers in Travel, Tourism, and Hospitality*, Lincolnwood, VGM Career Horizons, 1997.

Martin, B.S. : *The Efficacy of Growth Machine Theory in Explaining Resident Perceptions of Community Tourism Development*, Clemson University, 1996.

McNicol, B.J. : *Views of Residents, Developers and Government Planners About Tourists and Tourism Resort Developments in Canmore, Alberta*, The University of Galgary, Alberta, 1996.

Morrell, J. : *Employment in Tourism,* London: British Tourist Authority, 1985.

Murphy, P.E. : *Tourism: A Community Approach,* London: Methuen, 1985.

Nancy, N.: *Choosing a Career in Hotels, Motels, and Resorts,* New York, Rosen Pub. Group, 1997.

Paajanen, M. : *Assessing Local Income and Employment Effects of Tourism: Experience using the Nordic model of tourism,* Wiley, 1999.

Pearce, Douglas: *Tourism Today: A Geographical Analysis,* Harlow, Longman, 1995.

Peters, M: *International Tourism,* London, Hutchinson, 1969.

Robert C.: *Cases in Hospitality Marketing and Management,* New York, John Wiley, 1997.

Rocco, M.: *An Introduction to Hospitality Today,* Orlando, Educational Institute, 1998.

Sabharwal Rajiv : *Tourism and Hospitality Management in Liberalised Era,* Pacific, Delhi, 2011.

Sharma Sunil : *Planning and Development of Tourism and Hospitality,* Rajat Pub, Delhi, 2007.

Shrivastava Atul : *Modern Hospitality and Tourism Management,* Centrum Press, Delhi, 2010.

Simmons, D. : *Community Adaptation to Tourism: Comparisons between Rotorua and Kaikoura,* New Zealand. Tourism Management, 2002.

Slinn, Judy A: *Tourism: Management of Facilities,* London, Pitman: M & E, 1993.

Smith, G. : *International Tourism and Hospitality Careers through Education and Training,* CHRIE Annual Conference, Washington DC, 1996.

Smith, V.L. : *Hosts and Guests: The Anthropology of Tourism,* Oxford: Blackwell, 1978.

Swarbrooke, J.: *Marketing Tourism, Hospitality and Leisure in Europe,* London, International Thomson Business Press, 1996.

Tribe, John *Corporate Strategy for Tourism, London,* International Thomson Business Press, 1997.

Var, Turgut: *Tourism Planning,* London, Retailed, 2002.

Index

M

N

O

P

R

S

T

❑❑❑